# Infantry Training

## THE
# NATIONAL SERVICEMAN'S
# HANDBOOK

# Infantry Training

## THE

# NATIONAL SERVICEMAN'S HANDBOOK

Edited by Campbell McCutcheon

TEMPUS

First published 1951, this edition 2007

Tempus Publishing
Cirencester Road, Chalford
Stroud, Gloucestershire, GL6 8PE
www.tempus-publishing.com

Tempus Publishing is an imprint of NPI Media Group

Introduction © Campbell McCutcheon, 2007

British Library Cataloguing in Publication Data.
A catalogue record for this book is available from the British Library.

ISBN 978 0 7524 4423 9

Typesetting and origination by NPI Media Group
Printed and bound in Great Britain

# Introduction

The Second World War ended, literally, in a bang. The largest explosions the world had ever seen destroyed the Japanese cities of Hiroshima and Nagasaki, along with almost 400,000 lives. Within a few days Japan had capitulated, but the world had changed forever. Britain's Government was committed to demobbing the hundreds of thousands of men in the armed forces but the ending of war is never simple and minor conflicts were still underway in Greece and Trieste. A vacuum existed in the Dutch East Indies and French Indo-China and these countries had to be stabilised too. Britain also had its own problems as its Empire began to disintegrate. India had been promised its independence as a result of the help received during the war and other countries were demanding their independence too, some with words and others with violence.

With Churchill voted out of power in July 1945, and a new Labour Government under Clement Attlee in power on 27 July that year, demobilisation was well underway. However, it was soon realised that with so many men leaving the armed forces, Britain's worldwide commitments could no longer be guaranteed with the manpower available. The answer was conscription – something that had never been done in Britain in peacetime. It was first seen in the UK during the First World War, as volunteers dried up, and again in 1939 at the start of the Second World War. Economically, as well as politically, Britain could not afford the loss of manpower. The country had been brought to its knees as a result of the war and the men were needed to help convert Britain's industries from their wartime footings back to peaceful uses. With a shortage of decent housing, a need to manufacture goods for export to gain badly needed foreign currency and the need to help rebuild the infrastructure of our war-ravaged nation, Britain simply could not afford the loss of men to the armed forces, but they were needed for various reasons. An election promise was to bring home the five million men in uniform around the world, but Britain still needed an army to fulfil its worldwide commitments to its colonies, dominions and the devastated countries of Europe. Conscription, it was argued, was the only way.

Other world events were also making demands on the armed forces. Some were of Britain's own making, such as the conflict in Palestine that would lead to the setting up of the Jewish state of Israel, and the tensions between Muslims and Hindus that were leading to a near civil war in parts of India. There were also the simmering conflicts in Korea and Vietnam that would ultimately lead to major wars in both countries. In February 1946, conscription was considered in Parliament and opinion was divided. Manny Shinwell, Minister for Defence, was strongly against, as was Sir Stafford Cripps, who was in charge of Britain's economic reconstruction. Those for included Ernest Bevin, the Foreign Secretary, and Minister of Labour and National Service under Churchill's wartime cabinet. Many were against conscription. However it was an absolute necessity. There was no way around it: Britain needed an army to match its post-war commitments and it could only be provided by making men join it. The argument now was not whether men should be conscripted but the time they would be in the armed forces. Cripps advocated a year, the armed forces chiefs of staff wanted three. A compromise was set at eighteen months, with 5½ years reserve service.

In March 1947, the National Service Bill passed its first reading with few problems, but on its second, in April, many Labour MPs voted against it. The Act was passed, but only just. As a result, Attlee's Government panicked and reduced the period of service to twelve months. Northern Ireland was exempt from National Service but the men of Ulster could, if they wanted, volunteer. Unsurprisingly, few bothered!

In June 1948, the Soviets closed the roads to Berlin and the uneasy post-war alliance was over. Much of Eastern Europe was toppling to communism and there were communist insurgencies in countries like Malaya, while Hong Kong's garrison was bolstered against Chinese aggression. In December 1948, six months after the testing of Russia's atom bomb, the National Service Amendment Act came into force, raising conscription back to eighteen months and four years of reserve service. In June 1950, national service was raised to two years as a direct result of the manpower needed for the Korean War. As a trade-off, reserve service was reduced to 3½ years.

British national servicemen were involved in conflicts in Cyprus, Malaya, Suez, Korea, Kenya and a myriad number of other countries few in Britain had ever visited, let alone heard of. Some men got the posting of a lifetime to Christmas Island, only to be used as human guinea pigs during the dropping of Britain's atom bombs. Others went to Porton Down, where over 2,000 were deliberately infected with sarin nerve gas, all for an extra 15s and some extra days leave. At least three men died as a result. It was wilfully reckless and tantamount to murder. No national serviceman went to Korea before his eighteenth birthday, but many spent some months in Hong Kong awaiting their birthday before being thrown against the North Koreans and the Chinese. For some, though, the reality was different. They were sent to a rather peaceful Germany to protect the West against the USSR, while many ended in the UK, doing desk jobs. Of course national service was not just for soldiers; the navy and air force took their share of raw recruits, although to get into the RAF you had to be the pick of the bunch. Requiring men with real skills, the RAF could afford to be choosy. Seventy-two out of every hundred went to the army, twenty-six went to the RAF, with most of those never seeing an aircraft, while only two went to the navy. The navy could afford to be choosy, most of its jobs required real training and skills, and regulars signed up for seven years. With no representation at the interview boards, it managed without the steady influx of national servicemen that populated both army and air force.

However, after thirteen years the last conscript joined the army. He was Private Fred Turner who ended up in the Army Catering Corps, joining the army on 31 December 1960, the last day of call-up for national service. He was discharged from the army on 7 May 1963. The last national serviceman to leave was Lieutenant Richard Vaughan of the Royal Army Pay Corps, who was discharged a mere six days later on 13 May 1963. In all, about 2.5 million men, aged between seventeen and twenty-six had been conscripted. A whole generation had had two years of their lives taken by the Government. Some had fun, others hated every minute of it. Whatever the feelings of the men involved, it was a life-changing period of their lives. Many learned a career, or the direction of their lives changed totally as a result. Many saw parts of the world and experienced things they would never have experienced at home. We are unlikely ever to get national service in the UK again, but for that generation it has left many memories. For some it was of good mates killed in action in some foreign land, for others it was two years of square-bashing, and for some the chance to see the world. Of that 2.5 million who served, almost 400 died fighting for their country. It seems a small amount considering the number of conflicts they were involved in. With 6,000 being conscripted every two weeks, the number killed in action seems amazingly small. Thankfully, most men survived their 730 days of national service, even if many spent them marking the days till demob off the calendar.

Training for all was contained in a series of army publications, of which three are reproduced here. The raw recruit would have spent six weeks learning square-bashing and drill, a few more weeks learning to use his rifle and bayonet, and even more time on fieldcraft, before finally being turned into a fighting soldier.

26
GS Trg Publications
1857

WO Code No.
**8510**

WAR OFFICE

# DRILL

## (ALL ARMS)

# 1951

*This publication supersedes the Manual of Elementary Drill (All Arms) 1935 (Code No. 7959), Drill for Foot Guards and Infantry of the Line, 1939 (Code No. 7627) and Dismounted Drill for the Royal Artillery, 1939 (Code No. 7628) (formerly Military Training Pamphlets Nos. 18 and 18A).*

LONDON : HIS MAJESTY'S STATIONERY OFFICE
1951
PRICE 2s. 6d. NET

# GET THE BEST FROM YOUR BOOTS

New boots, when you receive them, still retain the preservatives applied to protect them during storage. The oily nature of these preservatives makes it difficult to obtain a brilliant shine without first preparing the surface of the boots. The following simple treatment will provide a hard foundation of the finest quality wax which will ensure a perfect, sparkling finish to your Army boots, quickly and easily.

- To new boots, apply 'Cherry Blossom' Boot Polish liberally with a little moisture added and work in well, using a cloth and an old tooth brush handle. *This ground-work is essential.*

- Leave to dry thoroughly before attempting to polish.

- Polish with brush, briskly.

- Apply a little more 'Cherry Blossom' on a slightly damp cloth, using a circular motion.

- Polish off lightly with soft cloth.

- Repeat last two operations daily and the boots will quickly develop the characteristic shine of the really polished soldier.

Also supplied in Tonette Dark Stain, Light Brown and Oxblood for your off-duty shoes

# DRILL

## (ALL ARMS)

# 1951

*By Command of the Army Council*

*[signature]*

THE WAR OFFICE
11*th January*, 1951

LONDON: HIS MAJESTY'S STATIONERY OFFICE
1951

## AMENDMENTS

| Amendment Number | By whom amended | Date of insertion |
|---|---|---|
| | | |
| | | |
| | | |
| | | |
| | | |
| | | |
| | | |
| | | |
| | | |
| | | |
| | | |
| | | |

## DISTRIBUTION

*(see Catalogue of War Office Publications, Part II)*

All Arms  ..  ..  ..  ..  ..  ..  ..  ..  Scale E

# CONTENTS

|  |  | Page |
|---|---|---|
| Definitions | .. .. .. .. .. .. .. .. .. | vi |
| Introduction .. | .. .. .. .. .. .. .. .. | vii |

### CHAPTER I—SQUAD DRILL AT THE HALT— WITHOUT ARMS

*Section*
| 1 | Attention | .. .. .. .. .. .. .. .. | 1 |
|---|---|---|---|
| 2 | Stand at ease | .. .. .. .. .. .. .. | 2 |
| 3 | Stand easy | .. .. .. .. .. .. .. | 2 |
| 4 | Forming up in three ranks | .. .. .. .. .. .. | 3 |
| 5 | Dressing | .. .. .. .. .. .. .. | 3 |
| 6 | Numbering and proving | .. .. .. .. .. .. | 4 |
| 7 | Open and close order march | .. .. .. .. .. | 5 |
| 8 | Getting on parade | .. .. .. .. .. .. | 5 |
| 9 | Turning and inclining | .. .. .. .. .. .. | 5 |
| 10 | Dismissing and falling out | .. .. .. .. .. | 7 |
| 11 | Sizing | .. .. .. .. .. .. .. .. | 7 |

### CHAPTER II—MARCHING

| 12 | Marching and halting in quick time | .. .. .. .. .. | 9 |
|---|---|---|---|
| 13 | Marching and halting in slow time | .. .. .. .. .. | 10 |
| 14 | Stepping out and Stepping short | .. .. .. .. .. | 11 |
| 15 | Paces forward and to the rear | .. .. .. .. .. | 11 |
| 16 | The side pace | .. .. .. .. .. .. .. | 12 |
| 17 | Wheeling | .. .. .. .. .. .. .. | 13 |
| 18 | Turnings and diagonal march in slow time | .. .. .. .. | 14 |
| 19 | Turnings and diagonal march in quick time | .. .. .. | 16 |
| 20 | Marking time, forward and halt—slow and quick time | .. .. | 18 |
| 21 | Changing step in slow and quick time | .. .. .. .. | 19 |
| 22 | Marching, marking time, and halting in double time | .. .. | 20 |
| 23 | Breaking into slow, quick and double time .. | .. .. .. | 21 |

### CHAPTER III—MARCHING IN LINE AND CHANGING DIRECTION

| 24 | Marching in line in slow time | .. .. .. .. .. | 23 |
|---|---|---|---|
| 25 | Taking open and close order | .. .. .. .. .. | 23 |
| 26 | Changing direction by forming, at the halt and on the march, in slow time | .. .. .. .. .. .. .. .. | 23 |
| 27 | Wheeling in line in slow time | .. .. .. .. .. | 24 |
| 28 | Marching in line and changing direction in quick time | .. .. | 24 |

### CHAPTER IV—FORMING SQUAD

| 29 | Forming squad from the halt in slow time .. | .. .. .. | 25 |
|---|---|---|---|
| 30 | Forming squad on the march in slow time .. | .. .. .. | 25 |
| 31 | Forming squad in quick time .. | .. .. .. .. .. | 26 |

### CHAPTER V—FORMING TWO RANKS

| 32 | To form two ranks from three ranks | .. .. .. .. | 26 |
|---|---|---|---|
| 33 | To form three ranks from two ranks | .. .. .. .. | 27 |

CONTENTS—*Continued*

*Section*                                                                 *Page*

CHAPTER  VI—MARCHING  OFF  IN  SINGLE  FILE

34  A squad facing a flank in threes marching off in single file    ..    27
35  A squad in line marching off in single file  ..    ..    ..    ..    28


CHAPTER  VII—COMPLIMENTS

36  Saluting at the halt    ..    ..    ..    ..    ..    ..    ..    30
37  Saluting on the march    ..    ..    ..    ..    ..    ..    31
38  Saluting  when  without  head-dress,  and  when  wearing  plain
      clothes, etc   ..    ..    ..    ..    ..    ..    ..    ..    33
39  Saluting with arms    ..    ..    ..    ..    ..    ..    ..    34
40  Saluting with the whip or cane    ..    ..    ..    ..    ..    34
41  Miscellaneous   ..    ..    ..    ..    ..    ..    ..    ..    35
42  Eyes right and left    ..    ..    ..    ..    ..    ..    ..    38
43  Compliments to the Colours ..    ..    ..    ..    ..    ..    38


CHAPTER  VIII—DRILL  WITH  THE  WHIP  OR  CANE

44  Attention    ..    ..    ..    ..    ..    ..    ..    ..    39
45  Stand at ease    ..    ..    ..    ..    ..    ..    ..    ..    39
46  Marching    ..    ..    ..    ..    ..    ..    ..    ..    39
47  Halting ..    ..    ..    ..    ..    ..    ..    ..    ..    40
48  Turning about ..    ..    ..    ..    ..    ..    ..    ..    40
49  Dismissing    ..    ..    ..    ..    ..    ..    ..    ..    40


CHAPTER  IX—RIFLE  EXERCISES  AT  THE  HALT
(LESS  SALUTING)

50  Attention    ..    ..    ..    ..    ..    ..    ..    ..    41
51  Getting on parade with rifles.   The short trail    ..    ..    ..    41
52  Stand at ease and Stand easy    ..    ..    ..    ..    ..    42
53  Slope from the order, Order from the slope    ..    ..    ..    42
54  Dressing at the order and the slope ..    ..    ..    ..    ..    45
55  Present from the slope, Slope from the present    ..    ..    ..    45
56  Ground arms, Take up arms    ..    ..    ..    ..    ..    46
57  Fix bayonets, Unfix bayonets    ..    ..    ..    ..    ..    47
58  Port from the order, Order from the port    ..    ..    ..    ..    49
59  Port from the slope, Slope from the port    ..    ..    ..    ..    50
60  For inspection port arms, Ease springs    ..    ..    ..    ..    50
61  Examine from the port, Ease springs; Port from the examine,
      Order from the examine    ..    ..    ..    ..    ..    ..    51
62  Trail from the order, Order from the trail ..    ..    ..    ..    53
63  Trail from the slope, Slope from the trail   ..    ..    ..    ..    53
64  Secure from the slope, Slope from the secure    ..    ..    ..    54
65  Secure from the order, Order from the secure    ..    ..    ..    54
66  Change arms at the slope    ..    ..    ..    ..    ..    ..    55
67  Change arms at the trail    ..    ..    ..    ..    ..    ..    56
68  Change arms at the secure    ..    ..    ..    ..    ..    ..    56
69  On guard from the slope, Slope from the on guard    ..    ..    57
70  On guard from the order, Order from the on guard    ..    ..    58
71  The cant from the order, The order from the cant..    ..    ..    59
72  The cant from the slope, The slope from the cant ..    ..    ..    59

CONTENTS—*Continued*

*Section*                                                                                          *Page*
73  The high port from the on guard ,from the slope, and from the
       order  ..  ..  ..  ..  ..  ..  ..  ..  ..  60
74  Recover from the slope, Slope from the recover  ..  ..  ..  61
75  Order from the recover, Recover from the order ..  ..  ..  61
76  Shoulder from the order, Order from the shoulder  ..  ..  62

CHAPTER X—RIFLE EXERCISES ON THE MARCH

77  Changing arms  ..  ..  ..  ..  ..  ..  ..  63
78  March at ease, March to attention—without slinging  ..  ..  63
79  March at ease—sling arms  ..  ..  ..  ..  ..  63
80  Double time—Cant and High Port ..  ..  ..  ..  ..  63

CHAPTER XI—FUNERAL EXERCISES WITH THE
                              RIFLE

81  Reverse arms from the present  ..  ..  ..  ..  ..  64
82  Change arms from the reverse  ..  ..  ..  ..  ..  64
83  Trail arms from the reverse ..  ..  ..  ..  ..  ..  65
84  Change arms from the trail ..  ..  ..  ..  ..  ..  65
85  Reverse arms from the trail ..  ..  ..  ..  ..  ..  65
86  Rest on your arms reversed from the reverse  ..  ..  ..  66
87  Attention from rest on your arms reversed  ..  ..  ..  66
88  Reverse arms from rest on your arms reversed  ..  ..  ..  66
89  Present arms from rest on your arms reversed and vice-versa  ..  67
90  Funeral exercises—simplified version  ..  ..  ..  ..  67

CHAPTER XII—PISTOL DRILL

91  For inspection draw pistols ..  ..  ..  ..  ..  ..  68
92  Examine pistols  ..  ..  ..  ..  ..  ..  ..  69
93  Return pistols after inspection  ..  ..  ..  ..  ..  70
94  Prove pistols  ..  ..  ..  ..  ..  ..  ..  ..  70

CHAPTER XIII—SENTRY DRILL

95  Single sentry paying compliments on his post  ..  ..  ..  71
96  Single sentry standing at ease  ..  ..  ..  ..  ..  72
97  Single sentry patrolling and paying compliments on his beat  ..  72
98  Double sentries paying compliments on their post  ..  ..  73
99  Double sentries patrolling  ..  ..  ..  ..  ..  ..  74
100  Double sentries paying compliments on their beat  ..  ..  74

CHAPTER XIV—GUARDS AND SENTRIES

101  General  ..  ..  ..  ..  ..  ..  ..  ..  75
102  Guard mounting  ..  ..  ..  ..  ..  ..  ..  75
103  Relieving, posting and dismissing a guard ..  ..  ..  ..  76
104  Guards turning out and turning in ..  ..  ..  ..  ..  77
105  Posting, relieving, marching and dismissing sentries and reliefs  ..  78
106  Challenging  ..  ..  ..  ..  ..  ..  ..  ..  79

CHAPTER XV—PLATOON DRILL

107  Formations and positions  ..  ..  ..  ..  ..  ..  82
108  Dressing  ..  ..  ..  ..  ..  ..  ..  ..  84

CONTENTS—*Continued*

*Section*                                                                                          *Page*

## CHAPTER XVI—COMPANY DRILL

109  Formations and positions of officers, warrant officer and platoon
    sergeants   ..   ..   ..   ..   ..   ..   ..   ..    84
110  Dressing   ..   ..   ..   ..   ..   ..    87
111  Forming up in close column of platoons, with and without the
    drum ..   ..   ..   ..   ..   ..   ..    89
112  Falling in and falling out the officers   ..   ..   ..    90
113  Close column of platoons forming column of threes   ..    91
114  Column of threes forming close column of platoons at the halt
    facing a flank   ..   ..   ..   ..   ..    92
115  Close column of platoons forming column   ..   ..    92
116  Column of platoons forming close column   ..   ..    93
117  Close column moving to a flank in threes ..   ..   ..    93
118  Column of platoons forming line facing a flank ..   ..    93
119  Line forming column facing a flank   ..   ..    94
120  Column of threes forming column facing a flank   ..    94
121  Column of platoons forming column of threes   ..   ..    94
122  Column of platoons forming line facing the same direction   ..    94
123  Line forming column facing the same direction ..   ..    95
124  Column of platoons, moving to a flank, forming column of threes
    by wheeling ..   ..   ..   ..   ..   ..   ..    95
125  Column of threes forming column of platoons, moving to a flank,
    by wheeling ..   ..   ..   ..   ..   ..    95
126  Column of threes forming column of platoons facing the same
    direction   ..   ..   ..   ..   ..   ..    95
127  Column of threes forming close column of platoons facing the
    same direction   ..   ..   ..   ..   ..    95
128  Column of platoons changing direction by forming   ..   ..    96
129  Close column of platoons on the march, forming line facing a flank    96
130  Close column of platoons, halted, forming line facing the same
    direction   ..   ..   ..   ..   ..   ..   ..    96

## CHAPTER XVII—BATTALION DRILL

131  Formations, positions of officers, warrant officers and platoon
    sergeants   ..   ..   ..   ..   ..   ..   ..    97
132  Dressing   ..   ..   ..   ..   ..   ..    101
133  Moving off in column of threes (route) from mass   ..   ..    101
134  Forming mass from column of threes (route)   ..   ..    102
135  Moving off in column of threes (route) from close column of
    companies   ..   ..   ..   ..   ..   ..    102
136  Forming close column of companies from column of threes (route)    102

## CHAPTER XVIII—DRILL FOR LIGHT INFANTRY
### REGIMENTS

137  General..   ..   ..   ..   ..   ..   ..   ..   ..    103
138  Squad drill   ..   ..   ..   ..   ..   ..   ..   ..    103
139  Rifle drill   ..   ..   ..   ..   ..   ..   ..    104
140  Saluting with the rifle..   ..   ..   ..   ..   ..    105
141  Sentries   ..   ..   ..   ..   ..   ..   ..    105

CONTENTS—*Continued*

*Section*                                                                  *Page*

### CHAPTER XIX—DRILL FOR RIFLE REGIMENTS

142 Squad drill         .. .. .. .. .. .. .. .. 106
143 Rifle drill         .. .. .. .. .. .. .. .. 107
144 Squad drill with arms    .. .. .. .. .. .. 110
145 Saluting with the rifle.. .. .. .. .. .. .. 111

### CHAPTER XX—INSTRUCTOR'S INFORMATION

146 Bearing of the instructors   .. .. .. .. .. .. 112
147 How to get the maximum out of a squad .. .. .. .. 113
148 Correction of faults  .. .. .. .. .. .. .. 113
149 Sequence of instruction   .. .. .. .. .. .. 113
150 Words of command    .. .. .. .. .. .. 114
151 Timing of words of command  .. .. .. .. .. 115
152 Communication drill and mutual drill .. .. .. .. 117
153 Calling out the time .. .. .. .. .. .. .. 117
154 Time and pace.. .. .. .. .. .. .. .. 118
155 Mechanical aids to drill  .. .. .. .. .. .. 118

## APPENDICES

A Notes on inspection  .. .. .. .. .. .. .. 112
B Sword drill    .. .. .. .. .. .. .. .. 124
C Funeral exercises with the pistol .. .. .. .. .. 132
D Specimen drill programmes .. .. .. .. .. .. 133

## LIST OF PLATES

*Plate*
1   Position of attention, without rifle .. .. .. .. .. 141
2   Stand at ease .. .. .. .. .. .. .. .. 142
3   Quick march, without rifle .. .. .. .. .. .. 143
4   Slow march, with rifle  .. .. .. .. .. .. 144
5   Saluting to the front .. .. .. .. .. .. .. 145
6   Position of attention, with rifle, bayonet fixed .. .. .. 146
7   Slope arms—first position  .. .. .. .. .. .. 147
8(*a*) Slope arms—second position   .. .. .. .. .. 148
  (*b*) Slope arms—third position  .. .. .. .. .. 148
9(*a*) Order arms—first position  .. .. .. .. .. 149
  (*b*) Order arms—second position  .. .. .. .. .. 149
10(*a*) Present arms—second position  .. .. .. .. .. 150
  (*b*) Present arms—third position  .. .. .. .. .. 150
11  Fix bayonets—first position .. .. .. .. .. .. 151
12  Fix bayonets—second position  .. .. .. .. .. 152
13(*a*) Unfix bayonets—first position  .. .. .. .. .. 153
  (*b*) Unfix bayonets—second position  .. .. .. .. 153
14(*a*) Sword drill—the carry  .. .. .. .. .. .. 154
  (*b*) Sword drill—position of the right hand  .. .. .. 154
15(*a*) Sword drill—the recover  .. .. .. .. .. .. 155
  (*b*) Sword drill—the salute  .. .. .. .. .. .. 155

# DEFINITIONS

**Alignment**—Any straight line on which a body of troops is formed or is to form.

**Column**—Bodies of troops one behind the other on parallel and successive alignments, at such a distance from one another as when formed to an angle of 90 degrees to either flank, will bring them into line with three paces interval between each.

**Close column**—A column with distance reduced to suit requirements.

**Column of route**—A column of threes with not more than three men abreast in any part of the column, including officers and supernumeraries. The normal formation for troops marching closed up on a road.

**Column of Threes**—A column with its officers and supernumeraries maintaining their places except for the officer in command who places himself at the head of the unit or sub-unit.

**Covering**—The act of a body placing itself directly in rear of another.

**Depth**—The space occupied by a body of troops from front to rear.

**Directing body**—The body, unit or subordinate unit on which the direction, pace and alignment or relative positions of the several parts of a formation depend.

**Distance**—The space between men or bodies of troops from front to rear.

**Dressing**—The act of taking up an alignment correctly.

**File**—A front rank man and his coverer or coverers.

**Blank file**—A file without a centre and rear rank man, or without a centre rank man. A blank file is the second file from the left.

**Flank**—Either side of a body of troops, as opposed to its front or rear.

**Directing flank**—That by which units march or dress.

**Inner flank**—That nearer the directing flank and serving as a pivot when a body is changing its direction.

**Outer flank**—That opposite to the inner or directing flank (often known as reverse flank).

**Forming**—A method of changing direction as opposed to wheeling.

**Front**—The direction in which troops are facing or moving at any given time.

**Frontage**—The extent of ground covered laterally by a body of troops.

**Incline**—A diagonal movement by which ground is gained to the front and flank simultaneously without alteration of the original alignment.

**Interval**—The lateral space between men or bodies of troops on the same alignment measured from flank to flank. Between dismounted troops intervals are measured from elbow to elbow. Each dismounted man is allotted a lateral space of 24 inches in two ranks ; in three ranks this lateral space is at arm's length with fist clenched.

**Line**—Troops formed on the same alignment.

**Markers**—Personnel employed, in certain circumstances, to mark points on which to direct a movement or by which to regulate a formation or alignment.

**Mass**—A battalion with its companies in line of close column of platoons, with 5 paces of interval between companies.

**Open order**—An increased distance between ranks for ceremonial or inspection purposes.

**Close order**—The normal distance between ranks in line.

**Pace**—A measurement of distance on foot, (*eg*, 30 inches (or 27 inches in the case of WRAC)) also rate of movement.

**Rank**—A line of men, side by side.

**Single file**—Men one behind the other on a frontage of one man at normal marching distance.

**Supernumeraries**—The NCOs etc, forming the third rank if in file, or the fourth rank if in threes.

**Wheeling**—A movement by which a body of troops changes direction, each rank or file pivoting on the inner flank but retaining its dressing.

# DRILL (ALL ARMS)

## INTRODUCTION

The object of drill is to develop in the individual soldier that sense of instinctive obedience which will assist him at all times to carry out his orders. That the foundation of discipline in battle is based on drill has been proved again and again.

Good drill, well rehearsed, closely supervised, and demanding the highest precision is an exercise in obedience and alertness. It sets the standard for the execution of any duty, both for the individual and the unit, and builds up that sense of confidence between commander and subordinate which is so essential to morale.

Good drill and a high standard are not learnt on the barrack square merely to be discarded in everyday life except for ceremonial occasions. It is the constant duty of those in command to insist on the standard they know to be right both on and off parade and in all circumstances. Once an idle action or bad turnout is allowed to pass, whether during the recruit stage or later, the standard is lowered and further bad habits will follow.

This manual is published for the information of all ranks of all arms of the Service, with special reference to drill instructors. It is laid out in chapters dealing with each phase of instruction, each chapter being in a logical sequence which has proved suitable in practice. Each phase is broken down into individual movements and the common faults are indicated. The detail is normally given for movement to the RIGHT only. Some notes for instructors are given in Chapter XX.

# Why are we waiting?

Jean sighed—"Men are funny —soldiers most of all!"

"You expect *me* to look smart all the time, but if I spent as long as *you* do on *my* shoes you'd soon grumble. Yet I'll match mine with yours any day."

Trust a woman to find the easy way—the WREN'S way— Jean's shoes were d-a-z-z-l-i-n-g!

### JEAN WAS RIGHT !

WREN'S *does* give the *brightest* possible shine with the *least* possible work.

Not only that—Bill also found that WREN'S stays fresh in the tin *and it is* *much more economical*.

In Black, Light Brown and Dark Tan Stain.

CHAPTER I

# SQUAD DRILL AT THE HALT—WITHOUT ARMS

Throughout this manual two distinct movements of the foot are referred to constantly. These are :—

(a) " *Bend the . . . knee* "—used when the body has to remain still or come to rest ; and

(b) " *Shoot the . . . foot forward* "—used to move the body forward from rest.

They are the basic movements of foot drill.

*To bend the . . . knee*—the leg that is on the ground is kept braced back with the foot firm and flat on the ground. The opposite knee is bent by raising it in front of the body so that the toe hangs directly below the knee and the foot is at a natural angle at least six inches from the ground. The leg is then straightened sharply so that when the foot reaches the ground the knee is braced back and the flat of the foot is firmly on the ground and in the required position.

*To shoot the . . . foot forward*—the opposite leg is braced back but allowed to flex at the ankle and toe while the detailed foot is shot forward with knee braced and ready to carry the weight of the body forward on to that foot.

In all movements of foot drill the following must be avoided :—

Scraping the foot on the ground.

Rising on the toes and clicking the heels.

Hopping or leaving the ground with both feet at once.

It is important that these movements (and faults) are demonstrated at the start and impressed on all recruits so that movements taught later are correctly done.

## SECTION 1 : **ATTENTION**

" Squad—attention " (pronounced *Shun*).

Move sharply to this position : Heels together and in line ; feet turned out to an angle of 30 degrees ; knees braced ; body erect and with the weight balanced evenly between the ball of the feet and the heels ; shoulders down and back (so as to bring the chest to a normal position without straining or stiffening), level, and square to the front ; arms hanging straight from the shoulders, elbows close to the sides, wrists straight, hands closed (not clenched), backs of the fingers close to the thighs, thumbs straight and to the front, close to the forefinger and just behind the seam of the trousers ; head up, neck feeling the collar, eyes open, steady and looking their own height.

*Common faults* :—

    (i) A strained and exaggerated position, causing breathing to be restricted.

   (ii) Unsteadiness and movement of the eyes.

  (iii) Feet and body not square to the front, heels not closed.

  (iv) Arms slightly bent and creeping forward.

   (v) Backs of the hands to the front, thereby opening the shoulder blades and constricting the chest.

  (vi) Wrists crooked and strained, knuckle of the forefinger projecting below the other fingers.

## SECTION 2 : STAND AT EASE

" Stand at—ease ".

Keeping the right foot still and leg braced back, " *bend the left knee* " and carry the left foot to the left so that the feet are about 12 inches apart ; at the same time force the arms by the nearest way behind the back, keeping them straight, and place the back of the right hand in the palm of the left, thumbs crossed, fingers and hands straight and pointing towards the ground ; at the same time transfer the weight of the body slightly to the left, so as to be evenly balanced.

*Common faults* :—

    (i) Failure to carry the foot off 12 inches and not square to the left.

  (ii) Bending the arms when bending the knee.

 (iii) Movement of the right foot with consequent loss of dressing.

 (iv) Bending at the waist when picking the foot up.

*Note.*—When a large pack is worn on the back and no rifle is carried the arms are kept to the side.

## SECTION 3 : STAND EASY

" Stand—easy ".

Relax the limbs, body and head.

*Common faults* :—

  (i) Moving the feet, thereby losing dressing.

 (ii) Slouching and talking.

*Notes.*—(i) Except on ceremonial parades, a handkerchief may be used and clothing adjusted on the instructor's orders.

     (ii) On the word of command " Squad " the position of *Stand at ease* will be resumed. This is the only executive word of command that has no cautionary word before it.

## SECTION 4 : FORMING UP IN THREE RANKS

" Form up in three ranks—move ".

The men position themselves in three ranks (front, centre, and rear), with 30 inches between ranks, and an interval of one arm's length (with fist clenched) between each man. The men stand at ease.

*Note.*—The above word of command is sufficient for the initial lesson. Section 8 must, however, be taught early during the instruction.

## SECTION 5 : DRESSING

Dressing includes not only being in line by the right or left but also being correctly covered off from front to rear, at the correct distance from the rank in front and at the correct interval from the man on the right or left.

Whenever a squad or unit halts in line, dressing will be taken up by word of command.

When a squad or unit gets on parade, dressing will be taken up automatically, *ie*, with no word of command.

To take up dressing by word of command :—

1. " Right—dress ". The squad, except the right-hand man, " *shoot the left foot forward* " 15 inches and " *bend the right knee* " to bring the right foot in to the left as for the position of attention, arms to the sides ; count a regulation pause (40 movements to the minute), turn head and eyes to the right (except the right-hand man of each rank) ; at the same time men in the front rank only extend the right arm, fist clenched, back of the hand uppermost, so that the knuckles touch the shoulder seam of the man on the right ; count a regulation pause ; each individual then dresses by taking short, quick steps until he can just see the lower part of the face of the man two away from him. The right-hand man of the centre and rear rank places himself 30 inches from the rank in front, each individual of these ranks covering off correctly by glancing out of the corner of his eye.

2. " Eyes—front ". Turn the head and eyes smartly to the front, and cut away the hands to the side, keeping the arms straight.

*Notes.*—(i) If this movement is carried out with rifles at the *Order*, the left arm will be raised, and the head and eyes turned to the right.

(ii) Trained soldiers are not required to raise the arm when dressing.

*Common faults* :—

(i) Jumping forward with both feet off the ground at once.

(ii) Feet and shoulders not held square to the front ; leaning forward when taking up the dressing.

(iii) Bending at the waist when moving the feet.

(iv) Incorrect distance, interval, and covering off.

## To take up dressing automatically

3. As above except that no short pace forward is taken, each soldier working independently.

When the squad has got its dressing, head and eyes are turned to the front (and hands cut away) in succession from the right, ranks in rear taking the time from the front rank.

## SECTION 6 : NUMBERING AND PROVING

### Numbering

1. In the early stages of training the instructor, who will not know the names of all men in his squad, may wish to speak to an individual as "*Number* —— of the —— rank". The squad will, therefore, always be numbered off.

2. " Squad—Number ".—The front rank only of the squad will number off sharply from right to left, the right-hand man calling out " *One* ", the next " *Two* ", and so on. Each man will keep his head and eyes steady to the front. Men in the centre and rear ranks take the number of the front rank man whom they are covering.

*Note.*—If an error is made in the numbering, the instructor will give AS YOU *WERE* and call out the last correct number. The soldier so named will call out his number again and the front rank will take up the numbering from him.

### Proving

3. The instructor may require to divide his squad into two parts. To do so he will select the left-hand man of the right half squad, call out his number, and explain what he is.

4. " **Number twelve** ". The man so indicated raises his left forearm parallel to the ground, keeping the left elbow still, palm of the hand to the right, fingers extended and close together.

*Note.*—If more than one part or division is required the instructor would order " **Numbers six, twelve and eighteen** " (etc), the men so indicated acting as above.

5. " **Left of the right half—squad** " (or " **Left of—divisions** "). On the executive word of command, *eg*, *Squad* or *Divisions*, the men who " proved " will cut their hands away to the side.

*Common faults* :—

    (i) Wrong numbering.

    (ii) Movement of the head and eyes.

    (iii) Failure to know the drill for proving.

## SECTION 7 : OPEN AND CLOSE ORDER MARCH

1. To inspect the squad and for squad drill, it is necessary for the squad to take " *Open Order*," *ie*, the front rank takes one and a half paces forward, the rear rank one and a half paces to the rear, and the centre rank stands fast.

2. " **Open order—march** ". The front rank " *shoot the left foot forward* " a full pace, and then " *shoot the right foot forward* " a short pace of 15 inches and " *bend the left knee* " to bring the two feet together ; arms to the side throughout.
The rear rank conforms to the rear.

*Common faults :—*

    (i) Failure to take a full pace to the front and, more particularly, to the rear.

    (ii) Arms not still to the side ; shoulders swinging.

    (iii) Eyes glancing towards the ground.

3. " **Close order—march** ". The reverse of the above takes place.

*Note.*—It is normal for " **Right dress** " to be given immediately after taking Open or Close order. It is not necessary to give right dress in Close Order immediately before taking Open Order, *eg*, when getting on parade or forming two deep for a guard of honour.

## SECTION 8 : GETTING ON PARADE

1. The squad form up in three ranks, and stand easy, on the edge of the parade ground, facing in the direction they will be when on parade. The right guide or right-hand man of the front rank acts as right marker.

2. " **Right—marker** ". On the command " **Right** " come properly to ease. On the command " **Marker** " the right marker comes to attention, marches in quick time 15 paces straight to his front (a lesser distance if there is not enough space), halts, and stands at ease.

3. " **Get on—parade** ". Marker and squad come to attention. The squad march forward straight to their front, halt on the 15th pace, dress automatically, look to the front and stand at ease in succession from the right.

*Note.*—A regulation pause will be made between each movement.

## SECTION 9 : TURNING AND INCLINING

1. " **Turnings by numbers : right turn—one** ". Keeping both knees straight, turn through 90 degrees to the right, on the right heel and left toe, raising the right toe and left heel in doing so, and keeping

the weight of the body on the right foot. On completion of this movement the right foot is flat on the ground, the left leg to the rear with heel raised, both knees braced back, and the body in the position of attention.

" Squad—**two** ". Bring the left foot in to the right by " *bending the knee* ".

*Notes.*—(i) The cautionary " *Turning by numbers* " should *not* be repeated for each turn done in succession by numbers.

(ii) In all turns the weight of the body must be kept on the forward foot.

2. " **About turn—one** ". As above but turn through 180 degrees, bracing the legs and maintaining the balance by locking the thighs together.

" Squad—**two** ". As above.

*Note.*—The about turn is always made right about.

3. " **Inclining by numbers : right incline—one** ". As above but turn through 45 degrees.

" Squad—**two** ". As above.

*Note.*—Point out at once the different aspect of dressing and covering. Each man's right shoulder must be in the centre of the next man's back, and in the case of centre and rear ranks the left shoulder must point to the centre of the back of the man originally covered off.

4. " **Turnings judging the time, right—turn** ". The squad carry out both movements of all turns, judging a regulation pause between each.

*Note.*—When ordering turnings at the halt, judging the time, the instructor's word of command " **Right—turn** " will be prefixed by " **Squad will move to the right** " (or " **left** " ) as the case may be and the cautionary words " **Squad will advance** " (or " **Retire** ") will be given whenever the squad is turning into line. When the squad turns to a flank, the cautionary indicates the direction in which the squad is to turn.

*Common faults* :—

(i) The weight being put on the rear foot ; allowing the heel of the forward foot to move over the ground instead of simply pivoting.

(ii) Moving the arms, particularly when bringing in the rear foot.

(iii) Bending at the waist when bringing in the foot.

(iv) Not making a square turn with the body and shoulder in the first motion.

## SECTION 10 : **DISMISSING AND FALLING OUT**

1. At the end of the first parade the squad must be taught how to dismiss.

" Dis—miss ". The squad, which will be in close order, turn to the right, salute, pause and then step off. After stepping off, the whole squad march straight forward for three paces and then break off gradually and carry on independently. (When marching independently they must keep the step until clear of the parade ground.)

*Notes.*— (i) If rifles are carried the butt salute will be given (*See* Sec. 39).

   (ii) If dismissing with the cane the cane must be placed under the arm before saluting (*See* Sec. 40). Those without canes will wait for those with canes.

   (iii) If no officer is present, similar movements will be carried out except that no salute will be given.

*Common faults :*—There is a tendency to regard the dismiss as the " last of a bad business ". This is the wrong attitude and will be checked at once. The dismiss is a compliment to the senior rank on parade and will be made as such. Squad instructors and commanders will at all times watch for a good turn and check the salute whether after a drill or any other parade.

2. Falling out differs from the dismiss in that it does not signify the end of the parade but only a break in it. The salute is not given. Troops fallen out will not leave the immediate vicinity of their place of parade or line of march.

" Fall—out ". The squad turn to their right and break off in quick time (or in double time if so ordered), counting a regulation pause between each movement.

*Note.*—The command " Fall—out " may be used in conjunction with open instructions, *eg*, " **Rifles against the wall and fall in again at the double, Fall out** ".

## SECTION 11 : **SIZING**

1. A well-sized squad, company or guard give much the best general impression to a spectator, and to the men the best chance to drill together. A recruit squad should therefore be sized at an early date.

2. Sizing can be either " *tallest on the right, shortest on the left* " or " *shortest in the centre* ". It can be done carefully by forming everyone into single rank and grading them for size or it can be done " *by inspection* " in threes or however many ranks are required, but this latter way should be confined to a small party such as a barrack guard.

3. " **Tallest on the right, shortest on the left, in single rank—size** ". The whole squad turn to their right, count a pause and then sort themselves out by size, remaining at attention. The exact grade is then checked by the instructor.

4. " **Squad—number** ". The squad number off from right to left.

5. " **Odd numbers one pace forward, even numbers one pace step back—march** ". The instructor must check this movement.

6. " **Stand fast the right-hand man, odd numbers to the right, even numbers to the left, ranks right and left—turn** ". All turn as ordered except the right-hand man, who remains facing his front.

7. " **Form three ranks. Quick—march** ". The squad forms three ranks, as laid down in Section 34, even numbers following on behind the odd numbers, *ie*, Number 1 remains Number 1 of the front rank, Number 3 becomes Number 1 of the centre rank, Number 5 becomes Number 1 of the rear rank, Number 7 becomes Number 2 of the front rank, and so on. On halting in position, each man turns to his front, takes up his own dressing, and remains at attention.

*Notes.*— (i) If it is required to size the squad finally with the tallest on the right and the shortest on the left, the word of command will be " **Stand fast the right-hand man, remainder right—turn** ". " **Form three ranks ; quick—march** ". The squad act as above.

(ii) If a small squad is to be sized, the word of command is " **In three (or single, etc) ranks—size** ". The squad turn to their right, pause and form up according to size.

CHAPTER II

# MARCHING

Marching plays its part in drill as a means to discipline; a unit marching with " style " is usually well-disciplined and of high morale. Similarly the slow march teaches balance and a good carriage, and is traditionally part of British Army ceremonial.

Although units continue to march at their traditional pace, the common pace for all arms and units when parading together is 116 paces to the minute in quick time. The recruit should, however, start marching at 140 paces to the minute, in order to inculcate agility, alertness, and an instinctive obedience to orders.

Slow time is 65 paces to the minute.

## SECTION 12 : MARCHING AND HALTING IN QUICK TIME

**The quick march**

1. The soldier will start to " march " only from the position of attention. (This applies to all occasions including " **Get on parade** " etc.) When the word of command " **Quick march** " is given so as to step off the squad in time with a band or another squad, it will be given on successive beats or paces, *ie*, " **Quick** " on the left foot, " **March** " on the right foot.

On the command " **March** " the soldier will always step off with the left foot and swinging his right arm.

2. In teaching recruits how to march, the following points will be emphasized :—

   (*a*)   The length of pace, which is 30 inches, from heel to heel.

   (*b*)   That the heel should come to the ground first and with the knee straight.

   (*c*)   That each leg must be swung forward naturally and in a straight line.

   (*d*)   That the arms must be swung freely and straight from front to rear, reaching the extremity of their swing each time the heel comes to the ground. The arms will be kept straight and swung from the shoulder, as high as the belt in front and behind (for recruits, as high in front as the breast pocket— *See* plate 3) ; wrist straight ; fingers curled up ; thumbs to the front ; shoulders still and square to the front.

3. When marching to his front, a soldier will select some mark in front and march on it. Each man in the squad is responsible for keeping his own dressing, cover, interval, distance, and correct step.

*Common faults :—*

   (i)   When marching in threes, incorrect distance between ranks.

   (ii)   When marching in line, incorrect interval between files.

   (iii)   At all times, lack of dressing, covering and style, unequal arm swinging, loss of the rhythm.

THE MAJORITY OF THESE FAULTS COME FROM STEPPING A PACE OF MORE THAN 30 INCHES. Instructors will constantly be on the alert for this and must check the pace frequently.

*Note.*—Instructors must be proficient in the use of metronome, drum and pace stick (*See* Section 155).

**The Halt**

4. " **Squad—halt** " will be given as the right foot passes the left. Check the forward movement as the right foot comes to the ground by placing the right foot flat on the ground and using the heel as a

" *brake* "; complete a short pace with the left foot, placing it flat on the ground in the same way; " *bend the right knee* " and bring the right foot in sharply to the left, to assume the position of attention. Swing the arms until the " *right knee is bent* ", then cut them away to the sides to the position of attention. The arms will be kept straight while doing this, as will the body and the left leg.

*Common faults :—*

   (i)   Bending the arms or the body.

   (ii)  Looking down.

  (iii)  Scraping the left foot on the ground.

  (iv)  Rising on the left toe instead of " *bending the right knee.* "

   (v)  Swaying about immediately after the halt.

  (vi)  Failure to " *bend the right knee* " sharply enough; this move-ment should be done in double time (count " one-two ").

## SECTION 13—MARCHING AND HALTING IN SLOW TIME

**The slow march**

1. Slow time is used to teach movements on the march before demanding them in quick time. It is taught by numbers by means of a " *balance step* " as follows :—

2. " **Slow marching by balance step. Left foot—front** ". Shoot the left foot forward 15 inches, toe turned out very slightly and point-ing towards the ground but just clear of it; upper part of the body erect; arms still to the sides; weight of the body on the right leg.

3. " **Squad—forward** ". Complete the pace of 30 inches by pushing the left foot forward another 15 inches; the toes must touch the ground first, NOT the heel nor yet the outside of the foot; bring the weight of the body on to the left leg, the right leg being to the rear and very slightly bent so as to bring the toes just clear of the ground.

4. " **Right foot—front** ". Bend the right knee further; swing the leg forward naturally before straightening and remaining 15 inches in front of the left foot, toe pointing downwards and just clear of the ground.

5. " **Squad—forward** ". Complete the pace with the right foot as detailed for the left foot, swinging the leg forward smoothly and without checking when the leg is straightened in front of the body. (Again the toe must touch the ground first and the body must be kept upright.) Arms still to the sides, elbows close in, legs swinging past the hands; shoulders still and square to the front. (At the completion of this movement the weight will be on the right foot, the left leg to the rear, toe just clear of the ground.)

This movement may be continued until the squad has got its balance, and until, instead of " **Forward** " after left foot front, the command " **Squad—halt** " is given.

### The Halt

6. Complete one full pace of 30 inches with the left foot, " *bend the right knee* "and bring the right foot in to the left in double time so as to assume the position of attention.

### " Slow—march "

7. In order to step off with a band or troops already marching in slow time, this command will be given on two following feet in time with the band or troops in front, " **Slow** " on the left foot, " **March** " on the right foot.

The movement is as described above, except there is no pause between the paces which will be taken at 65 to the minute.

*Common faults* :—

    (i) Heels touching the ground first.

    (ii) Elbows away from the sides.

    (iii) Hands gripped to the leg and therefore moving at each pace.

8. " **Squad—halt** ".—As above. The order is given just before the left foot comes to the ground.

*Common faults.*—A hop instead of completing the pace properly with the left foot and " bending the right knee " smartly and bringing the right foot in in double time.

## SECTION 14 : STEPPING OUT AND STEPPING SHORT

1. " **Step out** ".—The moving foot will complete its pace, and the soldier will lengthen the pace by three inches, leaning forward a little but without altering the time.

This step is used when a slight increase of speed, without an alteration of time, is required.

2. " **Step short** ".—The moving foot will complete its pace, after which the pace will be shortened by nine inches.

3. In both cases the normal length of pace will be resumed on the command, " Quick (or slow)—march."

## SECTION 15 : PACES FORWARD AND TO THE REAR

. . . paces forward (or " step back ")—march "

Paces forward and to the rear are always taken in quick time.

The fundamentals are as follows :—

    (*a*) The left foot must be " *shot forward* " or to the rear the required distance to get the body moving.

(b) Since the body will not be moving at full marching speed on that first pace it is possible to halt on that left foot (by " *bending the right knee* " and placing the right foot in line with the left, heels together) yet still to complete a pace of 30 inches.

(c) If more than one pace is taken, the right, and subsequently each leg in turn, is allowed to swing forward (or backward) naturally as in normal marching, stepping a full pace of 30 inches.

(d) When the body is moving at full marching speed and it is required to halt, it is natural to " *brake* " on the pace before halting as well as when the last pace is taken. Thus of necessity the last pace is a short one of 15 inches. Therefore, paces forward or to the rear can be : (i) one pace of 30 inches (or a short pace of 15 inches) ; (ii) Two or more paces the last of which must be 15 inches.

(e) The arms will be kept still to the sides, as in the position of attention, and the shoulders square to the front.

(f) The maximum number of paces that the man will be ordered to step forward or to the rear will be three.

*Note* : (i) These movements must be known before teaching " dressing " and " *open order—march* ".

(ii) A similar movement is carried out on the words of command " Right—dress ", " Open (or close) order—march ".

*Common faults :—*

(i) Hurrying the movement so that an incorrect length of pace is taken.

(ii) Bending the leg that is taking the step forward, and " hopping " with both feet off the ground.

(iii) Bending at the waist.

## SECTION 16 : THE SIDE PACE

1. The side pace (12 inches) is used to move the squad not more than eight paces to a flank—(If greater than eight paces the squad should be " *turned* " and moved in threes).

The exact number of paces, up to four, can be specified, when the squad will halt automatically; or the squad will continue moving until halted.

It is usual to teach the side pace to the left first as a direct " *follow on* " from the stand at ease.

2. " . . . . paces left close—march ".—" *Bend the left knee* " and carry the left foot off 12 inches to the left (as for the stand at ease), instantly closing the right foot to it, in a similar manner and in double time, thus completing the pace. Continue the movement until the

specified number of paces has been completed. Except for the movement of the feet the correct position of attention will be maintained.

3. " **Left close—march** ".—Number of paces being specified, continue the movement until halted.

4. " **Squad—halt** ".—The word of command will be given as the heels are together. The squad will complete one more pace and remain steady.

*Common faults* :—

(i) Uneven pace, loss of covering and dressing.

(ii) Failure to close the heels at each pace.

(iii) A tendency to " *hop* " instead of bringing the right foot in sharply as the left foot touches the ground.

## SECTION 17 : WHEELING

1. Whether marching in single file, threes, or sixes, the inner man will wheel on the circumference of a circle four feet in diameter and will change direction through 90 degrees.

The speed of the wheel is governed by the ability of the outside man to keep pace by stepping out. The man on the inner flank will glance outwards from the corner of his eye and will shorten his pace accordingly.

2. Files in rear will march straight to their front and will follow on the ground covered by the leading files. If the squad is halted or ordered to mark time when only a part of the men have wheeled into a new direction, the men who have not yet wheeled will cover off on those who have, moving to their places by the shortest route.

3. " **Right—wheel** ".—(There will be no cautionary " *Change direction* " or " *squad* ".)

If it is desired to wheel less than through a right angle, the word of command " **Forward** " will be given when the leading section is facing the required direction. They will then lead straight on.

If it is desired to wheel through more than a right angle, the word " **Right—wheel** " will be given a second time.

4. It is not a practical proposition to wheel more than six men in line, unless the wheel is a gradual one, *eg*, in a ceremonial procession through streets. With more than six men in line, a change of direction will be carried out by forming.

*Common faults* :—

(i) A tendency for the files in rear to swing out and away from the wheeling point.

(ii) Failure of the inner men to bring round each section.

(iii) Loss of distance due to the outer men not stepping out.

## SECTION 18 : **TURNINGS AND DIAGONAL MARCH IN SLOW TIME**

1. Turnings on the march are first taught in slow time. They are taught by numbers and by means of a balance step.

2. Throughout all turnings on the march, the correct position of marching must be maintained, the turn must be made squarely to the new direction and covering, dressing, distance, and interval must be corrected by each individual member of the squad immediately after turning.

3. When a band is playing or on ceremonial parades, the turns will be made so that the step is retained. In squad drill, the turn will be made as sharply as possible.

4. Turnings and inclines on the march comprise two movements ; action to check the forward movement and at the same time to change direction ; and a new movement to lead off in the new direction. Since most men are " *right-footed* " it is best to teach the left turn first.

5. " **Turning by numbers** ". " **Left turn—one** " (given as the right foot passes the left). " *Bend the right knee* " and remain balanced on the left foot with the " *right knee bent* " ; the upper part of the leg horizontal, foot hanging at a natural angle, toe pointing towards the ground, and vertically below the point of the knee ; the body and arms in the position of attention.

6. " **Squad—two** ". Keep the body in the position of attention, straighten the right knee sharply, keep the head up and chest raised ; force the shoulders square round (through 90 degrees) to the new direction, and at the same time turn the left foot through 90 degrees, bring the right foot in to the left to the position of attention.

7. " **Squad—three** ". Shoot the left foot forward, toe clear of the ground, as in slow marching by numbers.

" **Squad—forward** ". Complete the pace with the left foot and continue the slow march.

*Note.*—Turning by numbers is used to teach recruits initially and to check elementary faults in trained soldiers.

8. " **Balance step, left—turn** ". Given as the right foot passes the left. " *Bend the right knee* " and, as the right foot is placed on the ground, turn the body to the left, retaining the position of attention. At the same time " *shoot the left foot forward* " fifteen inches, toe just clear of the ground and pointing in the new direction ; remain in this position, with both legs well braced.

9. " **Forward** ". Complete the pace with the left foot and continue the slow march.

*Note.*—Turnings by balance step are used to smarten up the squad drill of trained soldiers and to teach balance and control.

*Common faults* :—

    (i) Not making a full and square turn with head and shoulders.

    (ii) Not checking the forward movement by "*bending the right knee*".

    (iii) Allowing the hands and arms to swing away from the position of attention.

    (iv) Not "*shooting the left foot forward*" so as to gain momentum in the new direction.

## Turnings

10. "**The squad will turn to the left, left—turn** ". Judging the time, the same action takes place but retaining the time of the marching.

11. "**Turning about by numbers** ". "**About turn—one** " (given just before the right foot touches the ground).

On the command " **One** " turn 90 degrees keeping the weight of the body on the right foot ; at the same time "*bend the left knee* " and bring the left foot into the right position of attention facing the new direction.

*Note.*—The "*bending of the knee* " must be done in quick time as this is what checks the forward movement and gives the power for the turn into the new direction. The squad should count out the time "*One stop* ". The movement is made sharply on the count of one followed by a pause.

12. "**Squad—two** ". Make a further turn through 90 degrees by "*bending the right knee* " and with the weight of the body on the left foot.

*Note.*—The squad count "*Two stop* ".

13. "**Squad—three** ". Mark time with the left foot.

*Note.*—The squad count "*Three stop* ".

14. "**Squad—four** ". The squad lead on in slow time with the right foot. Judging the time, the command TURN is given just before the right foot comes to the ground. The squad act as by numbers but in the marching time of 65 to the minute.

*Note.*—In case of a squad with a blank file, marching in line, the blank file will mark time two paces on the word " **About** ", thus gaining the position in the new front rank before the turn is completed. Guides should act in a similar manner. (This applies equally to a blank file or guide marching in quick time.)

*Common faults* :—

    (i) Not making a square turn with head, shoulders, body and feet.

    (ii) Moving the arms.

(iii) Turning at a pace quicker than 65 to the minute.
(iv) Failure to pick the knees up so that the upper part of the leg is horizontal.
(v) Allowing the foot to come up under the seat instead of with the toe vertically under the point of the knee.
(vi) Creeping forward during the second and third movements.

15. " **Diagonal march. Left in—cline** " (given as for left turn).
Diagonal march will be taught in the same way as turnings but emphasis will be laid on the covering and dressing.

16. When all these turnings have been taught and practised, instructors will explain to the squad the use of the cautionary words of command for turnings. These should be related to the position of the right hand man and the two basic formations of line and threes.

" Squad will advance "
" Squad will retire "  } Used whenever turning into line.

" Squad will move to the right (left) in threes ". Used to indicate the direction in which the squad will turn.

Examples :—
(a) *A squad moving to the right in threes :—*
(i) Required to turn to the left—" Squad will advance ".
(ii) Required to turn about—" Squad will move to the left in threes ".
(iii) Required to incline to the left—" Diagonal march ".

(b) *A squad retiring :—*
(i) Required to turn left—" Squad will move to the left ".
(ii) Required to turn right—" Squad will move to the right ".
(iii) Required to turn about—" Squad will advance ".

## SECTION 19 : TURNINGS AND DIAGONAL MARCH IN QUICK TIME

1. Before teaching turnings in quick time, the instructor must demonstrate again in slow time how the position of attention is maintained, the lift required to show this off, and how a turn is made square to the new direction. Thereafter he must demonstrate these points in quick time.
Turnings in quick time are first taught by numbers, the first movements in each case being the " check pace " required to stop forward movement preparatory to changing direction.

2. " Turnings by numbers ". " **Left turn—one** " (given as the left foot passes the right).

The soldier will " freeze " with the left foot forward, flat on the ground, and being used as a brake; the right foot 30 inches to the rear, heel raised; both legs braced, body balanced evenly between them; right arm swung forward, left arm swung back.

*Note.*—This movement, apart from teaching control and balance is a useful check on the position in marching.

3. " Squad—two ". Cut both arms to the side and at the same time " *bend the right knee* ", remaining raised with the toe at least six inches clear of the ground and under the point of the knee.

4. " Squad—three ". Straighten the right knee so as to force the body round into the new direction. As the foot comes to the ground " *shoot the left foot forward*", 15 inches, toe just clear of the ground. Hands still to the sides, body in the position of attention showing the lift of head and chest, shoulders back.

5. Squad for—ward ". Lead on in quick time with the left foot, swinging the arms.

6. " **Turnings by balance step** ". " **Balance step. Left—turn**".
Check the pace with the left foot; cut the hands to the sides; " *bend the right knee* "; force the body round to the new direction and as the right foot comes to the ground, " *shoot the left foot forward* " 15 inches and remain. Hands still to the side.

7. " Squad for—ward ". Lead on in quick time with the left foot, swinging the arms. Turnings judging the time are done as for the balance step except that the arms are swung as " *the foot is shot forward* " and a full pace of 30 inches is taken without any pause.

*Common faults* :—Failure to check the forward movement and failure to make a complete turn.

8. " **Turnings by numbers** ". " About turn—one " (given as the left foot passes the right).
The soldier will complete the pace with the left foot, take a half pace with the right foot and " freeze " with his left arm forward, right arm back, and left heel off the ground.

9. " Squad—two ". Cut the arms to the sides, make a turn to the right on the right foot and " *bend the left knee* " to adopt the position of attention.

10. " Squad—three ". Make another turn to the right, this time pivoting on the left foot, and " *bend the right knee* " to adopt the position of attention.

11. " Squad—four ". Mark time one pace with the left foot and resume the position of attention.

(*Note.*—The arms must be kept still to the side during movements two, three and four).

12. " **Squad—forward** ". Step off with the right foot and continue marching.

*Common faults :—*

    (i)   Bending the body forward when bending the knees.

    (ii)  Creeping forward on the second and third movements.

    (iii) Stamping the right foot on the fourth movement and failing to swing the arms, *ie*, failing to " *lead on* " with the right foot.

### SECTION 20 : MARKING TIME, FORWARD AND HALT —SLOW AND QUICK TIME

Marking time is done in the same cadence as marching and the position of attention must be maintained.

#### To slow mark time from the halt

1. " Slow mark—time ". Raise the left knee so that the top of the thigh is parallel with the ground, the lower leg perpendicular and the foot at a natural angle ; straighten the leg again directly to resume the position of attention and as the foot comes to the ground bend and straighten the right knee in a similar manner ; body erect, shoulders square to the front, arms still to the sides.

2. The position can be taught by numbers if necessary. On the command " **One** " raise the left knee. On the command " **Two** " lower the left knee, assume the position of attention and then immediately raise the right knee and remain. On the command " **Halt** " bring the right foot down to resume the position of attention.

*Common faults :—*

    (i)  Not remaining stationary on the same ground with consequent loss of dressing or interval.

    (ii)  Movement of the body, shoulders or arms.

    (iii) Looking down.

    (iv) Increasing the time above that of marching.

#### To slow mark time from slow marching

3. " **Mark—time** " (given with a long cautionary word and the executive just before the right foot reaches the ground).

Complete the pace with the right foot and begin the mark time with the left foot.

4. To move forward when slow marking time the word of command will be " **For—ward** ", this being given as the right knee is fully raised. The right knee will immediately be straightened and the left foot " shot forward " to take up slow marching.

**To quick mark time from the halt**

5. " Quick mark—time ".—The left knee is raised and the movement is the same as for slow time.

*Common faults* :—

As for the slow time, but in addition :—

    (i) A tendency to lean forward.

    (ii) Raising the foot so that it is too far back instead of with the toe under the point of the knee.

    (iii) Creeping forward instead of marking time on the same ground.

**To mark time from quick marching**

6. " Mark—time " (given with the cautionary well drawn out and the executive as the left foot passes the right).

Complete a short check pace of 15 inches with the right foot and begin the marking time with the left foot.

7. To move forward when quick marking time the word of command will be " Forward ".

This being given as the left foot is being raised. The right foot completes the next pace marking time and, as the right foot comes to the ground, the left foot is " shot forward " and the arms are swung, to take up the quick marching.

## SECTION 21 : CHANGING STEP IN SLOW AND QUICK TIME

*Note.*—This should be taught by numbers, starting with Slow Time.

**Changing step by numbers. Left foot leading**

1. " Change step—one " (given as the right foot reaches the ground). Complete the pace with the left foot so that the left foot is flat on the ground and 30 inches in front of the right foot.

2. " Squad—two ".—" *Bend the right knee* " so that the foot is placed flat on the ground with the hollow in the heel of the left foot.

3. " Squad—three ".—" *Shoot the left foot forward* " placing the foot flat on the ground 30 inches in front of the right foot.

4. Changing step with the right foot leading can be taught in a similar manner, except that for left read right in each case.

5. Having taught the movements by numbers the squad carry on without interruption. The first and third movements are done at the rate of marching. The second movement is done in double that time. The word of command is given on alternate and successive feet.

6. Changing step in quick time is taught by numbers in a similar way and the words of command and movements are identical except

that on " **One** " the right arm is raised in front, and the left arm in rear of the body (or *vice versa* if the right foot is leading), on " **Two** "— the arms are cut to the side, and on " **Three** "—the heel of the left foot is placed on the ground.

7. Changing step marking time—the word of command is given on alternate and successive feet. If " **Change** " is given on the left foot, and " **Step** " on the right foot, two beats will be made with the left foot in the same time as the marching, after which normal marking time will be resumed. If given on the opposite foot, two beats will be made with the right foot.

The movements are the same in slow and quick time.

*Common faults* :—

    (*a*) *When marching*

        (i) Swinging the shoulders.

        (ii) Not bending the knee.

        (iii) Not making a full pace for the third movement.

    (*b*) *When marking time*

        (iv) Body rolling.

        (v) Increasing the rate of marching.

## SECTION 22 : MARCHING, MARKING TIME, AND HALTING IN DOUBLE TIME

### The double march

1. " **Double—march** ".—Step off with the left foot and run on the balls of the feet with easy swinging strides, inclining the body slightly forward, but maintaining the correct carriage. The feet must be picked up cleanly from the ground at each pace, and the thigh, knee and ankle joints must all work freely. The body should be carried forward by a thrust from the rear foot without unnecessary effort. The heels must not be raised toward the seat, but the foot carried straight to the front and the ball of the foot placed lightly on the ground. The arms should be swung as in quick time except that they should be bent so that the forearm forms an angle of about 135 degrees with the upper arm.

The length of pace will be 40 inches and the rate of marching 180 paces to the minute.

*Common faults* :—

    (i) Swinging the shoulders.

    (ii) Looking down.

    (iii) Stepping too long at the head of the squad, thus causing straggling in rear.

    (iv) Running on the heels and loss of dressing, distance and interval.

    (v) Hurrying the rate of marching and a complete loss of military bearing.

Marking time

2. As for quick time, except that the ball of the foot only is put to the ground and the arms are kept to the side in the bent position. The rate of double marching is maintained.

Halting

3. As for quick time, at the same time cutting the arms to the side. The word of command " **Halt** " is given, in both cases, as the left foot leaves the ground, after which three more paces are taken. These three paces are required to check the more rapid movement of the body before gaining the position of attention. It is, however, normal to " *break into quick time* " before ordering " **Halt** " from double time.

*Common faults* :—

> (i) " *Hopping* " with both feet off the ground at once.
> (ii) Loss of precision in halting.

## SECTION 23 : BREAKING INTO SLOW, QUICK AND DOUBLE TIME

Breaking into quick time from slow time

1. " Break into quick time quick—march ". The executive words of command are given on successive paces, " **Quick** " as the left foot reaches the ground, " **March** " as the right foot reaches the ground. Swing the left leg and right arm forward, and the left arm to the rear, in the correct rate of marching ; continue marching in quick time.

*Common faults* :—

> (i) Making the first pace too hurriedly thereby failing to gain correct rhythm at the start.
> (ii) Stamping the left foot on the ground in the first pace, thereby losing height.
> (iii) Failing to swing the left arm to the rear.

Breaking into slow time from quick time

2. This is taught by numbers. The two movements are identical with the first two movements of changing step, left foot leading.

3. " Break into slow time by numbers " " Slow march—one " (given as the left foot is level with and passing the right). Complete the pace with the left leg, placing the flat of the foot on the ground as a " *brake* " ; keep the right foot on the ground, heel raised ; swing the right arm forward, and the left to the rear, stopping in the fully raised position.

4. " Squad—two ". *Bend the right knee* in double time placing the flat of the foot on the ground with the hollow against the heel of the left foot, cut both arms to the side.

5. " **Squad—three** ". *Shoot the left foot forward.*

6. " **Squad—forward** ". Carry on march in slow time.

7. Normally the word of command will be " **Break into slow time, slow—march** ". The change into slow time will be done without pause. The executive word of command " **March** " is given as the left foot is level with and passing the right.

*Common faults :—*

    (i) Failure to " *bend the right knee* " quickly enough thereby causing hopping.

    (ii) Swinging the right shoulder to the rear, caused by failure to " *bend the right knee* " high enough.

    (iii) Allowing the body to lean backwards.

    (iv) Failure to cut the arms into the side sharply enough.

### Breaking into double time from quick time

8. " **Break into double time, double—march** " (given as the left foot reaches the ground). Break into double time swinging the leg forward at the correct rate of marching, *ie*, 180 paces to the minute ; at the same time bend the arms.

*Common faults :—*

    (i) Immediate relaxation of control and rhythm.

    (ii) Allowing the head to loll forward.

### Breaking into quick time from double time

9. " **Break into quick time, quick—march** ". The executive words of command " **Quick march** " are given on successive paces, " **Quick** " as the left foot reaches the ground and " **March** " as the right foot reaches the ground.

Complete two more paces in double time, checking the pace to 30 inches, and then break automatically into quick time.

*Common faults : —*

Failure to march correctly at once.

CHAPTER III

# MARCHING IN LINE AND CHANGING DIRECTION

The importance of drill in line as carried out in present-day ceremonial is not only the fine show it makes for the public but also the fact that it requires a distinct effort from all taking part to execute it correctly. This individual effort is a specific means to build up the corporate spirit and discipline of a unit or sub-unit.

## SECTION 24 : **MARCHING IN LINE IN SLOW TIME**

Marching in line is taught first in slow time. The instructor must explain again the use of the cautionary words of command " **Advance** " and " **Retire** " and also the flank of direction. During practice the length of pace and distance between the ranks (one pace) must be checked frequently.

The following points must be demonstrated and practised :—

(*a*) Selecting an object and marching on it so as to keep a straight line of advance.

(*b*) How to keep interval and dressing.

(*c*) Regaining lost dressing gradually.

(*d*) Stepping off a full pace and halting so that dressing is not lost.

*Common faults :—*

(i) Failure to maintain correct interval, distance and dressing.

(ii) Making a sudden spurt or check to regain lost dressing instead of doing it gradually.

(iii) Stepping off and halting with an uneven and incorrect length of pace.

(iv) Stepping a pace of more than 30 inches.

## SECTION 25 : **TAKING OPEN AND CLOSE ORDER**

1. " **Open—order** " (given just before the right foot reaches the ground).

Centre rank :—Mark time two paces (left, right) and lead on with the left foot.

Rear rank :—Mark time four paces and lead on with the left foot. This makes three paces distance between each rank.

2. " **Close—order** "

Front rank :—Mark time four paces.

Centre rank —Mark time two paces.

## SECTION 26 : **CHANGING DIRECTION BY FORMING, AT THE HALT AND ON THE MARCH, IN SLOW TIME**

At the halt

1. " Change direction right, at the halt, right—form ".—The right-hand man turns to his right, the remainder of the front rank right incline ; the remainder of the squad stand still.

2. " **Squad, quick—march** ".—The right-hand man moves forward three paces and halts ; the two men in the file behind him conform, wheeling and halting behind him, facing the new direction at one pace

distance from each other ; the next files march forward, wheeling to face the new direction, and halt in line, dressed on the right-hand file.

*Note.*— (i) This movement is always used for changing direction when there are more than six men in line (*see* Sec **17**).

(ii) The command for this movement is the only one which is preceded by the cautionary " Change **direction** ".

(iii) The movement is normally taught from the halt to the halt by individual files in turn before the whole squad is practised together.

(iv) If the cautionary " **At the halt** " is not given the squad will take up marking time on the new alignment, from which they may be given " **For—ward** " or " **Squad— halt** ".

**On the march**

3. The right-hand man wheels square to his right and moves forward three paces in the new direction, halting or taking up the marking time. The remainder of his file follow.

4. The executive command will be given as for left turn. Each file will wheel and march to face the new direction, marking time or halting as may be ordered.

*Common faults :—*

(i) Failing to maintain the correct interval.

(ii) Increasing the rate of marching on the outer flank or when marking time.

(iii) Increasing the length of pace.

(iv) Failing to halt or take up the marking time on the correct foot.

## SECTION 27 : WHEELING IN LINE IN SLOW TIME

This move will not be undertaken with more than six men in line. The drill is as laid down in Sec **17**, but in line the individuals in each line must glance at the directing flank in order to keep dressing.

*Common faults :—*

(i) Allowing a bow to form in the centre of the line.

(ii) Bulging out from the point of wheel.

## SECTION 28 : MARCHING IN LINE AND CHANGING DIRECTION IN QUICK TIME

There is no difference in the basic detail, except that the " *Open order* " is not done in quick time.

One additional point to add is that, in line, it is most important for each individual to ensure that his arm is swung to the regulation waist height. In forming, the movement of cutting the arms to the side when halting or taking up the marking time must be emphasized.

## CHAPTER IV

# FORMING SQUAD

Forming squad is a movement whereby a squad, moving to a flank in threes, changes its formation to that of line but does not change its direction of march.

## SECTION 29 : FORMING SQUAD FROM THE HALT IN SLOW TIME

1. " **At the halt, on the left, form—squad** ".—The whole squad except the left-hand man of the leading section of threes (the pivot) make a left incline.

2. " **Slow march** ".—The pivot marches forward three paces and halts ; the remainder of the squad march round to their correct places in line and halt.

*Note.—* (i) If the cautionary is not preceded by " **At the halt** ", the squad marks time instead of halting.

(ii) It is advisable, the first time, to deal with the leading section of threes individually and the remaining sections in turn.

(iii) The same movement may be made " *On the right* ", in which case the pivot is the right-hand man of the leading section of threes and the incline is made to the right.

## SECTION 30 : FORMING SQUAD ON THE MARCH IN SLOW TIME

**Forming squad by balance step**

1. " **Balance step at the halt, on the left, form—squad** ".—The pivot man carries out the leg movement of the left incline but remains facing the original direction ; the remainder make a left incline by balance step.

2. " **Squad—forward** ".—The squad march forward to their positions in line and halt.

*Note.—*If " **At the halt** " is not given, the squad marks time instead of halting.

3. Having taught the movement by balance step, the normal word of command is " **On the left, form—squad** " preceded, if required, by " **At the halt** ". The squad then carry out the movement without pause : the pivot man need not bend the knee.

## SECTION 31 : **FORMING SQUAD IN QUICK TIME**

There is no difference in the basic detail.

The word of command is given as for right or left incline.

*Common faults :—*

   (i) The pivot man making a " change step " leg movement instead of a " turn " movement.

   (ii) Increasing the rate of marching and length of pace by the men in the rear sections of threes.

   (iii) Failing to halt or mark time on the correct foot.

## CHAPTER V

# FORMING TWO RANKS

It is often necessary in ceremonial for troops to march on to the parade ground in three ranks and there to form two ranks for the purposes of the parade. To effect this the only rank to move is the centre rank.

## SECTION 32 : **TO FORM TWO RANKS FROM THREE RANKS**

1. " Form—two ranks "

*First movement.*—The centre rank " *bend the left knee* " and carry the left foot a side pace of 24 inches to the left.

*Second movement.*—Odd numbers shoot the right foot forward a full pace of 30 inches; even numbers shoot the right foot to the rear a full pace of 30 inches.

*Third movement.*—The centre rank " *bend the left knee* " to resume the position of attention—odd numbers in the intervals of the front rank, even numbers in the intervals of the rear rank.

If there is a blank file in the centre rank, the left hand man of that rank will carry out the reverse of the above, *ie*, if an odd number he will act as an even number, and *vice versa*, except that in the case of a squad with an even number of men in the front rank and no centre or rear rank man in the blank file the left hand man of the centre rank will act in accordance with the detail for his even number.

*Common faults :—*

   (i) Centre rank not knowing their correct numbers.

   (ii) Incorrect interval in three ranks thereby not leaving room for the centre rank men to move into. This can be overcome by giving " **Right—dress** " before forming two deep.

   (iii) Not carrying the left foot far enough to the left in the first movement, thereby causing collisions and uneven covering.

(iv) Not reaching out far enough in the second movement, thereby failing to reach the correct new alignment.

(v) Failure to place the flat of the feet on the ground.

2. " In two ranks, right—dress ".—The normal drill movements are carried out except that dressing is without arms interval, each man being allowed 24 inches in the ranks, the rear rank remains two paces of 30 inches in rear of the front rank.

## SECTION 33 : TO FORM THREE RANKS FROM TWO RANKS

1. " Form—three ranks ".—The original centre rank men take up their original positions as follows :—

*First movements.*—If in the front rank they " *shoot the left foot* " to the rear a full pace of 30 inches. If in the rear rank they " *shoot the left foot forward* " a full pace of 30 inches.

*Second movement.*—All concerned will " *bend the right knee* " and carry the right foot a side pace of 24 inches to the right.

*Third movement.*—Centre rank men " *bend the left knee* " and resume the position of attention.

*Common faults :—*

(i) Not carrying the right foot off far enough in the second movement thereby failing to cover off.

(ii) Failure to place the flat of the feet on the ground.

2. " In three ranks, right—dress ".—Dressing will be carried out as normal at arms interval.

## CHAPTER VI

# MARCHING OFF IN SINGLE FILE

It is often necessary for a squad in three ranks to form single file, *eg*, when marching into a building.

## SECTION 34 : A SQUAD FACING A FLANK IN THREES MARCHING OFF IN SINGLE FILE

When halted

1. " Front rank, by the front—quick march". The front rank step off in single file in quick time.

2. " Centre rank, by the front—quick march".—Given as the tail of the front rank passes the head of the centre rank. The centre rank follow on behind the front rank.

3. " Rear rank, by the front—quick march".—Given as the tail of the centre rank passes the head of the rear rank. The rear rank follow on behind the centre rank.

**On the march**

4. " Form single file, centre and rear ranks, mark—time ".—The front rank carries on marching.

5. " Centre rank—forward ".

6. " Rear rank—forward ".

*Note*.—Similar movements can be done in a different sequence of ranks.

## REFORMING THREE RANKS

### When halted

7. " The squad will re-form three ranks on the front rank. Centre and rear ranks, by the front—quick march ".—The front rank stands fast. The centre and rear ranks lead on to their correct positions. **Centre (or rear) rank halt**.

### On the march

8. " The squad will re-form three ranks on the front rank, at the halt, front rank—halt ".—Front rank halts; centre and rear ranks continue marching to their positions. Centre (or rear) rank—halt.

*Note*.—If the first cautionary word of command is not followed by " At the halt ", the executive word of command at each rank in turn will be " Mark—time ".

## SECTION 35 : A SQUAD IN LINE MARCHING OFF IN SINGLE FILE

### When halted

1. " Advance in single file from the right—quick march ".—The right-hand section of threes march forward in quick time; the remainder mark time, going forward in quick time in succession of sections of threes from right to left, to form single file. The second and subsequent sections of threes wheel so as to cover off the right hand section.

### On the march

2. " Advance in single file from the right, remainder, mark-time ".— The right-hand section of threes leads on; the remainder mark time and go forward in succession to form single file.

## RE-FORMING THREE RANKS

### When halted

3. " The squad will re-form three ranks on the left, remainder, by the front—quick march ".—The original right-hand section of threes stand fast; the remainder march to their original positions in line and halt.

### On the march

4. " The squad will re-form three ranks on the left, at the halt. Right-hand sections of threes—halt ".—The right-hand section of threes halt; the remainder go to their original places in line and halt.

*Note.*—If the first cautionary word of command is not followed by " At the halt ", the executive word of command will be " Right-hand section of threes. Mark time ".

## CHAPTER VII

# COMPLIMENTS

Compliments in the armed forces derive from His Majesty The King, the highest being the Royal Salute to His Majesty and to those members of the Royal Family, Governors, Ministers, etc., to whom he delegates his authority. Formed bodies of troops on duty, being on The King's Business, are also entitled to compliments as are the standards, guidons or colours of units.

An officer is saluted as the King's representative and a holder of His Majesty's commission; the act of saluting an officer is to be civil, not servile, and is a mark of respect and good manners to a holder of His Majesty's commission. The right hand is raised palm to the front and open to indicate no weapon or offensive action; the position of the present arms and the salute with the sword have the same meaning.

A salute is, in fact, the normal greeting between comrades in arms. That a salute is given when a soldier meets an officer is a basic matter of discipline. That the salute is properly and smartly given is a matter of training. Failure to salute shows disrespect, idleness, and a low standard of discipline. Failure by an officer in uniform to insist on being saluted is a breach of discipline.

The details of which compliments must be paid are laid down in King's Regulations. It is the duty of all officers, warrant officers and NCOs to be familiar with the rules in general and especially with the simple details given below.

## SECTION 36 : **SALUTING AT THE HALT**

1. This is a basic lesson but must often be reverted to with trained soldiers, to correct any bad habits which have been picked up. Saluting at the halt to the front and to a flank is taught " by numbers ". To permit free movement this is best practised with the squad in open order and inclined diagonally.

### Salute to the front

2. " **Saluting by numbers** ". " **Salute to the front—one** ".—The right arm is kept straight and raised sideways until it is horizontal, palm of the hand to the front, fingers extended, thumb close to the forefinger.

Keeping the upper arm still and the hand and wrist straight, bend the elbow until the forefinger tip of the right hand is one inch above the right eye. Points to note are :—

(a) Upper arm horizontal and at right angles to the side; forearm, wrist and fingers all in one straight line.

(b) Palm of the hand vertical.

3. " **Squad—two** ".—To return to the position of attention the hand is cut the shortest way to the side by dropping the elbow towards the front. The fingers are curled up on the way down.

4. When judging the time, the hand will remain at the position of the salute for a regulation pause. The word of command will be : " **Salute to the Front—Salute** ".

*Common faults :—*
*In coming up to the salute :—*

- (i) Leaning to the left, straining the muscles and leaning backwards.
- (ii) Elbow forward; forearm, wrist and fingers not in a straight line.
- (iii) Hand too high or too far over towards the centre of the forehead; hand tilted forward; fingers *NOT* together; moving to the left arm; pushing the head forward.

*In cutting the hand away :—*

- (iv) Dropping the hand before the elbow.
- (v) Not straightening the arm and therefore not resuming a proper position of attention; moving the left hand when cutting the right arm away.

In general the most common fault in saluting to the front is that the movement is started before the soldier has halted, stopped speaking etc., and that the soldier starts speaking before the movement has been properly completed.

Salute to the flank

5. " Salute to the Right—One " or " Salute to the Right—Salute ".—
This is best taught from the correct position of the salute to the front.
Get the soldier to turn his head and eyes square off to the right and,
without upsetting the position of the right arm, wrist or hand, to shift
the hand so that the right eye can just look along the palm of the hand.
The soldier should look his own height or into the eyes of the officer
he is saluting. This must be practised until the movement of the
head, eyes, and hand become simultaneous.

*Common faults :*—

   (i) Leaning forward, looking along the back of the hand or
not looking the officer squarely in the face.

   (ii) Hand too high.

   (iii) Left shoulder allowed to come forward.

   (iv) Right elbow allowed to come forward and drop or fall to the
rear.

   (v) Not looking square off to the flank.

   (vi) Raising the wrist.

6. " Salute to the Left—One " or " Salute to the Left—Salute ",
—Taught as above, the right hand, wrist and arm being pushed further
over to the left to the correct position above the right eye.

*Common faults :*—

   (i) Turning the shoulder to the left and allowing the right elbow
to drop forward.

   (ii) Not allowing the right hand to move over to its correct
position.

   (iii) Dropping the wrist.

## SECTION 37 : **SALUTING ON THE MARCH**

Saluting on the march may be to a flank or to the front and may be
done in quick or slow time.

Saluting to the flank

1. " Saluting by **numbers** ". " **Salute to the right—one** " (given as
the left foot touches the ground).—Complete the next pace
with the right foot and freeze with right foot forward, heel on the
ground, toe raised, arms at the maximum extent of the swing.

" *Shoot the left foot forward* " and complete the next pace with the
left foot, heel on the ground, toe raised; bring the right arm smartly
to the position of the salute, turn the head and eyes to the right; cut
the left hand to the side as for the position of attention.

As the left foot comes to the ground and the salute is made, the
squad shout " Up ".

2. " **Squad—two** ". Keep the left arm still to the side, maintain the correct position of the salute and, without swinging the shoulder, complete the next pace with the right foot, and shout " **Two** ".

*Note*.—The orders **Two, Three, Four,** and **Five** may be given in quick succession, one pace being taken on each, and the appropriate number shouted each time the heel comes to the ground.

3. " **Squad—six** ".—Complete the pace with the right foot. As the heel touches the ground turn the head and eyes to the front, cut the right arm away to the side, and shout " **Down** ".

4. " **Squad—seven** ".—Continue marching in quick time, swing the arms and shout " Swing " on the first pace.

5. Judging the time the word of command will be :—

" **Saluting** ". " **Salute to the right—salute** " (Given as the left foot comes to the ground). Come up to the salute the next time the left foot touches the ground and cut the hand away on the sixth pace (right foot).

*Note*.—Recruits will continue to call out the time.

### When passing an officer

6. When a soldier passes an officer, he will salute on the third pace before reaching him, and lower the hand on the third pace after passing him; if carrying a cane he will place it under the left arm, cutting away the hand before saluting (*see* Sec 40). During the salute the soldier will look the officer full in the face.

*Note*.—Recruits will be practised in marching two or three together, saluting " points " being placed on either side. When several men are together, the man nearest the " point " will give the time.

They should be practised in saluting " points " on the move as well as fixed saluting " points ".

### *Common faults :—*

In addition to the faults already mentioned, there is a tendency to swing the shoulders and to stray from the direction of marching in the direction of the salute. This latter fault is corrected in instruction by getting an instructor to act as a guide to the squad.

### Saluting to the front

7. The word of command is given as the right foot passes the left, *ie*, as for the " *Halt* ". The squad halt, salute to the front, wait for a regulation pause, salute to the front again, pause, turn about, pause and lead off in quick time.

*Note*.— (i) This is the drill movement to teach how to approach an officer.

(ii) Instructors will insist on the correct counting of the regulation pause ; the whole drill should be carried out at the rate of 40 movements to the minute.

# SECTION 38 : SALUTING WHEN WITHOUT HEAD-DRESS AND WHEN WEARING PLAIN CLOTHES, Etc.

This section covers the case of the individual soldier who passes an officer, is spoken to by an officer or who is passed by an officer, when the individual soldier either has no hat or is dressed in plain clothes. As part of a recruit's training, these movements will be explained, demonstrated and practised on the square.

**Without head-dress**

1. At all times when without head-dress a soldier :—

(a) When passing an officer will cut his hands to his sides and turn his head and eyes to the flank on the left foot and so remain for six paces, when he will turn his head to the front.

(b) When spoken to by an officer—will stand to attention.

(c) When passed by an officer—will stand to attention.

**When in plain clothes**

2. A soldier will remove his head-dress well clear of his head and look the officer in the eye. He will stand to attention if speaking to or spoken to by the officer.

**When sitting**

3. A soldier, if sitting when an officer approaches, will stand to attention facing the officer, and salute with the hand ; if two or more men are sitting or standing about the senior warrant officer, NCO, or oldest soldier will face the officer, call the whole to attention, and alone will salute.

**When addressing or delivering a message to an officer**

4. A soldier will march smartly towards the officer in quick time, halt two paces from him, salute, address the officer or deliver his message, salute again, turn about, and march off in quick time. (*See* Sec **41**.)

*Note.*—When appearing before an officer in a room a soldier will salute. He will not remove his head-dress.

*Common faults* :—

(i) Failure to pay the necessary compliment.

(ii) Saluting with no hat on.

## SECTION 39 : SALUTING WITH ARMS

1. The salute with the sword is given at Appendix B.

2. The salute with the rifle is normally carried out at the slope. The salute requires the same action of the hand for a salute to the front as to a flank ; the head and eyes only being turned to a flank if the salute is to be given to one side or the other.

3. " **Salute to the front—salute** ".—Retain the position of the slope with the left hand ; bring the right hand across the front of the body by the shortest way to strike the butt with the palm of the hand just below the small, thumb in line with the knuckle of the butt ; hand flat on the butt, fingers extended and together, thumb close to the forefinger so that fingers, wrist and forearm are in a straight line, base of the fingers resting on the edge of the butt nearest the sling, forearm horizontal.

Make a regulation pause and cut the hand away to the side.

*Note.*— (i) This movement can be taught by numbers if required.
(ii) Words of command for saluting with the rifle are given in exactly the same way as for saluting with the hand.

*Common faults :—*

(i) Hand not far enough over to the left.
(ii) Elbow drooping.
(iii) Moving from the correct position of the slope, particularly moving the butt of the rifle to the right to meet the right hand.

## SECTION 40 : SALUTING WITH THE WHIP OR CANE

1. The action of saluting is the same as given above but with additional movements added to transfer the cane to and from the right hand. All movements are done at the rate of 40 to the minute.

**At the halt**

1. Take the cane by the right hand from the position of attention and place it horizontally underneath the left armpit, ferrule to the rear. Keep the left hand to the side and cut the right hand away to the side before saluting. As soon as the salute is completed reach across the body with the right hand and, seizing the cane, return it to the position of attention.

**On the march—saluting to a flank**

2. The word of command will be normal. As the left foot first comes to the ground, place the cane under the left arm ; as the left foot again comes to the ground, cut the right hand away to the side start the salute as the left foot next comes to the ground.

*Note.*—The salute lasts for six paces. On the eleventh pace (left foot) seize the cane by the right hand ; on the 13th pace cut it away to the side ; on the 15th pace swing the arms again.

## On the march—salute to the front

3. The word of command is given as for " *Halt* ".

Halt ; put the cane under the left arm ; cut the right arm away ; salute ; salute again ; turn about ; step off seizing the cane with the right hand ; as the left foot comes to the ground cut the cane to the side on the third pace ; start swinging the arms on the fifth pace.

*Common faults :—*

   (i) Failure to keep the cane horizontal under the arm.

   (ii) Failure to grasp the cane at the point of balance after saluting.

## SECTION 41 : MISCELLANEOUS

The following detail is given for the use of instructors. The information should be put over by " question and answers " when the squad is standing easy.

## National Anthem

1. All ranks in uniform not under the orders of an OC on parade will stand to attention, officers, warrant officers and NCOs saluting. When on parade or in an organized party the salute will be given only by officers and warrant officers, except that an NCO will salute if in charge of the party. If in plain clothes, all ranks stand to attention and take off their hats. An officer, or NCO commanding a party on the move will halt the party which will remain at the slope or attention ; the officer or NCO will salute. If carrying a drawn sword the officer will remain at the carry.

Sentries will slope arms.

## Acknowledging salutes

2. Officers will receive and return a salute with the courtesy it deserves. When two or more officers are together, the senior will return the salute.

## Left hand salute

3. Where, through physical incapacity, a salute with the right hand is impossible, the salute will be given with the left hand.

## Military funerals

4. Officers and soldiers passing a military funeral will salute the bier by giving eyes right or left. The senior in charge of a party will salute.

**When riding a horse**

5. An officer riding without arms will salute with the right hand. A soldier mounted without arms will salute as follows :—

(a)   When riding with both hands on the reins will give an eyes right or left without moving his hands.

(b)   When holding the reins in one hand only, will drop the right hand to the full extent of the arm, behind the right thigh, fingers half closed, back of the hand to the right, and give an eyes right or left.

(c)   When riding a horse of a team in a wagon or limber, *see* Manual of Horsemastership, Equitation and Animal Transport, 1937, Sec 89, para 2.

(d)   When driving a horsed vehicle :—*See* Manual of Horsemastership, Equitation and Animal Transport, 1937, Sec 106, para 4.

**When driving a mechanical vehicle (including bicycles)**

6. The rider of a bicycle (pedal or motor) or driver of a mechanical vehicle, will not salute when the vehicle is in motion, owing to the danger of taking the eyes off the road.

When the vehicle is stationary, he will salute by giving an eyes right or left but will not remove his hands from the handlebar or steering wheel.

7. When seated on or in a horsed or mechanical vehicle as a passenger, officers will pay compliments by saluting with the right hand, if possible, otherwise they will follow the instructions laid down for soldiers. Soldiers will sit to attention and, if facing the direction in which the vehicle is moving, will salute by giving an eyes right or left. If seated facing in any other direction, they will look straight to their own front.

**Special instruction for saluting with the rifle**

8. *At the halt.*—A soldier will salute as follows :—

(a)   If at the " *Order* " when an officer passes he will turn towards the officer and stand to " *Attention* ".

(b)   If at the slope when an officer passes he will salute as laid down in Sec 39.   The salute will begin three paces before the officer passes the soldier and the hand will be cut away on the third pace after he has passed him.

9. *On the move.*—When a soldier passes an officer, he will do so at the " *Slope* ", and will salute and look him full in the face.   He will salute on the third pace before reaching him, and will cut the hand away and turn the head to the front on the third pace after passing him.

10. *When addressing or delivering a message to an officer.*—When a soldier, carrying a rifle, delivers a written message to or addresses an officer he will do so at the " Slope ". Unless the officer is on the move, the soldier will halt two paces from the officer, salute and deliver the message; if no reply is needed or when the reply is received, he will salute as before, turn about and march off in quick time. (*See* Sec **38**.)

### Compliments on the march

*Note.*—The following paragraphs refer mainly to the procedure in peace, since compliments during a march on service will not be paid unless specially ordered.

11. When a body of troops passes :—

(*a*)  The King, The Queen and other members of the Royal Family.

(*b*)  Armed bodies of troops on the march, commanded by an officer.

(*c*)  Guards and escorts.

(*d*)  Their own brigade commander (or CRA in Artillery), general officers and officers of the Royal Navy and Royal Air Force of equivalent rank, when in uniform, the commander will give the order " **March to attention** " and compliments will be paid in succession by the sub-units on parade, respective commanders giving the command " **Eyes right** " (or " **Left** "). All officers will salute as will such other ranks as may be in command of sub-units.

*Note.*—In horsed artillery the commands are repeated in succession by Nos. 1.

12. Small bodies of troops not commanded by an officer will pay compliments to all officers.

13. An officer in command of an armed party will return the salute of a NCO in charge of an unarmed party of less than 20 men, but will not call the armed party to attention.

When in command of a party, armed or unarmed, an officer will salute any officer senior to him provided he is a Field Officer or higher or of equivalent rank in the other Services.

14. Compliments paid by guards and sentries will be returned as detailed above.

15. Bodies of troops on the march or on training will only pay compliments to the same higher commander once a day. At other times the commander only will salute his seniors.

16. When persons entitled to salutes approach from the rear, compliments will not be paid, but officers will salute.

This will not apply in the case of those members of the Royal Family to whom the compliments are paid; in this case troops will be ordered to march to attention and give " *eyes right* " *or left*.

17. Troops will march to attention until clear of as well as when approaching their parade ground, and when entering or leaving barracks.

## SECTION 42 : EYES RIGHT AND LEFT

A formed body requiring to pay a compliment to a flank will receive the order to march by the desired flank and will then get " Eyes—right ".

The guide will look to his front in order to keep direction. All officers, warrant officers and those NCOs in command will salute. The remainder will turn their head and eyes to the desired flank.

The executive word of command will be given as the left foot touches the ground in quick time or as the right foot touches in slow time. In either case the whole will work when the left foot next comes to the ground.

" Eyes—front " is given in a similar manner.

These commands will be given so that the officer in front is at the salute as he comes level with the near end of the saluting base and so that the rear rank is just clear when they get " Eyes—front ".

*Common faults :—*

(i) Looking down.

(ii) Closing in to the flank of direction.

(iii) Shortening the length of pace.

(iv) When in column of route failure of the commander to give his order from a position in which the rear of his command can hear. The commander must drop back to the flank to do this if necessary.

## SECTION 43 : COMPLIMENTS TO THE COLOURS

His Majesty is represented in most units by his standard, guidons, or colours. These are therefore entitled to compliments.

The following rules are for general guidance and are not intended to supersede the orders which may exist in regiments for compliments to be paid to their own colours.

(i) An individual soldier on seeing the colours will stop working or halt, face the colours and salute.

(ii) A party of men working, drilling or marching will halt, face the colours and stand to attention. The officer or NCO commanding the party will salute. If the party has rifles, bayonets will be fixed and arms will be presented.

(iii) Guards will turn out and "*present arms*".

(iv) On marching on or off parade, colours will be received in "*open order*", with bayonets fixed and arms at the "*present*". The band or drums will play "The Point of War".

(v) Two units, both carrying colours, will give "Eyes right" to each other as they pass.

(vi) The only times when a colour is not saluted are :—

    (*a*) When the colours are carried by a unit forming a part of the escort at a military funeral. (The salute is given to the bier.)

    (*b*) When the colour is cased.

## CHAPTER VIII

# DRILL WITH THE WHIP OR CANE

The detail of cane drill is given for the information of those officers, warrant officers and NCOs who carry a cane or pace stick, and for mounted troops who carry a whip.

For saluting with the whip or cane *see* Sec **40**.

### SECTION 44 : ATTENTION

Hold the cane firmly in the right hand, in a perpendicular position close to the right side of the body, first joint of the forefinger of the right hand underneath the knob of the cane and pointing towards the thigh, thumb down and to the front, the knob of the cane pointing towards the ground, the remaining three fingers grasping the cane.

### SECTION 45 : STAND AT EASE

Adopt the position of stand at ease with the back of the right hand in the palm of the left ; the right hand holds the cane as at attention ; the cane is kept between the crook of the right arm and the body, ferrule end up and pointing obliquely to the right front.

### SECTION 46 : MARCHING

Step off and as the left foot first comes to the ground, move both hands at the same time to grasp the cane in the middle, keeping the cane upright into the right shoulder with the left hand ; as the left foot again comes to the ground straighten the right arm with the cane horizontal, and cut the left hand to the side. As the left foot comes to the ground for the third time swing the arms as in marching, holding the cane between the thumb and first two fingers of the right hand and keeping it parallel to the ground throughout the swing, which must be straight from the front to rear.

*Note.*— (i) The cane in this position is " *at the trail* ".

(ii) Should the squad be dressed at less than arms interval and moved to a flank, the cane will be kept at the position of attention and both arms will be swung.

## SECTION 47 : **HALTING**

" Squad—halt ".—Keep the cane at the " *trail* ". After a regulation pause, bring the cane to the position of attention as follows :—

*First movement :* Grasp the cane with the left hand at the centre and bring it to a perpendicular position at the right side, at the same time move the right hand to the knob of the cane as in the position of attention.

*Second movement :* Cut the left hand away to the side.

## SECTION 48 : **TURNING ABOUT**

1. *When halted.*—Keep the cane in the position of attention.

2. *On the march.*—On the first movement of the turn bring the cane to a perpendicular position in front of the right shoulder, upper part of the arm close to the side, forearm horizontal, hand in line with the waist-belt. On the first pace after the completion of the turn, bring the cane to the trail as the right foot reaches the ground.

## SECTION 49 : **DISMISSING**

1. When an officer is present, the squad will salute with the cane as given in Sec **40**, *ie*, turn to the right; cane under the left arm; right hand cut away; salute; cut the hand away; step off, cutting the cane to the trail as the left foot comes to the ground.

*Note.*— (i) Men not carrying a cane will wait for those in the squad who are.

(ii) Movements will be at 40 to the minute.

2. If no officer is present the squad will turn to the right, pause and break off, bringing the cane to the trail working on the left foot.

## CHAPTER IX

# RIFLE EXERCISES AT THE HALT
## (less Saluting)

The training that rifle exercises give in co-ordinating the brain and limbs and the "balance " they afford to foot drill make them an essential part of any drill programme.

All rifle exercises are taught by numbers. When judging the time all movements are made as sharply as possible, counting a regulation pause between each movement. (Movements are at 40 to the minute.)

The word of command for the movement judging the time will be as for numbers but the word " ARMS " becomes the executive, *eg*, " **Slope arms—One** " becomes " Slope—arms".

The most common fault in rifle exercises is lack of control over the rifle which causes movement of the body. In rifle exercises the upper arm and elbow are kept close to the body and there should be no movement of the head or body except where specifically given in the following detail.

Rifles and bayonets on parade should be clean and dry as for inspection.

## SECTION 50 : **ATTENTION**

The normal position of attention is maintained except that the right hand will hold the rifle perpendicularly at the right side; thumb on the left of the rifle and touching the leg; fingers together on the right of the rifle, slanting towards the ground; back of the hand to the right and the wrist well behind the rifle; butt of the rifle flat on the ground, toe of the butt in line with the rear seam of the toecap of the boot, magazine to the front.

*Note.*—When demonstrating, the instructor will fix his bayonet and show how the line of the rifle, when prolonged by the bayonet, comes up outside the arm and not between the arm and the body. This position is a natural one and is the only position that will guarantee the bayonet being free of the clothing when " *sloping arms* " with bayonets fixed.

*Common faults :—*

   (i)   Butt in the wrong position.

  (ii)   Rifle not perpendicular and sling not square to the front.

 (iii)   Back of the hand turned to the front.

 (iv)   Wrist not behind the rifle and elbow away from the side.

  (v)   Fingers not together and allowed to curl onto the front of the rifle.

## SECTION 51 : **GETTING ON PARADE WITH RIFLES—THE SHORT TRAIL**

As for Sec 8 except that the right arm will not be swung but will be slightly bent to raise the butt of the rifle about one inch from the ground *ie*, to the position of the short trail.

As soon as the squad halts, the butt is placed on the ground in the correct position of attention.

When taking up the dressing, the front rank raise the left arm instead of the right and the rifle is again raised to the position of the short trail when moving.

*Common faults :—*

    (i)  Putting the fingers round the front of the rifle     ⎱   When marching
    (ii)  Letting the rifle swing about at the side   ⎰   or dressing.
    (iii)  Banging the butt on the ground when halting or dressing.

## SECTION 52 : STAND AT EASE AND STAND EASY

**Stand at ease**

1. " Stand at—ease ".—" *Bend the left knee* "; and carry the left leg to the left so that the feet are about 12 inches apart, keep the left arm to the side; force the rifle straight out to the front, by keeping the right arm straight; shoot the right hand forward to its fullest extent but without moving the hand on the rifle, the toe of the butt, or allowing the right shoulder to droop. . The weight of the body is transferred slightly to the left so as to be evenly balanced.

*Common faults :—*

    (i)  Moving the butt.
    (ii)  Allowing the rifle to swing to the right or left.
    (iii)  Moving the left arm.
    (iv)  Putting the fingers round the front of the rifle.
    (v)  Lack of co-ordination between right arm and left leg.

**Stand easy**

2. " Stand—easy ".—Force the right hand up to the nosecap of the rifle, the fingers and thumb curling round the rifle; bend the right arm so that the angle of the rifle is not altered.

**Stand at ease from stand easy**

3. " Squad ".—Force the right hand down the rifle to the correct position of stand at ease; brace the body.

**Attention from the stand at ease**

4. " Squad—attention ".—Pull the rifle into the side keeping the butt on the ground; " *bend the left knee* "; keep the left arm to the side.

*Common faults :—*

    (i)  Moving and banging the butt on the ground.
    (ii)  Lack of co-ordination between foot and arm-bending forward from the waist.

## SECTION 53 : SLOPE FROM THE ORDER, ORDER FROM THE SLOPE

**The slope from the order**

1. " Slope arms—one ".—Throw the rifle straight up the right side with a vigorous flick of the wrist, keeping the elbow still, and release it before the right hand reaches the level of the waist belt jerking the

right arm straight again; at the same time move the left arm across the body and catch the rifle just below the upper sling swivel, hand in line with the right armpit, knocking the rifle back into the right shoulder strike the rifle with the palm and heel of the hand, closing the fingers and thumb of the left hand round the rifle, and as the left hand strikes the rifle catch the butt with the fingers and thumb of the right hand.

*Note.*—The fingers and thumb of the right hand will be in the same position as at attention, but will hold the butt so that the forefinger is about in line with the knuckle of the butt, rifle perpendicular with the magazine to the front.

2. " **Squad—two** ".—Force the rifle across the body so that the muzzle passes just in front of the face ; as soon as the muzzle has passed the face and the left hand is about in line with the left breast pocket, let go of the rifle with the left hand and drop the hand so that the elbow is against the side (as at attention), forearm parallel to the ground and at right angles to the body, wrist straight ; at the same time move the fingers and thumb of the right hand round the rifle and drive the butt into the heel of the left hand just before the magazine touches the left shoulder ; close the fingers and thumb of the left hand round the butt so that the thumb is round the toe of the butt and about one inch above the butt plate and the fingers, from the centre knuckles to the tips are together on top of the butt, and point towards the muzzle.

*Note.*—The magazine will now point to the left and be flat on the shoulder just below the collar bone.

3. " **Squad—three** ".—Cut the right hand the nearest way to the position of attention ; keep the wrist stiff and curl up the fingers on the downward travel ; keep the rifle still.

*Common faults :—*

*First movement*

   (i) Failing to release the rifle with the right hand soon enough to allow both hands to grasp the rifle at the same time.

   (ii) Dropping the right shoulder to the rear.

   (iii) Letting the upper part of the arms and elbows leave the body.

*Second movement*

   (iv) Holding the rifle too long with the left hand, thereby causing the magazine to hit the shoulder before the butt hits the hand.

   (v) Moving the head and body.

   (vi) Letting the upper part of the arms and elbows leave the side.

*Third movement*

(vii) Moving the right elbow away from the body, thereby bringing the hand out in front of the body.

(viii) Moving the rifle on the shoulder.

## The order from the slope

4. " Order arms—one ".—Pull the rifle down to the full extent of the left arm, retaining the original grip with the left hand, so that the rifle is perpendicular and bearing against the inner part of the left elbow ; at the same time move the right arm across the body so that the right hand meets the rifle slightly above the level of the left shoulder; fingers and thumb round the rifle.

*Note.*—This must be brought out in the instructor's demonstration.

5. " Squad—two ".—Pull the rifle down and across the body with the right hand to a position slightly forward of the position of attention, magazine to the front, and butt about one inch above the ground ; at the same time move the left hand and forearm upwards and across the body, so that the heel of the hand strikes the rifle just below the nose cap, fingers and thumb together, with the hand cupped round and in front of the rifle ; at the moment of impact cut the fingers and thumb of the right hand away from the front of the rifle to the correct position of attention.

6. " Squad—three ".—Cut the left hand to the left side to the position of attention, and resume the position of attention.

*Note.*—The rifle will be lowered gently to the ground and the muzzle pulled slightly to the rear as the right arm is straightened.

*Common faults :—*

*First movement*

(i) Moving the head.

(ii) Releasing the grip with the left hand.

(iii) Making a circular movement with the right hand in front of instead of upward and close across the body.

(iv) Not reaching far enough up with the right hand.

*Second movement*

(v) Waving the butt out in front of the body.

(vi) Dropping the right shoulder to the rear.

(vii) Failure to synchronize the arrival of the left hand on the rifle with the movement of the fingers of the right hand.

*Third movement*

(viii) Banging the butt on the ground.

(ix) Cutting the left arm away in a circular movement and allowing it to go too far to the rear.

## SECTION 54: **DRESSING AT THE ORDER AND THE SLOPE**

When dressing is done at the *order* the front rank will raise the left arm. When done at the *slope* the right arm will be raised.

When getting on parade with the rifle, the movements will be as laid down in Sec 8 except that having come to *attention* arms will be *sloped* before stepping off, and will be *ordered* immediately after halting on the marker, and before taking up the dressing.

## SECTION 55: **PRESENT FROM THE SLOPE, SLOPE FROM THE PRESENT**

**Present from the slope**

1. " Present arms—one ".—Bring the right hand smartly the nearest way upwards and across the body to seize the rifle just below the small of the butt, back of the hand on top, thumb underneath forefinger just above the knuckle of the butt.

2. " Squad—two ".—Pull the butt in and towards the centre of the body ; push out the small of the butt and pull it towards the centre of the body with the right hand, so that the rifle is perpendicular and about three inches in front of the nose ; at the same time take the left hand away from the butt and drive it onto the rifle sling, so that the fingers and thumb are extended, palm, wrist and forearm against the sling, wrist opposite the magazine, elbow forced into the side of the butt and tip of the thumb in line with the mouth.

3. " Squad—three ".—Pull the rifle straight down in front of the body to the fullest extent of the right arm, turning the magazine to the front, keeping the rifle perpendicular and about three inches in front of the body. (The position of the fingers and thumb of the right hand will be as when at the order, except that they will be in position on the butt so that the hand is just below and clear of the cocking piece.) At the same time quit the rifle with the left hand and, forcing the elbow into the side, strike the rifle and seize it in line with the belt buckle. (The movement of the left forearm should be downwards and outwards from the second position until the forearm is horizontal and pointing to the front changing to a circular horizontal movement, parallel with the belt.) On seizing the rifle strike it with the heel of the hand, fingers outside the sling, close together and round the rifle, thumb perpendicularly up the left side of the rifle, wrist straight ; at the same time " *bend the right knee* " placing the flat of the foot on the ground with the hollow touching the heel of the left foot.

*Common faults :—*

*First movement*

    (i) Making a circular movement with the right arm and letting the right elbow leave the body.

  (ii) Not gripping the rifle with the fingers of the right hand round the butt.

  (iii) Moving the butt to the right to meet the right hand.

*Second movement*

  (iv) Raising the original level of the right hand.

  (v) Failure to have the left elbow along the butt.

  (vi) Focusing the eyes on the rifle, causing a tendency to lean backwards.

  (vii) Moving the head.

*Third movement*

  (viii) Pushing the rifle upwards before starting the downwards movement of the right arm.

  (ix) Failure to release the rifle with the left hand, thereby causing the hand to be too high.

  (x) Rearing back from the rifle.

  (xi) Turning the right toe out, therefore dragging the right shoulder to the rear.

  (xii) Unco-ordinated movement with arms and foot.

**The slope from the present**

4. " Slope Arms—one ".—Except that the rifle has not so far to travel, the movement is the same as the second movement of the *Slope* from the *Order*. (Sec 53.) At the same time " *bend the right knee* " to close the heels.

5. " Squad—two."—As for the third movement of the *Slope* from the *Order* ; cut the right hand to the side.

## SECTION 56 :—GROUND ARMS. TAKE UP ARMS

**Ground arms**

1. " Ground arms—one ".—Keep the body straight but inclined forward ; and bend down by bending and opening the knees ; lay the rifle gently on the ground at the right side, magazine to the right, muzzle pointing straight to the front, right hand in line with the right toe, left arm straight and against the body and hip. The head is kept as erect as possible with the eyes looking to the front.

2. " Squad—two ".—Release the rifle with the right hand and resume the position of attention.

**Take up arms**

3. " Take up arms—one ".—Bend down as in the first movement of the *ground arms* ; seize the rifle with the right hand in the original position by the right toe ; raise the muzzle sufficiently to put the thumb and fingers between the rifle and the ground.

4. " **Squad—two** ".—Resume the position of attention, bringing the rifle to its correct position at the order.

*Note.*—If a squad is stood to attention with rifles and it is required to stand the rifles against a wall, tree, etc, instead of grounding arms, the order will be " **Rifles against the wall (etc)—move** ". On this command the squad will turn to the right, pause, break off, place their rifles against the wall and fall in again in the same places as before the order was given.

*Common faults :—*

In both movements :—

   (i) Looking on the ground thereby causing some types of head-dress to fall off.

   (ii) Banging the rifle on the ground.

## SECTION 57 : FIX BAYONETS. UNFIX BAYONETS

*Notes.*—(i) Only done in open order.

   (ii) The cautionary word " **Squad** " is only normally given when an instructor is correcting faults, etc.

**Fix bayonets**

1. " **The squad will fix bayonets** ".— " **Squad—fix** ".—Force the rifle out with the right arm as for the position of the stand at ease, and bend the left elbow to the left rear: seize the bayonet handle with the left hand, back of the hand against the body, thumb curled round and over the ring of the bayonet, forefinger curled round and under the cross-piece, the remaining fingers curled round the grooves of the handle. Straighten the left arm downwards, arm against the side, scabbard turned upwards in an anti-clockwise direction, left wrist bent so that the bayonet blade is perpendicular on the left buttock, left hand behind the left leg sufficiently far so as not to be visible from the front.

*Common faults :—*

   (i) Bending the body to the right.

   (ii) Failure to get the left thumb and forefinger under the cross-piece.

   (iii) Lack of co-ordination in the movement of the right and left arms.

   (iv) Trying to pull the bayonet out of the scabbard with an up-wards movement.

2. " **Squad—bayonets** ".—Turn the head downwards and far enough to the right to enable the eyes to see the muzzle of the rifle, bring the bayonet between the body and the arm, and fix it on the rifle ; strike the bayonet handle so that the left arm is nearly straight,

the forearm, wrist and hand in one straight line, fingers and thumb together and extended ; the whole arm, wrist and fingers pointing in the direction of the right toes.

*Note.*—The thumb should run along the top of the cross-piece of the bayonet.

*Common faults :—*

    (i) Taking the left arm too far away from the side.

    (ii) Leaning the body forward from the hips when fixing.

3. " Squad—attention ".—Resume the position of attention by pulling the rifle into the right side, cutting the left arm the nearest way to the left side, and turning the head to the front.

*Common faults :—*

    (i) Lack of co-ordination between arms and head.

    (ii) Moving the butt on the ground.

    (iii) Cutting the left arm away with a loose wrist.

### Unfix bayonets

4. " The squad will unfix bayonets ". " Squad—unfix ".

With the right hand lift the rifle over the right instep and place the butt on the ground between the feet so that the toe of the butt is in line with the toes of the boots and the butt flat on the ground ; grip the rifle between the knees (which should be slightly bent) and strike the rifle on the stock with the left hand just below the nosecap, hand cupped as for the second movement of the *order arms*. Maintain the grip with the left hand and, with the right hand, strike the bayonet handle with the hand cupped ; press the retaining spring with the middle finger of the right hand, twist the bayonet to the left, forcing it off the rifle muzzle, turn it to the right, and lift it clear of the nosecap so that the blade is perpendicular with the ring to the rear.

*Common faults :—*

    (i) Failing to grip the rifle between the knees.

    (ii) Opening the heels.

    (iii) Leaning the body forward from the hips in order to clear the bayonet from the rifle.

    (iv) Looking down at the bayonet.

5. " Squad—bayonets ".—With a flick of the right wrist, turn the bayonet over to the left so that the flat of the blade strikes the left hip, and seize the scabbard with the left hand, pushing it as far forward as possible for the mouth to receive the bayonet ; force the bayonet fully home in the scabbard ; left elbow straight to the rear, shoulders square to the front, right elbow close to the front of the body ; as the right wrist flicks the bayonet over in the initial movement turn the head downwards and to the left, so that the eyes can just see to insert the bayonet into the scabbard.

*Common faults :—*

(i) Dropping the left shoulder to the rear.

(ii) Bringing the left elbow to the front.

(iii) Allowing the right elbow to leave the body.

6. " Squad—attention ".—Strike the rifle with the right hand in the exact position in relation to the stock as at the position of attention ; at the same time return the head to the position of attention ; count a regulation pause and, by lifting the rifle over the right instep, resume the position of attention.

*Common faults :—*

(i) Opening the heels.

(ii) Lack of co-ordination between head, arms and knees.

## SECTION 58 : PORT FROM THE ORDER, ORDER FROM THE PORT

### The port from the order

1. " Port—arms ".—With a flick of the right hand, wrist, and fore-arm, throw the rifle diagonally across the body, muzzle leading, magazine to the left and downwards, barrel crossing opposite the point of the left shoulder. (Do not allow the right hand to rise above the level of the waist belt.) Catch the rifle at the point of balance with the left hand, thumb and fingers round the rifle, in line with the left breast-pocket button. As the left hand catches the rifle, strike the rifle with the right hand so that the forefinger is outside the trigger guard, the remaining fingers and the thumb curled round the small of the butt, thumb nearest to the body.

*Common faults :—*

(i) Transferring the rifle from one hand to the other.

(ii) Leaning the body backwards as the rifle is thrown across the body.

### The order from the port

2. " Order arms—one ".—Strike the rifle with the right hand at the place at which it is held at the *order*, with the fingers and thumb round the rifle so that the thumb is nearest to the body, right forearm and elbow close on to the rifle.

3. " Squad—two ".—With the right hand force the rifle down to the right side and strike the stock with the left hand as for the second movement of the Order Arms from the Slope. (Sec 53.)

*Common faults :—*

As for the second movement of the *order* from the *slope*. (*See* Sec 53.)

4. " Squad—three ".—As for the third movement of the *order* from the *slope*.

## SECTION 59 : **PORT FROM THE SLOPE, SLOPE FROM THE PORT**

**Port from the Slope**

1. " Port arms—one ".—Seize the rifle with the right hand as in the first movement of the *present arms* (Sec 55), except that the hand will be round the small of the butt, with the right forefinger outside the trigger guard.

2. " **Squad—two** ".—Pull the rifle downwards across the body with the right hand, releasing it with the left; move the left hand inwards and upwards to receive the rifle in front of the left breast pocket.

*Common faults :—*

*First movement :*—(i) As for the first movement of the *present*.

*Second movement :*—(ii) Allowing the rifle to fall into the left hand instead of being pulled.

**Slope from the port**

3. " **Slope arms—one** ".—Drive the rifle into the left hand as in the second movement of the *slope* from the *order*. (Sec 53.)

4. " **Squad—two** ".—Cut the right hand to the right side as for the third movement of the *slope* from the *order*.

## SECTION 60 : **FOR INSPECTION PORT ARMS, EASE SPRINGS**

*Note.*—The squad having been ordered to Port Arms, the following movements are taught :—

**For inspection port arms**

1. " **For inspection port arms—one** ".—Push the safety catch forward with the right thumb.

2. " **Squad—two** ".—Seize the knob of the bolt between the thumb and first two fingers of the right hand, remaining fingers curled up, right elbow against the body.

3. " **Squad—three** ".—Turn the bolt handle upwards with the right hand and draw back the bolt to its full extent.

4. " **Squad—four** ".—Strike the butt with the right hand so that the butt is held in the palm of the hand; fingers together in front of the butt and extended towards the ground; the thumb horizontal and on the inside of the butt, nail in line with the cocking piece; right elbow against the body.

*Note.*—When judging the time, the word of command, which may be given from the *slope* or the *order*, is " **For inspection port—arms** ".

*Common faults :—*

    (i)  Allowing the rifle to move, owing to lack of control with the left hand.

    (ii)  Allowing the right hand to stray from one movement to the next without pause.

    (iii)  Having the back of the right hand and the wrist arched in the final position.

**Ease springs**

5. " **Ease springs—one** ".—Seize the knob of the bolt between the thumb and first two fingers of the right hand, remaining fingers curled up, right elbow against the body.

6. " **Squad—two** ".—With the right hand, close and open the bolt fully five times, or until all rounds or cases are ejected. Leave the bolt fully drawn back.

7. " **Squad—three** ".—Force the bolt home with the right hand and turn the bolt handle downwards.

8. " **Squad—four** ".—Press the trigger with the right forefinger.

9. " **Squad—five** ".—Strike and force down the bolt handle with the fingers of the right hand; turn the safety catch over to the rear with the forefinger.

10. " **Squad—six** ".—Return the right hand to the small of the butt, forefinger straight, and outside the trigger guard.

*Common faults :—*

    (i)  Allowing the rifle to move owing to lack of control with the left hand.

    (ii)  Allowing the right hand to stray from one movement to the next without pause.

### SECTION 61 : EXAMINE FROM THE PORT, EASE SPRINGS, PORT FROM THE EXAMINE, ORDER FROM THE EXAMINE

**The examine from the port**

1. " **Examine—arms** ".—" *Bend the left knee* ", placing the flat of the foot on the ground about 16 inches to the left front, and force the muzzle downwards with the left hand keeping the arm slightly bent so that the rifle is in front of the right shoulder, muzzle at eye level, butt pressing against the outside of the right thigh; place the right thumb in the charger guide with the nail uppermost and at an angle to reflect the light up the barrel; fingers together on the right of the rifle and extended towards the ground.

_Common faults :—_

(i)   Bending the body forward from the hips.
  (ii)  Turning the left toe to the front.
  (iii) Left thumb at an incorrect angle.

### Ease springs
2. " Ease—springs ".—(_See_ Sec 60.)

### The port from the examine
3. " **Port**—arms ".—Pull the rifle towards the body with the left hand into the correct position of the _port_ ; strike the rifle at the small of the butt with the right hand, forefinger outside the trigger guard; " _bend the left knee_ " to close the heels as in the position of attention.

### The order from the examine
4. " Order arms—one ".—Strike the rifle with the right hand in the same place as that held at the _order_, fingers and thumb curled round the rifle, forearm and elbow on the stock ; " _bend the left knee_ " to close the heels.

5. " Squad—two ".—Pull the rifle down to the right side, striking it with the left hand just below the nosecap as for the second movement of the _order_ from the _slope_ (Sec 53).

6. " **Squad—three** ".—Cut the left hand away as in the third movement of the _order_ from the _slope_.

_Common faults :—_
  _First movement :_
    (i) Not reaching up far enough with the right hand.
    (ii) Pulling the rifle towards the body with the left hand.

  _Second and third movement :_
    (iii) As in the _order_ from the _slope_.

_Notes :_  (i)  When a man in a squad has had his rifle inspected, he will wait until the man next but one to him is being inspected. He will then _ease springs, order arms_, and _stand at ease_.
       (ii)  If the squad are in the position of " _for inspection port arms_ " and one or more men are ordered individually to examine arms, they will return to the original position before easing springs, etc.
       (iii) If the squad have collectively received the order " Examine arms " they will ease springs and order arms from that position.

# SECTION 62 : TRAIL FROM THE ORDER, ORDER FROM THE TRAIL

**Trail from the order**

1. " **Trail—arms** ".—With a flick of the wrist throw the muzzle forwards and downwards, catching the rifle at the point of balance with the right hand, fingers and thumb round the rifle, back of the hand to the right, arm straight, so that the rifle is horizontal, muzzle pointing to the front and the magazine underneath.

*Common faults :—*

    (i) Rifle not horizontal.

    (ii) Muzzle pointing to the right or left.

    (iii) Right thumb on the right of the rifle instead of round it.

**Order from the trail**

2. " **Order—arms** ".—With the right hand force the butt to the ground and raise the muzzle to assume the correct position of the *Order*.

*Common faults :—*

    (i) Failing to get the butt in the right place.

    (ii) Banging the butt on the ground.

# SECTION 63 : TRAIL FROM THE SLOPE, SLOPE FROM THE TRAIL

**Trail from the slope**

1. " **Trail arms—one** ".—Seize the rifle at the point of balance with the right hand, fingers and thumb round the rifle with the back of the hand uppermost.

2. " **Squad—two** ".—Pull the rifle downwards and across the body with the right hand to the correct position of the *trail*, and release the rifle with the left arm, forcing the arm down the left side to the position of *attention*.

*Common faults :—*

    *First movement :* Failing to reach high enough up the rifle.

    *Second movement :*

        (i) Taking the elbow away from the side, thereby losing control.

        (ii) Moving the head.

**Slope from the trail**

3. " **Slope arms—one** ".—Force the rifle across the body driving the butt into the heel of the left hand as in the second movement of the *slope* from the *order* (Sec 53).

4. " **Squad—two** ".—Cut the right arm to the side as in the third movement of the *slope* from the *order*.

*Common faults :* Failing to reach up high enough in the first movement.

## SECTION 64 : SECURE FROM THE SLOPE, SLOPE FROM THE SECURE

**Secure from the slope**

1. " Secure arms—one ".—As for the first movement of the order from the *slope* (Sec 53).

2. " Squad—two ".—Turn the magazine to the front, move the left hand from the butt and seize the rifle in line with the left armpit, fingers and thumb round the rifle, back of the hand to the left, elbow forced downwards and to the rear.

3. " Squad—three."—Swing the muzzle down to the front with the right hand so that the rifle is pointing slightly downwards and in the same direction as the right toe, with the bolt action under the left armpit ; release the rifle with the right hand ; cut the right hand to the position of *attention*.

*Common faults :—*

  (i) *First movement :* As in the *order* from the *slope*.

  (ii) *Second movement :* Failing to reach up high enough with the left hand, thereby making it impossible to have the bolt action under the armpit in the final position.

  (iii) *Third movement :* Bringing the left hand forward thereby causing the bolt action to be forward of the arm pit.

**Slope from the secure**

4. " Slope arms—one".—Flex the left wrist and without moving the position of hand or arm bring the rifle to a perpendicular position in front of the left shoulder, magazine to the front ; at the same time seize the rifle at the small of the butt with the right hand, back of the hand to the front, fingers and thumb curled round the small.

5. " Squad—two ".—Drive the butt into the heel of the left hand as in the second movement of the *slope* from the *order* (Sec 53).

6. " Squad—three ".—Cut the right hand to the side as in the third movement of the *slope* from the *order*.

*Common faults :—*

  (i) Failing to get the magazine square to the front.

  (ii) Letting the left elbow move outwards and forwards.

  (iii) Putting the fingers of the right hand in front of the sling.

## SECTION 65 : SECURE FROM THE ORDER, ORDER FROM THE SECURE

**Secure from the order**

1. " Secure arms—one ".—Throw the rifle upwards and in front of the right shoulder with a flick of the right wrist, keeping the elbow into the side ; catch the rifle with the right hand at the point of balance so

that the forearm is parallel to the ground, hand in line with the waist belt, and the rifle perpendicular, magazine to the front.

2. " Squad—two ".—Throw the rifle across the body, catching it at the point of balance with the left hand so that the rifle is in the same position as in the first movement, except that it is in front of the left shoulder ; at the same time cut the right arm to the side.

3. " Squad—three ".—Force the bolt action under the left armpit in the position of the *secure*.

*Common faults :—*

    (i) *First movement :* Looking at the rifle.

    (ii) *Second movement :* Transferring the rifle from one hand to another.

    (iii) *Third movement :* Failing to pull the bolt action back under the armpit.

**Order from the secure**

4. " Order arms—one ".—Seize the rifle with the right hand in the place it is held at the *order* (Sec 53).

5. " Squad—two ".—Force the butt down and pull the rifle to the right side striking it with the left hand as in the second movement of the *order* from the *slope*.

6. " Squad—three ".—As in the third movement of the *order* from the *slope*.

*Common faults :—*

    (i) *First movement :* Right elbow away from the body and heel of the hand not against the stock.

    (ii) *Second movement :* Swinging the butt too far in front of the body.

    (iii) *Third movement :* As in the third movement of the *order* from the *slope* (Sec 53).

## SECTION 66 : CHANGE ARMS AT THE SLOPE

1. " Change arms—one ".—Seize the butt at the plate with the right hand, back of the hand uppermost, fingers underneath, thumb round the toe of the butt ; at the moment of impact seize the small of the butt with the left hand, fingers and thumb on top with the fingers between the butt and the sling, and the back of the hand underneath ; keep both elbows against the body.

2. " Squad—two ".—Force the rifle muzzle forwards in front of the centre of the body, pulling the heel of the butt against the pit of the stomach ; turn the magazine to the front, with the left thumb touching

the jacket ; force the rifle on to the right shoulder, turning the magazine to the right so that a correct slope is obtained.

3. " Squad—three ".—Cut the left hand to the side.

*Common faults :—*

*First movement*
  (i) Allowing the butt to move upwards.
  (ii) Having the fingers of the left hand round the sling.

*Second movement*
  (iii) Moving the head.
  (iv) Failing to pull the butt into the pit of the stomach thereby allowing the muzzle to describe a semi-circle instead of a " V ".
  (v) Putting the rifle on the right shoulder with the butt too far to the right.

*Third movement*
  (vi) Moving the right elbow away from the body, thereby bringing the hand out in front of the body.
  (vii) Moving the rifle on the shoulder.

*Note.*—The change arms from the right shoulder to the left is exactly the reverse procedure.

## SECTION 67 : CHANGE ARMS AT THE TRAIL

1. " Change arms—one ".—Force the rifle to a perpendicular position in front of the right shoulder without moving the upper arm, as in the first movement of the *secure* from the *order*   (Sec 65).

2. " Squad—two ".—Throw the rifle across the body as in the second movement of the *secure* from the *order*.

3. " Squad—three ".—Straighten the left arm to the side to bring the rifle to the *trail*.

*Common faults :—*

Ponderous movement of the rifle and movement of the body.

*Note.*—The change back to the right side is exactly the reverse procedure.

## SECTION 68 : CHANGE ARMS AT THE SECURE

1. " Change arms—one ".—Force the rifle to a perpendicular position in front of the left shoulder, magazine to the front, forearm parallel to the ground.

2. " Squad—two ".—Throw the rifle across the body as detailed in Sec 67.

" Squad—three ".—Force the bolt action under the right armpit in the correct position of the *secure.*

*Common faults :—*

    (i)  *First movement :*—Turning the magazine to the left.

    (ii)  *Second and third movements :*—As for the *secure.*

*Note.*—The change from right to left is exactly the reverse.

## SECTION 69 : ON GUARD FROM THE SLOPE, SLOPE FROM THE ON GUARD

*Note.*—Bayonets will be fixed and ranks will be opened to eight paces.

**On guard from the slope**

1. " **On guard—one** ".—Seize the rifle at the small of the butt with the right hand as in the first movement of the *port* (Sec **59**).

2. " Squad—two ".—" *Bend the left knee* " and place the foot flat on the ground 30 inches in front of the right foot; keep the knee slightly bent and incline the body a little forward so that the weight is over the left leg, with the left shoulder forward; keep the right leg braced back with the foot flat on the ground; force the head forward. At the same time force the rifle down in front of the right shoulder, seizing it as high up as possible with the left hand so that the upper arm is against the body with the arm slightly bent; bayonet at throat level, butt outside the right hip, magazine underneath, the right fore-finger outside the trigger guard with the hand just in front of the right thigh and the forearm pressing on the top of the butt.

3. " **Squad—three** ".—Push the safety catch forward.

4. " **Squad—four** ".—Seize the knob of the bolt as in the *For Inspection port arms* (Sec **60**).

5. " **Squad—five** ".—Open and close the bolt.

6. " **Squad—six** ".—Apply the safety catch with the forefinger, the remaining fingers pushing down the bolt lever.

7. " **Squad—seven** ".—Return the right hand to the small of the butt, forefinger outside the trigger guard.

*Common faults :—*

    (i)  Failing to reach up high enough with the left hand

    (ii)  Shortening the pace forward with the left leg.

    (iii)  Bending the right knee and raising the heel from the ground.

    (iv)  Having the butt between the forearm and the body.

    (v)  Finger on the trigger.

} Second movement

The slope from the on guard

*Note.*—Before arms are sloped the squad will be ordered to *ease springs*. This will be done in the *on guard* position in the sequence given in Sec **64**. For practice purposes this may be left until the end of the instruction.

8. " Slope **arms—one** ".—" *Bend the left knee* " and place the left heel against the right, straightening the body and head to the position of attention. At the same time pull the rifle back across the body driving the butt into the heel of the left hand as in the second movement of the *slope* from the *order*.

9. " Squad—**two** ".—Cut the right hand to the side.

*Common faults :*—

    (i)   Lack of co-ordination between right leg and arm.

   (ii)   Failing to straighten the body quickly enough.


## SECTION 70 : ON GUARD FROM THE ORDER, ORDER FROM THE ON GUARD

### On guard from the order

1. " **On** guard ".—Throw the rifle up in front of the right shoulder and adopt the *on guard* position, bringing both hands on to the rifle at the same time; cock the action in the correct sequence.

*Common faults :*—

Transferring the rifle from the right to the left hand in two movements.

### The order from the on guard

*Note.*—Before arms are ordered the squad will *ease springs* in the correct sequence. For practice purposes this may be left until the end of the instruction.

2. " **Order arms—one** ".—" *Bend the left knee* " and place the left heel against the right, straightening the body to the position of *attention*. At the same time seize the rifle with the right hand at the position held at the *order* in the same way as in the *order* from the *examine*.

3. " Squad—**two** ".—Bring the rifle to the right side as in the second movement of the *order* from the *examine* (Sec **61**).

Cut the left hand to the side.

*Common faults :*—

As in the *order* from the *examine*.

## SECTION 71 : THE CANT FROM THE ORDER, THE ORDER FROM THE CANT

*Note*.—The *cant* is always used when doubling with a rifle when the bayonet is *not* fixed.

**The cant from the order**

1. " Cant—arms ".—With a jerk of the right hand throw the rifle across the body as in the *port* from the *order* (Sec 58), except that the magazine points to the front; cut the right hand to the side and catch the rifle in the left hand at the point of balance, fingers and thumb round the rifle, elbow into the side.

*Common faults :—*

Transferring the rifle from one hand to the other.

**The order from the cant**

2. " Order arms—one ".—As for the *order* from the *port* (Sec 58), except that the back of the right hand is on top of the rifle.

3. " Squad—two " and " Squad—three ".—As for the *order* from the *port*.

*Common faults :—*

As for the *order* from the *port*.

## SECTION 72 : THE CANT FROM THE SLOPE, THE SLOPE FROM THE CANT

**The cant from the slope**

1. " Cant arms—one ".—As for the first movement of the *port* from the *slope* (Sec 59).

2. " Squad—two ".—As for the second movement of the *port* from the *slope* except that the magazine is turned to the front.

3. " Squad—three ".—Cut the right hand to the side.

*Common faults :—*

(i) *First and second movements*.—As for the *port* from the *slope*.

(ii) *Third movement*.—As for the *slope* from the *order*.

**The slope from the cant**

4. " Slope arms—one ".—Seize the rifle at the small of the butt with the right hand.

5. " Squad—two ".—Release the rifle with the left hand and drive the butt into the heel of the hand as in the first movement of the *slope* from the *port* (Sec 59).

6. " Squad—three ".—Cut the right hand to the side.

## SECTION 73 : **THE HIGH PORT FROM THE ON GUARD, FROM THE SLOPE, AND FROM THE ORDER**

*Note.*—The *high port* is always used when doubling with a rifle with bayonet fixed.

### High port from the on guard and vice versa

1. " High—port ".—" *Bend the right knee* " and place the right heel against the left, straightening the left knee and the body to the position of attention. At the same time force the rifle in front of the body without moving the position of the hand on the rifle, which is held diagonally across the front of the body, magazine to the front, left hand in front of the left shoulder and sufficiently far in front of the body for the butt to be brought instantly to the firing position.

*Common faults :*—

Rifle held too close to the body.

2. " On—guard ".—" *Bend the left knee* " and adopt the *on guard* position.

*Common faults :*—

Failing to adopt a fighting attitude immediately.

### High port from slope and vice versa

3. " High port—one ".—Seize the rifle at the small of the butt with the right hand as for the *port* from the *slope* (Sec 59).

4. " Squad—two ".—Force the rifle to the *high port* position in front of the body, turning the magazine to the front and seizing the rifle with the left hand.

5. " Slope arms—one ".—Bring the rifle to the shoulder as in the second movement of the *slope* from the *order* (Sec 53).

6. " Squad—two ".—Cut the right hand away.

*Common faults :*—

As detailed in similar movements.

### High port from the order and vice versa

7. " High—port ".—With a flick of the right wrist throw the rifle diagonally across the front of the body, seizing it simultaneously with both hands in the correct *high port* position.

8. " Order arms—one ".—Seize the rifle with the right hand as for the *order* from the *cant* (Sec **71**).

9. " Squad—two ".—Force the rifle down to the right side as for the *order* from the *cant*.

10. " Squad—three ".—Cut the left hand to the side.

*Common faults :*—

As detailed in similar movements.

## SECTION 74 : RECOVER FROM THE SLOPE, SLOPE FROM THE RECOVER

Recover from the slope

1. " Recover arms—one ".—Seize the rifle with the right hand at the small of the butt as for the first movement of the *port* from the *slope* (Sec 59).

2. " Squad—two ".—Bring the rifle to a perpendicular position in front of the body, magazine pointing to the rear, right hand round the small of the butt, back of the hand to the front and in line with the mouth. At the same time release the rifle with the left hand and seize it again so that the palm is round and underneath the butt plate, thumb round the heel 1 inch above the butt plate and the fingers together on the right of the butt ; elbows against the body.

*Common faults :—*

(i) Muzzle inclining towards the body.

(ii) Rifle held too low.

Slope from the recover

3. " Slope arms—one ".—Release the rifle with the left hand and drive the butt into the heel of the hand.

4. " Squad—two ".—Cut the right hand to the side.

*Common faults :—*

(i) Moving the head.

(ii) Failing to get any " crack " from the rifle.

## SECTION 75 : ORDER FROM THE RECOVER, RECOVER FROM THE ORDER

Order from the recover

1. " Order arms—one ".—Pull the rifle down in front of the left shoulder to the full extent of the left arm, releasing it with the right hand, keeping the magazine to the rear. Immediately seize the rifle with the right hand as in the first movement of the *order* from the *slope* (Sec 53).

2. " Squad—two ".—Force the rifle down across the body, turning the magazine to the front and striking it with the left hand as in the second movement of the *order* from the *slope*.

3. " Squad—three ".—Cut the left hand to the side.

*Common faults :—*

As for the *order* from the *slope*.

Recover from the order

4. " Recover arms—one ".—Throw the rifle perpendicularly up the right side as for the first movement of the *slope* from the *order* (Sec 53).

5. " **Squad—two** ".—Force the rifle upwards with the right hand to the correct position of the recover. At the same time seize the butt with the left hand.

*Note*.—The above movements are cumbersome, and it is more normal for arms first to be sloped in each case.

## SECTION 76 : **SHOULDER FROM THE ORDER, ORDER FROM THE SHOULDER**

### Shoulder from the order

1. " **Shoulder arms—one** ".—Throw the rifle perpendicularly up the right side as in the first movement of the *slope* from the *order* (Sec 53), except that the left arm comes across the body to seize the rifle in line with the waist belt, and the middle finger of the right hand is slipped inside the trigger guard, the first and middle fingers being round the magazine, thumb and remaining fingers pointing downwards, the upper part of the barrel resting in the hollow of the shoulder.

2. " **Squad—two** ".—Cut the left hand to the side.

*Common faults :—*

As for the first movement of the *slope* from the *order*.

*Note*.—The rifle must be caught about 2 inches lower than in the *slope*, otherwise the trigger will be too high and the right arm bent.

### Order from the shoulder

3. " **Order arms—one** ".—Release the rifle with the right hand and allow it to drop till the butt is 1 inch from the ground ; seize the rifle with both hands as in the second movement of the *order* from the *slope* (Sec 53).

4. " **Squad—two** ".—Cut the left hand to the side.

*Common faults :—*

Letting the butt crash to the ground.

## CHAPTER X

# RIFLE EXERCISES ON THE MARCH

Though some movements may be of practical use in moving about buildings or on the line of march, the main use of rifle exercises on the march is as a variant in the form of drilling trained soldiers. They are also an effective form of drill for drill displays.

Except in changing arms from the right shoulder to the left, all movements on the march are made on successive beats of the left foot. Words of command are given as the left foot comes to the ground. The movement starts the next time the left foot comes to the ground.

## SECTION 77 : **CHANGING ARMS**

" Change—arms "

1. When the rifle is at the *slope* on the left shoulder the word of command " **Arms** " is given as the left foot reaches the ground. The three movements are done on successive beats of the left foot.

2. When the rifle is at the *slope* on the right shoulder the word of command is given as the right foot reaches the ground the three movements are done on successive beats of the right foot.

## SECTION 78 : **MARCH AT EASE—MARCH TO ATTENTION WITHOUT SLINGING**

1. " **March at—ease** "

*1st beat*.—Seize the small of the butt with the right hand as in the first movement of the *port* from the *slope*.

*2nd beat*.—Push the rifle up, turning the magazine to the front, cocking piece on the shoulder, butt against the left breast pocket, muzzle inclining slightly to the rear.

*3rd beat*.—Cut the right hand to the side.

*Common faults :—*

(i) Butt away from the body.

(ii) Catching the sights in the clothing.

2. " **March to—attention** "

*1st beat*.—Seize the small of the butt with the right hand.

*2nd beat*.—Pull the rifle down to the correct position of the *slope*.

*3rd beat*.—Cut the right hand to the side.

*Common faults :—*

(i) Moving the head.

(ii) Catching the sights in the clothing.

## SECTION 79 : **MARCH AT EASE—SLING ARMS**

" **March at—ease** ".—Pull the rifle down the left side as in the first movement of the *order* from the *slope*.

*Note*.—Slings are loosened and the rifle slung on the right shoulder with the sling in front, rifle behind, in the men's own time.

## SECTION 80 : **DOUBLE TIME—CANT AND HIGH PORT**

On successive beats of the left foot do the movements already given in Secs **71** to **73**.

*Note*.—The *cant* is used when bayonets have not been fixed.

## CHAPTER XI

# FUNERAL EXERCISES WITH THE RIFLE

The following rifle exercises are required only by the firing party and troops lining the streets at a military funeral.

### SECTION 81 : REVERSE ARMS FROM THE PRESENT

1. " Reverse **arms—one** ".—*Bend the right knee* and place the foot alongside the left as in the *slope* from the *present* (Sec 55). At the same time force the rifle out in front of the body to the full extent of both arms, keeping the left hand as low as possible.

2. " **Squad—two** ".—Turn the rifle over slowly, by bringing the butt between the arms in the direction of the body (changing the grip of the hands) until the position of the rifle is reversed, with the muzzle pointing to the ground, magazine towards the body and in line with the chest ; arms straight ; fingers and thumb of both hands curled round the rifle.

3. " Squad—**three** ".—Interchange the position of the hands by seizing the small of the butt with the left hand, back of the hand to the left and immediately seizing the rifle at the point of balance with the right hand.

4. " Squad—**four** ".—Release the rifle with the right hand and force it under the left armpit, so that the magazine is uppermost and in front of the body, muzzle to the rear, rifle against the side, elbow against the rifle, rifle at an angle of 45 degrees. At the same time force the right arm behind the body in line with the waist belt and seize the rifle near the outer band, back of the hand downwards.

*Common faults :—*

| | |
|---|---|
| *First movement :* | (i) Raising the level of the left hand too much. |
| *Second movement :* | (ii) Loss of timing. |
| | (iii) Bending the arms. |
| | (iv) Rifle too high. |
| *Third movement :* | (v) Butt held too low causing the rifle to be nearly horizontal. |

*Note.*—The rifle is carried at the *reverse* only when marching in slow time.

### SECTION 82 : CHANGE ARMS FROM THE REVERSE

1. " Change arms—one ".—Release the rifle with the right hand and cut the right arm to the side. At the same time, hold the rifle at the small of the butt with the left hand and allow the muzzle to swing forward so that the rifle is perpendicular. Keep the left hand at the level of the breast pocket.

2. " Squad—two ".—Throw the rifle across the body and catch it at the small of the butt with the right hand level with the breast pocket. At the same time cut the left hand to the side.

3. " Squad—three ".—Force the rifle under the right armpit and seize it near the outer band with the left hand, arm behind the body, in the position of the reverse.

*Common faults :—*

| | |
|---|---|
| *First movement :* | (i) Forcing the left hand too far out in front of the body. |
| *Second movement :* | (ii) Allowing the rifle or hand to drop too low. |
| *Third movement :* | (iii) Butt held too low causing the rifle to be nearly horizontal. |

*Note.*—On the march, the movements are done on successive beats of the left foot and the same rules for rifle exercises on the march apply.

## SECTION 83 : TRAIL ARMS FROM THE REVERSE

*Note.*—Only done when breaking into quick time from slow time and when the rifle is under the left armpit.

1. " Trail arms—one ".—Release the rifle with the left hand and seize it again at the point of balance.

2. " Squad—two ".—Release the rifle with the right hand and force it down to the position of the trail, butt to the front, magazine uppermost.

*Common faults :—*

| | |
|---|---|
| (i) *First movement :* | Failing to bring the left hand far enough back to seize it at the point of balance. |
| (ii) *Second movement :* | As in the *trail.* |

## SECTION 84 : CHANGE ARMS AT THE TRAIL

As already detailed except that the position of the rifle is completely reversed.

## SECTION 85 : REVERSE ARMS FROM THE TRAIL

1. " Reverse arms—one ".—Force the rifle under the left armpit with the left hand to the correct position of the reverse, and at the same time seize it near the outer band with the right hand.

2. " Squad—two ".—Seize the rifle at the small of the butt with the left hand.

*Note.*— (i) Only done when the rifle is at the left side.

(ii) On the march the first movement is done as the left foot reaches the ground immediately after *bending the right knee* on the command " Slow—march ". The rules for rifle exercises on the march apply.

## SECTION 86 : REST ON YOUR ARMS REVERSED FROM THE REVERSE

*Note*.—Only done when the rifle is under the left arm.

1. " Rest on your arms—reversed ".—Cut the right hand to the side and bring the rifle to a perpendicular position with the left hand ; lower the muzzle on to the left boot, between the toecap and the lace-holes, so that the butt is in front of the centre of the body ; turn the head and eyes to the right and shoot the right arm to the right at shoulder level, arm straight, fingers extended, back of the hand uppermost ; bring the right arm round to the front keeping the arm straight until it has traversed 45 degrees ; bend the arm and place the right hand on the butt plate, back of the hand uppermost, fingers extended down the left side of the butt, thumb round the toe ; keep the right elbow away from the body and as high as possible ; pause and turn the head and eyes to the front.

To repeat the above movements with the left arm, turn the head and eyes to the left, and shoot the left arm to the left, placing the left hand over the right ; pause and look to the front, pause and drop both elbows against the body and lower the chin on to the breast.

In performing the above movements the time should be taken from the right or left hand man as the case may be.

*Common faults :—*

Doing the movement too hurriedly, thereby losing the dignity of the occasion.

## SECTION 87 : ATTENTION FROM REST ON YOUR ARMS REVERSED

" Squad—attention ".—Raise the head.

*Note*.—This command is always given before any other when resting on arms reversed.

## SECTION 88 : REVERSE ARMS FROM REST ON YOUR ARMS REVERSED

1. " Reverse arms—one ".—Seize the small of the butt with the left hand, back of the hand to the left.

2. " Squad—two ".—Force the rifle under the left armpit and seize it with the right hand behind the back as for the reverse.

*Common faults :—*

    (i) *First movement :* Dropping the left shoulder.

    (ii) *Second movement :* As detailed in similar movements.

## SECTION 89 : PRESENT ARMS FROM REST ON YOUR ARMS REVERSED AND VICE VERSA

To present arms from rest on your arms reversed

1. " Present arms—one ".—Raise the rifle about six inches with the right hand. At the same time seize it with the left hand in the relative position held when at the *present*, back of the hand downwards and towards the body, thumb to the left

2. " Squad—two ".—Seize the rifle just below the small of the butt with the right hand in the relative position held when at the *present*, thumb on the left, fingers on the right, back of the hand to the front.

3. " Squad—three ".—Turn the rifle over by lowering the butt towards the body and come to the *present* ; " *bend the right knee* " and move the foot to its correct position.

To rest on your arms reversed from the present

4. " Rest on your arms reversed—one ".—Bring the right foot smartly up to the left, raise the rifle about six inches, and place the left hand underneath the butt plate, thumb round the toe of the butt, the first two joints of the fingers grasping the right side of the butt.

5. " Squad—two ".—Turn the rifle over to the front, muzzle leading, butt kept close to the body so that the position of the rifle is reversed, *ie*, the muzzle is now pointing towards the ground. Place the muzzle on the toe of the left boot.

The left hand will be allowed to turn with the rifle so that on the completion of the movement it will be resting on top of the butt plate, fingers and thumb being in the same position as in *one*. At the same time lower the head on to the breast.

6. " Squad—three ".—Place the right hand on top of the left.

## SECTION 90 : FUNERAL EXERCISES—SIMPLIFIED VERSION

1. When time and standard of training do not allow of the full detail above to be taught, the following simplified drill will be observed.

(*a*) All marching will be at the *slope*.

(*b*) A simplified form of *rest on your arms reversed* will be used. This is done only from the *present* and will be followed by " *Attention* " and return to the *present*.
This form is also used by all troops lining the streets who may have to present arms after the bier has passed.

(*c*) If time does not even permit this being taught the compliment of the *present* will be paid.

**Rest on your arms reversed**

2. " Rest on your arms reversed—one ".—" *Bend the right knee* " and bring the right foot in to the left. At the same time force the rifle out in front of the body to the full extent of both arms, keeping the left hand as low as possible.

3. " Squad—two ".—Turn the rifle over slowly by bringing the butt between the arms in the direction of the body (changing the grip of the hands) until the position of the rifle is reversed, with the muzzle pointing to the ground, magazine towards the body and in line with the chest ; arms straight : fingers and thumbs of both hands curled round the rifle.

4. " Squad—three ".—Interchange the position of the hands by seizing the small of the butt with the left hand, back of the hand to the left and immediately seizing the rifle at the point of balance with the right hand.

5. " Squad—four ".—Place the muzzle on the left toe so that the butt is in front of the centre of the body. At the same time place the right hand on the butt plate, back of the hand uppermost, fingers extended down the left side of the butt, thumb round the toe : elbow against the body.

6. " Squad—five ".—Place the left hand on top of the right : lower the chin on the breast.


## CHAPTER XII

# PISTOL DRILL

Each movement is described for the 9-mm automatic and for the ·38-inch revolver.

For funeral exercises with the pistol *see* Appendix C.

### SECTION 91 : FOR INSPECTION—DRAW PISTOLS

**9-mm. automatic**

1. " For inspection draw pistols—one ".—Using both hands, unfasten the case in the most convenient way ; raise the flap, keeping it open and held between the right wrist and the body : keep both hands on the pouch.

2. " Squad—two ".—Seize the grip with the right hand, fingers and thumb round it, forefinger outside the trigger guard, back of the hand to the front ; draw the pistol and hold it so that the pistol is about 12 inches in front of the centre of the body, muzzle pointing to

the ground, magazine to the right ; right hand in line with the waist belt. At the same time seize the sliding portion with the left hand, thumb straight, nearest to the body and pointing upwards with the ball on the grooves, fingers in front of the slide, forefinger on the grooves ; both elbows against the body.

3. " Squad—three ".—With the left hand, force the sliding portion up until it is locked in the rear position.

4. " Squad—four ".—Cut the left hand to the side.

·38-inch revolver

5. " For inspection draw pistols—one ".—Bring both hands to the case and unbutton it as detailed above.

6. " Squad—two ".—Draw the pistol with the right hand, forefinger outside the trigger guard, and bring the pistol to a vertical position about 12 inches in front of the centre of the body at breast pocket level, muzzle downwards, barrel upright. At the same time grasp the barrel with the left hand, thumb pressing against the comb and cylinder fluting.

7. " Squad—three ".—Open the pistol ; keep the left hand and barrel stationary.

8. " Squad—four ".—Cut the right hand away to the side.

## SECTION 92 : EXAMINE PISTOLS

*Note.*—Done from the *for inspection draw pistols* position.

9-mm automatic

1. " Examine pistols—one".—Seize the pistol with the left hand round the barrel so that the back of the hand is to the left, and the trigger guard is resting on the thumb and forefinger.

2. " Squad—two".—Release the pistol with the right hand and cut that arm to the side. At the same time force the pistol just above the left shoulder, bottom of the butt resting on the shoulder, trigger guard to the right, ejector opening uppermost, barrel horizontal, muzzle to the front, back of the hand to the left, elbow against the body.

After the barrel has been inspected and the inspecting officer has passed the next file the final position of the " *draw* " will be resumed as follows :—

3. " Squad—one".—Bring the pistol down in front of the body and seize the butt with the right hand, forefinger outside the trigger guard, as in the second position of the *for inspection draw pistols*.

4. " Squad—two".—Cut the left hand to the side.

·38-inch revolver

5. " **Examine pistols—one**".—Grasp the butt of the pistol with the right hand.

6. " Squad—two".—With the right hand, force the pistol to the right side and in line with the shoulder, barrel pointing to the front ready for inspection, the left hand grasping the top of the barrel, left elbow in line with the shoulder, right elbow close to the side.

7. " Squad—three".—Cut the left hand away to the side.
After the barrel has been inspected and the inspecting officer has passed the next file, the final position of the " *draw* " will be resumed as follows :—

8. " Squad—one".—Bring the pistol to the correct position with the right hand, grasping it with the left hand.

9. " Squad—two".—Cut the right hand away to the side.

## SECTION 93 : **RETURN PISTOLS AFTER INSPECTION**

**9-mm automatic**

1. " **Return pistols—one**".—Depress the long catch to the right with the right thumb.

2. " Squad—two".—Operate the trigger with the right forefinger.

3. " Squad—three".—Return the pistol to the case ; fasten the case, using both hands.

4. " Squad—four".—Cut both hands to the side to assume the position of attention.

·38-inch revolver

5. " **Return pistols—one**".—Close the pistol by raising the butt to the barrel, with the right hand ; keep the left hand stationary.

6. " Squad—two".—Return the pistol to the case using both hands and fasten the case.

7. " Squad—three ".—Cut the right hand away and adopt the position of attention.

## SECTION 94 : PROVE PISTOLS

1. " **Prove pistols—one** " " **two** " and " **three**".—Draw the pistol as detailed above.

2. " Squad—four."—Turn the breech of the pistol towards the front keeping the elbows stationary.

*Note.*—If some men are armed with rifles and others with pistols, the latter will *prove* on the command " *for inspection port— arms.*" When arms are ordered they will return pistols.

## CHAPTER XIII

# SENTRY DRILL

Sentry drill is necessary to teach the movements required by men on guard duty. The movements themselves incorporate a large number of the movements of elementary drill. As a preliminary, picquet sentry drill may be taught which is the same as sentry drill but without rifles.

All movements start from and finish at the position of *stand at ease*. (This represents the sentry on his post.) Movements start therefore by coming to attention and then taking a pace forward (so that, when sloping arms, the bayonet does not hit the sentry box).

When on their beat double-sentries will :—

   (a) move in quick time at the *slope* ;

   (b) turn inwards to the left or right about on arrival at the end of the beat ;

   (c) not halt except in front of the sentry box, unless to pay compliments or when challenging ;

   (d) turn to the right and left correctly.

When standing on their post sentries will :—

   (e) face their front and stand properly *at ease* ;

   (f) not stand in their boxes in good or even moderate weather. Except in the execution of their duty sentries will not quit their post or converse with anyone.

The cautionary words " **As on sentry** " will precede each word of command.

## SECTION 95 : SINGLE SENTRY PAYING COMPLIMENTS ON HIS POST

*Notes* : (i) The following drill is described as for drilling a squad but indicates the correct action for the single sentry.

   (ii) The two compliments that can be paid are the *salute* and the *present*. Before either is made the sentry must first come to the *slope*.

   (iii) A sentry on his post will be alert to observe an officer approaching so that he can be at the *salute* or *present* as the officer comes within three paces of his post. He will cut his hand away or return to the *slope*, when the officer is three paces past him.

   (iv) A sentry in his box will come to attention but will not salute.

   (v) A " roaming sentry " with rifle slung will halt, turn to his front and stand to attention until the officer has passed.

   (vi) A sentry with pickhelve or small fire-arm will salute with the hand.

**The salute**

" As on sentry, to the front—salute".—The squad, which will be standing properly *at ease* and acting individually as for a sentry on his post, will :—

Come to attention ; take a pace forward of 30 inches ; slope arms ; make the butt salute and remain.

Movements will be at the rate of 40 to the minute.

**The present**

" As on sentry, present—arms ".—Action will be as above except that the squad will *present arms*.

*Common faults :—*

    (i)   Movements too hurried.

    (ii)  Rifle allowed to swing out of control in the pace forward.

    (iii)  Too short a pace forward.

## SECTION 96 : SINGLE SENTRY STANDING AT EASE

" As on sentry, stand at—ease "

The reverse process is carried out. The squad will cut the hand away (or *slope arms*), *order arms*, take a pace to the rear and stand at ease.

## SECTION 97 : SINGLE SENTRY PATROLLING AND PAYING COMPLIMENTS ON HIS BEAT

*Note.*—The number of paces or extent of a sentry's beat will always be defined in the orders for that post.

1. " As on sentry, to the right (or left)—march ".—The squad will come to attention, take a pace forward, *slope arms*, turn to the right (or left) and step off in quick time.

2. " As on sentry, about turn ".—On reaching the end of his beat the sentry will turn about. If marching to the right he will turn left about, if marching to the left he will turn right about.

3. " As on sentry, stand at—ease ".—This will be given as for " *halt* ". The squad will halt (as a sentry would in front of his sentry-box), turn to face their front, *order arms*, take a pace to the rear and stand at ease.

*Common fault :—*

A tendency to quicken the pace during the about turn.

4. While on patrol a sentry may be required to salute or present. Provided that there is time he will move to his post otherwise he will pay the compliment directly. In each case he will halt, face his front, and salute or present.

He will then either continue his patrol or stand at ease.

5. For the squad the word of command will be :—

" As on sentry, to the front—salute " ⎫ This will be given as for "halt".
        or       ⎬ The squad will halt, face their
" As on sentry, present arms " ⎭ front and act accordingly.

6. The next word of command will be :—

" **As on sentry, to** the right (or left)—**march** " ⎫
        or       ⎬ The squad will act
" As on sentry, stand at—**ease** " ⎭ accordingly.

The squad can now practise patrolling a set number of paces. The instructor will give his orders before getting the squad on the march by telling them to patrol, out and in, a number of times and finally to pay a compliment, or to stand at ease. The only word of command needed is " As on sentry to the right (or left)—march ".

*Note.*— (i) The word of command " About—turn " is always given as the left foot is level with and passing the right, ensuring that the turn about, whether to the left or right, is done in the sequence already taught. This method of turning about applies at all times throughout sentry drill. When counting a set number of paces, the beat is always an odd number, so that the end of the beat is reached as the left foot comes to the ground. The right arm and right leg are then cut in and the turn finally completed by leading on with the right leg. The paces are again counted from when the foot next reaches the ground.

(ii) If the beat of a single sentry is both to his right and left and the total gives an even number of paces, one pace must be subtracted from the total, so that when doing a complete patrol the turn about may be done correctly.

## SECTION 98 : **DOUBLE SENTRIES PAYING COMPLIMENTS ON THEIR POST**

1. A double sentry comprises two men who act together, taking the time from the right hand and senior one. The right hand and senior sentry is the " old soldier " and is in command of the post. His position of authority must be emphasized.

The only exception to this is when, standing *at ease* on their post, an officer appears from the left, when the left hand sentry will give the time.

The time is signalled by tapping the butt on the ground. These movements are taught first by word of command.

2. To teach the movements of a " double sentry " the squad is first practised, as a whole, as the right hand or old soldier and then as the left hand or junior. The squad is then divided in half by numbering, proving the right of the left half; then giving the left half the order " **Four paces left close—march** ".

3. When the signal is given by tapping the butt a regulation pause will be counted by both sentries before starting the movement. This is to ensure that the junior sentry does not " jump the pistol ". The taps with the butt will be given in quick succession.

When at the halt and after paying a compliment, the sentries will " look in " towards each other. The signal to *stand at ease* as on sentry is taken as from when the old soldier turns his head to the front. A regulation pause will be counted before the sentries move.

4. Signals when on patrol can only be given when the sentries are marching inwards.

### To patrol (Signal—1 tap)

5. " As on sentry, outwards—march ".—The squad come to *attention*, *slope arms*, turn outwards, and patrol in quick time.

*Note.*— (i) The extent of the beat must have already been pointed out.

(ii) " As on sentry, about—turn " is not given.

(iii) To practise the squad the command can be given by signal by the instructor or a man of the right half detailed by him.

### To salute (Signal—2 taps) or present arms (Signal—3 taps)

6. " As on sentry, to the front—salute " (or " present—arms "). *See* Sec 95.

7. " As on sentry, stand at—ease " (Signal—Sentries " look in " and the old soldier turns his head to the front). *See* Sec. 100. The sentries work together.

## SECTION 99 : DOUBLE SENTRIES PATROLLING

" As on sentry, stand at—ease " (Signal—Extend one finger of the right hand). *See* Sec 100.

The signal will be given so that both sentries will halt in front of their sentry-box or post.

The signal is shown as the left foot comes to the ground, is repeated as the left foot comes to the ground again and the halt is made as the left foot comes to the ground the third time. The sentries proceed to face their front.

## SECTION 100 : DOUBLE SENTRIES PAYING COMPLIMENTS ON THEIR BEAT

Salute (Signal—Extend two fingers of the right hand)

1. " As on sentry, to the front—salute ".—The right hand sentry will, if possible, time his signal so that they halt on their post. This may not always be possible.

Present arms (Signal—Extend three fingers of the right hand)

2. " As on sentry, present—arms ".—As above but presenting arms.

3. To move in, sentries " look in ". After paying a compliment from patrolling, a double sentry will always continue patrolling. If they are more than three paces from their posts they will turn inwards. If they are three paces, or less, from their posts, they will turn outwards.

## CHAPTER XIV

# GUARDS AND SENTRIES

The object of this chapter is to lay down a simple routine that will ensure the effective mounting and relief of guards and sentries under peace-time conditions. The detail gives the normal system laid down for the Army for ceremonial purposes, but units which have their own regimental customs may continue in their tradition.

## SECTION 101 : GENERAL

1. The following instructions are generally applicable to guards mounted for ceremonial purposes (as opposed to tactical), with the exception that, in paying and returning compliments, commanders of guards and sentries will salute with the hand instead of presenting arms.

2. During guard mountings officers armed with the sword will be at the " Carry ".

3. The personal weapon for guards and sentries of units of the Royal Armoured Corps is the pistol.

4. Mounted troops, if on guard dismounted with the sword, will adjust the following instructions to sword drill.

5. Guards, including reliefs, rounds and patrols will march with sloped arms and bayonets fixed. (Except for the senior warrant or non-commissioned officer of the guard, who will not fix bayonet.)

6. Guards, rounds, sentries and reliefs will pay compliments as laid down in King's Regulations.

## SECTION 102 : GUARD MOUNTING

Parading

1. All guard or picquet duties will be paraded and inspected on the regimental/battalion, squadron/battery or company parade ground.

Duties will be formed up in line, the guards on the right, picquets on the left, with the spare man two paces in rear of and covering the right hand file of his guard or picquet.

2. If the guard is commanded by an officer, his place will be three paces in front of the centre, and the senior NCO on the right of the guard.

If the guard is commanded by a NCO, he will be on the right of the guard and will not be covered ; the next senior NCO (if any) being on the left will not be covered off. If a drummer or trumpeter is mounting with the guard his position will be on the right of and in line with the senior NCO of the guard. Guards and duties will be inspected by the adjutant or orderly officer. After inspection the adjutant (or orderly officer) will fall in the officers (if any) and order the guards and picquets to be marched off and spare men for duty to be dismissed.

### Formation of a barrack guard

3. The normal formation for a barrack guard will be as follows :—

Two NCOs and three other ranks in single rank. (The junior NCO marches on the right, the senior in rear.)

Two NCOs and six other ranks, in two ranks.

Two NCOs and nine other ranks, in three ranks.

4. In the event of more than two NCOs being on any one guard, the senior NCO marches two paces in rear of and in the centre of the rear rank, the next senior on the right, the junior on the left.

5. When the new guard is halted opposite the old guard, they will be dressed by the sergeant in charge of the guard, who will then place himself on the right of the guard before giving his words of command.

### SECTION 103 : RELIEVING, POSTING, AND DISMISSING A GUARD

1. When the ground admits, the new guard will advance in line towards the front of the old guard and be halted, when possible, 15 paces in front of it. When this is not possible, the new guard will halt six paces from the left of the old guard facing the same direction.

2. The old guard will then *present arms*, and the new guard will return the salute. Commanders of guards, if officers, will salute : if NCOs, they will *present arms* at the same time as the men.

On a barrack or quarter guard the senior NCO of the guard will, while still at the *present* (after the new guard have *presented arms*) state the number of sentry posts, *eg*, " One by day, two by night ".

3. Both guards will then *slope arms*, *order arms*, and *stand at ease*.

The new guard will be told off and the first relief sent out. When the first relief of the new guard is sent out, a NCO (normally a corporal) of the old guard, will accompany it to bring in the relieved sentries. If the relief move in line, the NCO will be on the left flank, if in file (or single file) he will be at the head of the file or rank. As soon as all the sentries are relieved, the two NCOs will change places and the NCO of the old guard will assume command. While the relief is marching round, the commander will take over the property in charge of the guard according to the list on the inventory board, at the same time checking the list in the old guard report.

4. When the reliefs have returned, and all the men of the old guard have fallen in, both guards will be called to attention and ordered to *slope arms*.

5. In every case the word of command will be given by the old guard first, followed by the new guard, *eg*, " **Old guard, slope—arms** "— " **New guard, slope—arms** ", etc.

6. The old guard will then move off, in line if possible, otherwise in threes or file, the new guard *presenting arms*, the commander of the old guard giving " **Eyes right** " (or **Left**) as he marches off and after changing direction.

7. When the old guard has left, the new guard will be addressed by its title, *eg*, " barrack guard ". The new guard will *slope arms* and will receive the command " **Move to the right (or left) in file quick— march** ". It will be marched to the position previously occupied by the old guard. Here will be explained the detail for turning out. The guard will dismiss to the guard-room, where the orders for the guard will be read out. These orders will also be read and explained to the men of the first relief when they come off sentry.

8. If it is necessary to pay compliments during guard mounting, words of command will be given to both guards by the senior officer or NCO on parade.

9. The old guard will be marched to the regimental parade ground and, after inspection of weapons and ammunition, will be dismissed.

## SECTION 104 : **GUARD TURNING OUT AND TURNING IN**

1. " **Guard—turn out** ".—(Given by the sentry on the guard-room.) The guard will turn out at the double, with rifles at the high port if bayonets are fixed, and fall in at the slope, in open order, taking up their own sizing and dressing. The trumpets or bugles (if on parade) will be two paces to the right of the senior NCO.

When the guard is commanded by an officer he will be three paces in front of the centre of the guard.

2. " **To the guard-room, dis—miss** ".—Given by the senior NCO. The guard will dismiss in open order and file into the guard-room. The sentry will salute in time with the guard and will state his post " **No. 1 post and all's well, Sir** ", if he is visited by the officer.

B

3. The guard commander will accompany the inspecting officer round the guard-room premises, cells, etc.

*Notes* : Guards and picquets turn out under peace-time conditions :—

(i) To pay compliments to members of the Royal Family, to certain distinguished persons, to senior officers, and to armed parties, etc (*See* Kings Regulations) except that after retreat and before reveille a barrack guard will not turn out to pay compliments except to " rounds " or an armed party.

(ii) As a routine at reveille, retreat, and tattoo, when they will be inspected by the guard commander.

(iii) When called upon to do so by visiting or other " rounds ".

(iv) When the guard is turning out to the brigade commander or a still more senior officer, the NCO will remain on the right of his guard and will not accompany the inspecting officer.

(v) In paying compliments, the NCO commanding the guard will handle his arms in like manner with the guard.

(vi) Between retreat and reveille the NCO on duty may be inside the guard-room. The sentry on the guard-room must call out the NCO as soon as he observes rounds or an armed party approaching.

## SECTION 105 : POSTING, RELIEVING, MARCHING AND DISMISSING SENTRIES AND RELIEFS

### Posting sentries

1. When a sentry, who is to be posted on a new post as yet without a sentry, reaches a point just short of the post assigned to him, he will be halted. The sentry will then step off without further order and will halt and face in the required direction on his exact post. The NCO (normally a corporal) will then read and explain to him his orders, the object for which he is posted, the front of his post, and the extent of his beat.

### Relieving sentries

2. " Relief—halt ".—On the approach of the relief, the sentry, with his rifle at the *slope*, will place himself in front of the sentry box. The NCO of the relief will halt the relief at about two paces from the sentry. The new sentry will then move out from the relief, and fall in on the left of the old sentry turning to face in the same direction. The NCO will read the orders to the new sentry and ensure that the sentry understands them.

3. " Sentries—pass ".—The old sentry will move to his place in rear of the relief, and the new sentry will close two paces to his right.

4. " **Relief quick—march** ".—The relief will be marched off. The relief will give " **Eyes—right** " to the sentry and the sentry will salute working on the command " **Eyes—right** " and " **Eyes—front** ".

### Marching reliefs

5. Reliefs of fewer than four men will be formed in single rank ; when of four men or upwards, they will be formed into two ranks.

When marching in line, the NCO will be two paces in rear of the centre ; when in file (or single file) he will be on the right of the rear file (or man). The exception to this is when guards are changing.

### Dismissing a relief

6. When dismissing a sentry or relief he will be dismissed to the guard-room without permission being obtained from an officer or senior NCO. If an officer is in sight, the sentry will salute.

## SECTION 106 : **CHALLENGING**

1. A sentry will challenge a person or party approaching his post when he is doubtful of whether that person or party is authorized to pass or suspicious of his or their reasons for approaching. Challenging is also necessary when it is ordered or in special cases, such as that of a sentry posted on a fortress or prison, or when a password has to be delivered.

2. When it is necessary to challenge the sentry will act as follows :—

(a) He will come to the *on guard* position when a person or party approaches the post, and will, as soon as the person or party is within speaking distance, call out " **Halt** " and when the person or party has halted, " **Advance one** "; if, and when, the sentry is satisfied as to the identity of the person or party, he will say " **Pass, friend—all's well** " then *slope arms* and pay the required compliment as the person or party goes past.

(b) If a password is to be given, the sentry will come to the *on guard* " position and will halt the party approaching at about ten paces from him. Although it is normal for a NCO of the guard to be on duty at the same time as the sentry, if he is not there then the sentry will call him from the guard room. The sentry will order " **Who goes there** " at which the party will identify itself. Thereafter the sentry will order " **Advance one and give the countersign** ". The individual will then give the password and, if correct, the sentry will call out " **Advance friend, all's well** ". The party will then be stepped off by their officer or NCO who will order " **Eyes—left** " (or **right**) to the sentry. The guard and/or sentry will then pay the appropriate compliment.

(*c*) In the event of his challenge being disregarded, or his orders disobeyed, a sentry will turn out the guard or take such other action as is laid down in his guard orders.

*Note*.—This procedure is altered in the case of tactical guards. " Advance one " means that one person only is to advance for identification. If in answer to the challenge the sentry receives the reply " *Grand* (or *Visiting*) *rounds* ", he will call out " **Stand, grand (or Visiting) rounds—advance one**," the sentry remaining *on guard*, etc, until he has identified the person approaching or until he has received the password. When satisfied the sentry will say " **Pass, grand (or visiting) rounds—all's well** " ; presenting arms, etc., or turning out the guard or saluting as the case requires.

When challenging is unnecessary, grand or visiting rounds will inform the sentry as to their identity on approaching his post, the sentry presenting arms, in the case of grand rounds, and remaining at the *slope* in the case of visiting rounds.

# KEY TO DIAGRAMS
## (*See* Chapters XV-XVII)

| | |
|---|---|
| Commanding officer .. .. .. .. .. | ☦⊙ |
| Unit second in command .. .. .. .. | ⊙ |
| Adjutant .. .. .. .. .. .. | ⊕ |
| RSM .. .. .. .. .. .. .. | ⊞ |
| Drill Sergeant .. ..′ .. .. .. .. | ⊞ |
| | |
| Company commander (or equivalent) .. .. | ⊙ |
| Company second in command .. .. .. | ⊙ |
| CSM .. .. .. .. .. .. .. | ⊟ |
| CQMS .. .. .. .. .. .. .. | ⊡ |
| | |
| Platoon commander (or equivalent) .. .. | ○ |
| Other officers .. .. .. .. | ○ |
| Platoon Sergeant ⎤<br>⎬ .. .. .. .. ..<br>or other Sergeant ⎦ | ⊡ |
| Section Commander .. .. .. .. .. | ⊠ |
| Rank and file .. .. .. .. .. .. | ☐ |
| Front, centre and rear ranks .. .. .. .. | ▭ |

## CHAPTER XV

# PLATOON DRILL

Platoon drill is taught as an essential preliminary to company drill. It is the first occasion on which a specific sub-unit is drilled together and is therefore of particular importance in building up the identity of the platoon.

### SECTION 107 : FORMATIONS AND POSITIONS

There are three formations, *Line, Column of Threes, and Column of Route.*

#### Line

1. The platoon will form up with each section forming one rank, section commander on the right, second in command of the section on the left. The platoon commander will be three paces in front of the centre of the platoon and the platoon sergeant three paces in rear of the centre. The platoon commander, centre file and platoon sergeant will all cover off, the centre man of the front rank guiding the officer as required.

#### Column of threes

2. A platoon in column of threes is in exactly the same formation as line but facing a flank. Positions are only changed when the flank of direction changes. The officer and platoon sergeant then change places, the officer always being on the directing flank. The officer and sergeant will move round the head and tail of the platoon in a clockwise direction. This is the normal formation for drill, when moving to a flank in threes.

#### Column of route

3. Column of route is as above except that the officer and sergeant move to the head and tail respectively of the platoon, moving in a clockwise direction, the move taking place after completing the turn and before the platoon steps off. When changing places from the halt the officer and sergeant will move in quick time, if on the march they will move at the double.

Column of route demands that all supernumerary ranks form within the column of threes. This formation is only used when on the line of march.

*Common faults :—*

    (i) Not keeping closed up on the march.

    (ii) Bulging out from the wheeling point when wheeling.

*Note.*—The instructor must explain the meaning of the cautionary words of command " **Advance (or retire) in column of threes** "

## A PLATOON IN LINE

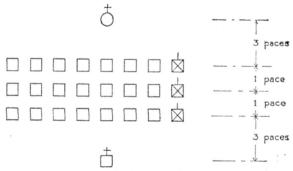

*Note.*—The men will fall in with their own sections.

## A PLATOON IN COLUMN OF THREES
## BY THE LEFT

For column of route, the platoon commander would be an arm's distance in front of the centre section commander and the platoon sergeant an arm's distance behind the second in command of the rear section.

4. "No. . . . **Platoon will advance in column of threes from the right**". "**Right—turn**", "**Left Wheel, by the left, quick—march**".

The term "Advance" or "Retire" in column of threes means that, on stepping off, the leading section of threes will wheel at once in the direction indicated.

As in squad drill the cautionary word of command "**Right**" or "**Left**" will indicate the direction in which the platoon will turn.

## SECTION 108 : DRESSING

1. Whenever the platoon halts in line, it will receive the command " Right—dress " and will act as in squad drill. The platoon sergeant will move out five paces to the right of the platoon. He will dress all three ranks in the order—front, centre, rear and will return to the front rank and give the command " Eyes—front ". He will then return to his position in quick time.

2. During training or out of barracks and in order to save time, the platoon commander may order " By the—right ". Every man will turn his head and eyes off to the front in succession from right to left, as soon as he has got his dressing.

## CHAPTER XVI

# COMPANY DRILL

The movements required in company drill incorporate most of the basic duties detailed in this manual.

Company drill, well conducted, is of great value in building up the morale and confidence of the company. It also provides an opportunity to practise junior leaders in giving words of command and in asserting their power of command.

Company drill should at first be preceded by a lecture to the officers, NCOs and guides to ensure that they understand the formations and movements to be done. Officers, NCOs and guides should change places during drill so that all are practised.

## SECTION 109 : FORMATIONS AND POSITIONS OF OFFICERS, WARRANT OFFICERS AND PLATOON SERGEANTS

1. The following are the formations in company drill :—

| | |
|---|---|
| Line | Column of route |
| Column of threes | Column of platoons |
| Close column of platoons | |

**Line**

2. The three platoons form up side by side with three paces interval between each platoon. Each platoon is drawn-up as for platoon drill. The company commander is in the centre of his company three paces in front of the centre platoon commander (who will guide him to ensure he is covered off). The second in command of the company will be three paces in front of the right-hand man of the company. The CSM will be level with the centre platoon sergeant but one file on his right and the CQMS one file to his left.

85

A COMPANY IN LINE

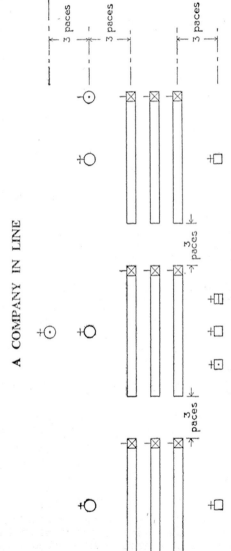

*Note.*—A company in column of threes is an identical formation but facing a flank.

# A COMPANY IN COLUMN

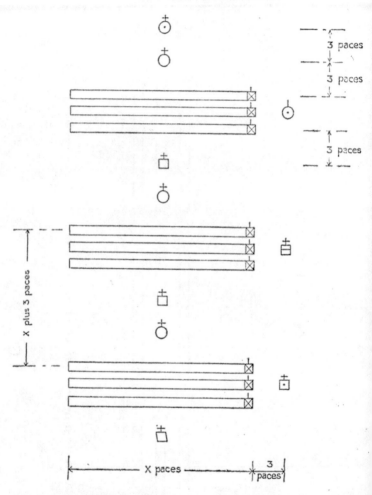

A company in close column is exactly the same formation except that the distance between platoons is shortened to any convenien number of paces.

**Column of threes**

3. Column of threes is the same as line but facing a flank. The officers will be on the directing flank. If this flank is changed officers and the supernumerary rank will move clockwise round platoons to gain their positions; on the march in double time, at the halt in quick time.

**Column of route**

4. Column of route is the same as column of threes except that all officers and supernumeraries are in the ranks, the company commander leading, the CSM level with the platoon commander of the leading platoon, and the second in command and CQMS in rear of the rear platoon. Platoon commanders will be in front and platoon sergeant in rear of their platoons.

*Notes.*—(i) Company and platoon commanders will break ranks to supervise the marching and, if necessary to give a word of command or pay a compliment.

(ii) Where an officer is in front, it is the duty of the man behind him to keep him at his correct distance and place. Such men in the ranks must not hesitate to raise their voices to say " Forward ", " Right ", " Left " or " Correct ", etc.

**Column and close column of platoons**

5. Column of platoons is the formation in which the platoons are one behind the other at a distance equal to their own length plus three paces, *eg*, the distance between the first and second platoons is the frontage of the second, plus three paces.

In close column the distance between each platoon is the same.

In column the distance will vary with any variation in the strength of platoons.

6. For normal purposes close column of platoons will be formed at 12 paces distance. This is measured between the heels of the rear rank of the leading platoon and those of the front rank of the next platoon. This distance is based on the room required to open ranks for inspection. For drill, seven paces is more convenient.

## SECTION 110 : DRESSING

1. On being halted in line, column or close column a company will always be dressed.

**The company in line**

2. On the command " Right—dress "

(*a*) The men dress by the right.

(b)    The officers in front of the company turn about together as the men turn off their heads, and supervise the dressing and covering off. They take up their own dressing by the flank of direction under the supervision of the second in command of the company.

(c)    The second in command turns to his right to dress the officers and turns again to face the company when done.

(d)    The CSM turns to his right and marches out five paces to the flank of the company, wheels left, halts in line with the front rank and five paces from it, turns left and dresses all three ranks in rotation. He will return to the line of the front rank, having completed the dressing of the rear rank, and will give " Eyes—front ".

On this command :—

(e) The men will act as taught.

(f) The officers turn about.

(g) The CSM turns left and marches back to his place.

## The company in column or close column

3. On the command " Right—dress "

(a) The men dress by the right.

(b) The officers, except the second in command of the company, turn about as the men turn their heads.

(c) The platoon sergeants turn right and move out five paces to the flank of their platoons, wheel left, halt five paces away from and level with their front rank ; turn left and carry on with the dressing. Having dressed all three ranks they will return to their position five paces from and level with their front rank, facing inwards.

*Note.*—In order that the platoon sergeants may work together it is usual to lay down the number of paces they will take when marching out.

(d) The CSM steps off and halts six paces to the front of and facing the right-hand man of the company, from which position he can check the covering of the right-hand man of each platoon. He then turns left, moves out five paces and checks the dressing of the platoon sergeants.

(e) When dressing is complete, the platoon sergeant of the leading platoon will give " No . . . platoon, eyes—front ". The centre platoon sergeant repeats the order but omits the word *platoon.* The rear platoon sergeant gives the cautionary command in full.

On the command " Eyes—front ", given by the rear platoon commander :—

(f) The officers turn about.

(g) The platoon sergeants and CSM step off and return to their places.

## SECTION 111: FORMING UP IN CLOSE COLUMN OF PLATOONS, WITH AND WITHOUT THE DRUM

1. Before markers are called for, the platoons will stand on the edge of the parade ground on the reverse flank opposite the positions they are to occupy when formed up.

2. " Right—markers " (given by the CSM).—The markers come forward as detailed in Sec 8 ; but turn to their left after halting, and order arms and stand easy.

*Note*.—The distance between markers may be checked by the CSM, who will then face the parade opposite the right marker of the centre platoon.

3. " Company get on—parade " (given by the CSM).—The men get on parade in the normal way except that they turn to their left before ordering arms.

Forming up with the drum

4. The CSM gives the orders :—

" Company ".—The company stand properly at ease.

" Fall in ".—The drummer, standing three paces behind the CSM and facing the parade, beats a double flam upon which the markers come to attention, take one pace forward and cover off.

" Steady ".—The drummer beats a flam, upon which the company come to attention. After a regulation pause he beats a roll, upon which the company take one pace forward, look to their right, and take up their dressing, remaining looking to their right. When dressing is completed the drummer ceases the roll. After a regulation pause the drummer beats a flam, upon which the company look to their front.

5. The senior officer on parade, standing five paces to the CSM's right rear, then orders :—

" Company stand at—ease ".—" Call the—roll ".

On the command " Call the—roll ;" platoon sergeants who will have formed up in front of their platoons, come to attention, slope arms, turn about, call the roll and prepare their platoons for inspection.

Officers, who will have been standing at ease seven paces in rear of the senior officer, come to attention and march forward to inspect their platoons. On completion of this duty, they report to the company commander and then continue marching up and down on the front of the parade.

6. As soon as all platoons have been inspected, the CSM calls the company to attention and tells off for drill.

This is a drill procedure to ensure that everyone knows the number of his platoon and section.

7. The CSM's word of command will be " **Company, tell off by—platoons** ".

The platoon sergeants, in turn from the front, will call out " **No ... platoon** ". The centre platoon commander will omit the word **platoon**.

8. The CSM then orders " **Tell off by—sections** ".

The section commanders tell off in turn from the front, No. 1 Section, No. 2, No. 3, etc, until No. 9 Section.

The commanders of the first and last platoons only use the word " section ".

### Forming up without the drum

9. The procedure is similar. The CSM gives the order " **Fall in** " upon which the markers come to attention, take a pace forward and cover off.

The CSM orders " **Steady** " (on which there is no movement). " **Right—dress** ". The company comes to attention, take a pace forward and take up their dressing in the normal way. He then orders " **Eyes—front** ".

10. The company commander takes over and carries out the same procedure as already detailed.

*Common faults* :—

  (i) Anticipating the drum thereby causing " heavy ", ragged movements.

  (ii) Failing to cover off from front to rear throughout the company.

  (iii) Watching the drummer when looking to the right.

## SECTION 112 : FALLING IN AND FALLING OUT THE OFFICERS

1. Whenever officers are to parade with the troops and there is more than one officer, the senior officer will fall in the remainder. This is done after the unit has had the roll called, has been inspected and has been told off.

While waiting to be fallen in, officers will march up and down in quick time on the flank or front of the parade. When the unit is called properly at ease, they will halt approximately opposite their positions, face the men on parade and stand properly at ease.

2. The senior officer on parade will order " **Fall in the—officers** ".

The officers will come to attention and march off in quick time to their places, where they will halt and turn to face their front, and will then stand at ease.

The platoon sergeants come to attention, turn to face the officers approaching them and report their platoons. Having done this they turn about and move at the short trail by the reverse flank to the place in rear of their platoons.

3. After falling in the officers the company commander will order "Tell off by—platoons". The platoon commanders will tell off as detailed above.

4. Similarly, when the parade is over and after bayonets have been unfixed the parade will be stood at ease. The senior officer on parade will then order "Fall out the—officers".

The officers will come to attention and march up to the senior officer whom they will salute. As soon as they have done this they will march on and halt in line seven paces behind him, turn about and stand at ease.

## SECTION 113 : CLOSE COLUMN OF PLATOONS FORMING COLUMN OF THREES

1. ". . . *Company move to the right in column of threes*, right — turn".

The whole company will turn to the right and the leading platoon commander will order "No. . . . platoon by the left, quick—march".

2. The remaining platoon commanders will, in succession, give "No. . . . platoon—left wheel, by the left, quick—march". The leading platoon will lead straight on. The other platoons will be stepped off in step with the leading platoon so as to form into column of threes at three paces distance from the platoon in front. The platoon commanders in rear will give "Right—wheel" to bring their platoons into column of threes behind the leading platoon.

3. The movement may be varied by ordering "Advance" or "Retire in column of threes from the right". In this case the leading platoon will wheel at once, without further order, into the required direction.

4. "From the right" or "From the left" indicates the direction in which the men are to turn. When the former is ordered, the right of the leading platoon will lead, and when the latter is ordered, the left of the platoon in rear will lead.

5. Platoons may be ordered to move off in a different order, eg, "Advance in column of threes from the right, in the following order", "No. 2 Platoon, No. 3, No. 1 Platoon, Company, right—turn". Platoon commanders march off their platoons in the order named, the platoons in rear following on behind the leading platoon.

*Common faults :—*

    (i) Failure to use the correct cautionary—"Advance" or "Move to the right . . .", etc.

    (ii) Bulging out at the wheels.

    (iii) Failure to judge the time at which to give "March" to the platoons in rear, in order to achieve the correct three paces distance between platoons.

## SECTION 114 : COLUMN OF THREES FORMING CLOSE COLUMN OF PLATOONS AT THE HALT FACING A FLANK

" . . . Company, at the halt, facing left, form close column of—platoons ".

The leading platoon commander will immediately halt his platoon, advance and give " Right—dress ". The commander of the second platoon will give " Right—wheel ". The third platoon commander will wheel his platoon on the same ground. Both platoon commanders will wheel left so as to bring their platoons to close column distance. They will halt their platoons, advance and give " Right—dress ". The right-hand man of each platoon will turn and face the new front immediately his platoon is halted. These guides will have their position checked by the CSM who will pace out the distance between platoons. Dressing will be carried out as given in Sec 110.

*Note.*—It is important that platoons should wheel square onto their new alignment and before the point where the left-hand man will halt ; this allows the platoon to halt covered off and properly closed up after the second wheel.

*Common faults :—*

    (i) Failure to wheel correctly, squarely and soon enough.

    (ii) Platoons not closed up.

    (iii) Ranks marching at more than one pace apart.

## SECTION 115 : CLOSE COLUMN OF PLATOONS FORMING COLUMN

**From the halt**

1. " At the halt, on No. . . . platoon, form column, remainder, quick—march ".

The platoon in rear stands fast. The platoons in front are halted by the commanders so as to achieve column distance. The company is dressed.

2. To form column on the centre or leading platoon, the platoons in rear must first be retired. The platoon commanders in rear will advance their platoons again before dressing.

**On the move**

3. " . . . Company will form column on No. . . . platoon, remainder, double—march " (or " Mark—time. ").

This can be done either by the company commander ordering the leading platoons to double, when they will be broken into quick time by the platoon commanders at column distance or by his ordering the platoons in rear to mark time. The platoons in rear would then be given " For—ward " by the platoon commanders so as to achieve column distance.

For a close column halted required to step off in column

4. " . . . Company, advance in—column ". The leading platoon commander orders " No. . . . platoon will advance, by the right, quick—march ". Platoon commanders in rear step off their platoons in succession so as to achieve column distance, in step with the leading platoon.

## SECTION 116 : COLUMN OF PLATOONS FORMING CLOSE COLUMN

At the halt

1. " On No. . . . platoon, form close column, remainder, quick—march ".

The platoons in rear are halted by their platoon commanders on reaching close column distance. The company is dressed.

On the march

2. The company commander's word of command will be as above except that he will order " Double—march ".

The platoon commanders will break their platoons into quick time on reaching close column distance.

*Note.*—The company commander may order this movement at the halt,

3. " At the halt, form close—column ". The leading platoon commander will at once order his platoon to halt. The following platoons will be halted on reaching close column distance. The company will be dressed.

## SECTION 117 : CLOSE COLUMN MOVING TO A FLANK IN THREES

" . . . Company will move to the right, in close column of platoons in threes. Company, right—turn " " Company, quick—march ".— The platoons will work as in squad drill.

As soon as the movement is completed, the company commander will order " The platoon on the right (left) will direct ".

## SECTION 118 : COLUMN OF PLATOONS FORMING LINE FACING A FLANK

" Platoons, change direction left, into line, left—form ".

Platoons work on the company commander's word of command. The command may be given " At the halt " in which case the men will halt as they come into line. The company will be dressed.

*Note.*—If the movement is started from the halt, platoons work as in squad drill and the company commander orders " Quick—march ".

## SECTION 119 : LINE FORMING COLUMN FACING A FLANK

1. At the halt

" Platoons, change direction right, into column, right—form. Quick march ".

2. On the march

The words of command are the same as above except that " Forward " will take the place of " Quick march ".

## SECTION 120 : COLUMN OF THREES FORMING COLUMN FACING A FLANK

1. " Facing left, advance in—column ".—The leading platoon commander orders " No. . . . platoon will advance. Left—turn ". Platoon commanders in rear give " Left—turn " on reaching the same spot, and immediately after turning, the flank of direction.

2. The distance of three paces between platoons in column of threes allows this movement to take place without the platoons in rear marking time.

3. When advancing in column, platoon commanders and guides take their correct distance from the platoon in front. They must check this distance constantly by selecting a mark on the ground and counting the number of paces they take to reach it after the platoon in front passes it.

## SECTION 121 : COLUMN OF PLATOONS FORMING COLUMN OF THREES

This is the reverse process of Sec 120.

" In succession. Move to the right in—column of threes ".

The leading platoon commander orders " No. . . . platoon right—turn ". The remaining platoons will follow suit on reaching the same spot.

*Note*.—The company commander may order " Advance " (or " Retire ") if desired, and platoons will wheel accordingly directly after turning.

## SECTION 122 : COLUMN OF PLATOONS FORMING LINE FACING THE SAME DIRECTION

At the halt

1. " On the left form line. Remainder, left in—cline ". " Remainder, quick—march ".

The platoon commanders give " Right in—cline " as they come opposite their place in line and then halt their platoons in line. The company is dressed.

On the move

2. The company commander orders " Double—march " and platoon commanders break into quick time on arriving at their position in line.

## SECTION 123 : LINE FORMING COLUMN FACING THE SAME DIRECTION

**At the halt**

1. " At the halt on No. . . . platoon, form column, remainder, right—turn ". " Remainder, quick—march ". The leading platoon stands fast. The centre platoon wheels right immediately and then wheels left at column distance. The rear platoon follows and in turn wheels at column distance. Platoon commanders halt their platoons at their place in column and turn them to the front.

The company is dressed.

**On the march**

2. " Advance in column. Remainder, right—turn ".

The right platoon continues to march to its front. The platoons in rear are ordered to advance by their commanders as they reach their position in column.

## SECTION 124 : COLUMN OF PLATOONS, MOVING TO A FLANK, FORMING COLUMN OF THREES BY WHEELING

" Advance in column of threes. Platoons, left—wheel ". Each platoon wheels at once.

## SECTION 125 : COLUMN OF THREES FORMING COLUMN OF PLATOONS MOVING TO A FLANK, BY WHEELING

" Move to the right in column. Platoons right—wheel ". This is the reverse of Sec 124.

## SECTION 126 : COLUMN OF THREES FORMING COLUMN OF PLATOONS FACING THE SAME DIRECTION

" Platoons, on the left, into column, form—platoons. Company, for—ward ". Platoons act as in squad drill.

## SECTION 127 : COLUMN OF THREES FORMING CLOSE COLUMN OF PLATOONS FACING THE SAME DIRECTION

" At the halt, on the left, form close column of—platoons ".

The leading platoon commander gives " No. . . . platoon, at the halt, on the left, form—platoon ". The platoons in rear are given similar orders so as to reach their position in close column. The company is dressed.

## SECTION 128 : COLUMN OF PLATOONS CHANGING DIRECTION BY FORMING

" Change direction—right "

1. The leading platoon commander gives " No . . . platoon, right—form " and then " For—ward ". Platoons in rear conform on reaching the same ground.

2. The company commander will order the flank of direction to be the same as the direction of the change, *eg*, if the company is by the right, he will order " By the—left " before ordering " Change direction —left ".

*Common faults* :—

Delay by platoon commanders in giving " For—ward ", with consequent crowding on the forming point and loss of the correct column distance.

## SECTION 129 : CLOSE COLUMN OF PLATOONS, ON THE MARCH, FORMING LINE FACING A FLANK

" At the halt, facing left form—line ". The rear platoon commander gives " No . . . Platoon. At the halt, left—form ". In succession from the rear, the platoons in front will receive a similar order to bring them into line. The company is dressed.

## SECTION 130 : CLOSE COLUMN OF PLATOONS, HALTED, FORMING LINE FACING THE SAME DIRECTION

". . . Company will form line. Remainder, left—turn ".

" Remainder, quick—march "

The platoons in rear wheel right and then left so as to bring themselves into their position in line, where they are halted and turned to the front by platoon commanders. The company is dressed.

*Common faults* :—

Failure to make the wheels early enough to bring the platoons on to the alignment in time to be covered off before halting.

### CHAPTER XVII

# BATTALION DRILL

The following movements of battalion drill are the minimum necessary for a battalion to parade, to move off, and to reform.

The movements within the companies are the same as for company drill.

The detail is shown in skeleton as for four companies of equal size. This detail will be used as a basis for unit drill by units of all arms.

# SECTION 131: FORMATIONS, POSITIONS OF OFFICERS, WARRANT OFFICERS, AND PLATOON SERGEANTS

(a) The following are the formations in battalion drill :—

| | |
|---|---|
| Line | Column of companies |
| Column of threes | Close column of companies |
| Column of route | Mass |

### Line

1. The four companies form up side by side with three paces interval between platoons and companies.

The positions of officers, warrant and non-commissioned officers, are as in company drill, and in addition : the battalion commander is 15 paces in front of the centre of the battalion, the second in command of the battalion is six paces in front of the right-hand man of the battalion, the adjutant is six paces in front of the left-hand man of the battalion, the RSM is three paces in rear of the centre of the rear rank, covering off the battalion commander.

### Column of threes

2. Column of threes is the same as line but facing a flank, except that the battalion commander is nine paces in front of the centre rank of the leading platoon, the second in command is three paces in rear of the centre rank of the rear platoon, the adjutant is two paces to the right rear of the battalion commander, and the RSM three paces in front of the centre rank of the leading platoon.

### Column of route

3. Column of route is the same as column of threes except that all officers, warrant and non-commissioned officers are in the ranks as in company drill.

### Column of companies

4. Column of companies is a formation in which each company is formed up as for a company in line in company drill, with the companies one behind the other on parallel and successive alignments at a distance apart equal to their own frontages plus three paces. The positions of officers, warrant and non-commissioned officers are the same as in company drill, and in addition : the battalion commander is 15 paces in front of the centre of the leading company, the second in command is six paces in front of the right-hand man of the front rank of the leading company, the adjutant is six paces in front of the left-hand man of the front rank of the leading company, and the RSM is two paces behind the platoon sergeant of the second company from the front.

### Close column of companies

5. The detail for close column of companies is the same as for column, except that the distance between companies is reduced to any suitable number of paces, and is the same between all companies.

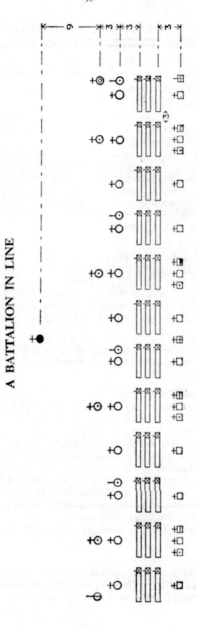

A BATTALION IN LINE

# A BATTALION IN COLUMN OF COMPANIES

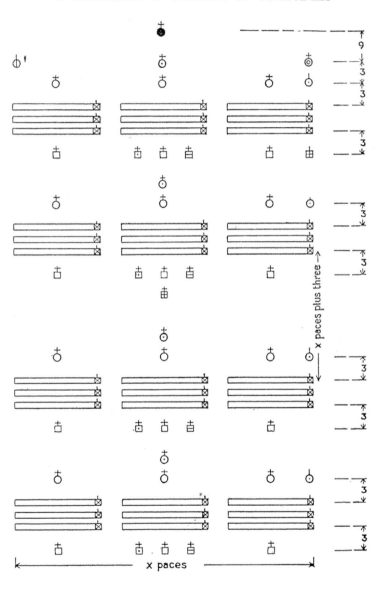

A BATTALION IN MASS

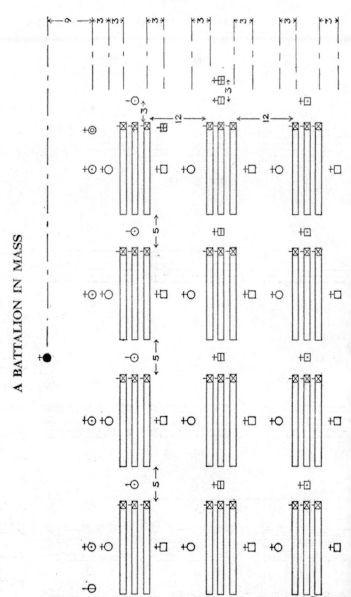

**Mass**

6. In mass the battalion forms up with its companies in line, each in close column of platoons, with five paces interval between companies. The positions of the company officers, warrant and non-commissioned officers are the same as for a company in close column of platoons, and in addition : the battalion commander is 15 paces in front of the centre of the battalion, the second in command is six paces in front of the right-hand man of the battalion, the adjutant is six paces in front of the left-hand man of the front rank of the leading platoon of the left-hand company, and the RSM is six paces to the right of the centre rank of the second platoon of the right-hand company.


## SECTION 132 : DRESSING

**In line**

1. As in company drill except that the RSM performs the duties as laid down for the CSM. The dressing of the officers will be supervised by the second in command.

**In column and close column**

2. As in company drill except that the CSM performs the duties as laid down for the platoon sergeant. Distances between companies will be paced out by the RSM who carries out the movements detailed for the CSM in company drill.

**Mass**

3. As in column or close column in company drill. In the cautionary word of command before " Eyes—front ", the word " **platoon** " will be used only by platoon sergeants of the leading platoon of the right-hand company, and of the rear platoon of the left-hand company. The RSM will supervise generally.


## SECTION 133 : MOVING OFF IN COLUMN OF THREES (OR ROUTE) FROM MASS
### (Battalion standing at ease)

1. " **Advance (retire) in column of threes (route) from the right (left)** . . . **company—leading** ". The battalion second in command, company commanders, and adjutant come to attention and turn about. The company commander of the named company then calls his company to attention, slopes arms and gives the appropriate command as in company drill. Each company acts similarly to gain their correct positions in column of threes (route).

2. The movement may also be done in a special order of march in which case instead of ordering ".... **Company—leading** ", the battalion commander must specify the order required, *eg*, " **Advance in column**

of route from the right, in the following order, ' C ', ' A ', ' D ' and ' B '
—companies ".

The second in command, company commanders and adjutant act
on the command " Companies ".

## SECTION 134 : FORMING MASS FROM COLUMN OF THREES (ROUTE)

" At the halt facing left (on the left), form—mass ".—The company
commander of the leading company immediately orders " ... Company,
at the halt facing left (on the left), form close column of platoons ".
The company acts as in company drill. The remaining company
commanders conform to gain their correct positions in mass, irre-
spective of the order of march.

## SECTION 135 : MOVING OFF IN COLUMN OF THREES (ROUTE) FROM CLOSE COLUMN OF COMPANIES

(Battalion standing at ease.)

1. " Advance (retire) in column of threes (route) from the left (right),
. . . Company—leading ".—The second in command, company commanders and adjutant come to attention and turn about. The company
commander of the leading (rear) company calls his company to
attention, slopes arms and orders ". . . . Company, left (right) wheel,
by the left, quick—march ". The remaining company commanders
conform to gain their correct positions in column of threes (route).

2. Similar movements may be done without advancing or retiring.
They may also be done in a specified order of march as in company
drill, the battalion commander giving the order of march as in mass.

If the battalion is in column the battalion commander would call the
battalion to attention, slope arms, right (left) turn and give the command " Companies, left (right) wheel, by the left, quick—march ".

3. If the movement does not involve the leading (rear) company
wheeling the battalion commander would order " Move to the right
(left) in column of threes, by the left, quick—march ". The company
first in the order of march would move straight ahead, the remainder
wheeling to gain their correct positions.

## SECTION 136 : FORMING CLOSE COLUMN OF COMPANIES FROM COLUMN OF THREES (ROUTE)

"At the halt, facing left (on the left) from close column of—companies".
Companies will act in exactly the same way as do the platoons in
similar movements in company drill.

CHAPTER XVIII

# LIGHT INFANTRY DRILL

" The Service of Light Infantry does not so much require men of stature, as it requires them to be Intelligent, Hardy and Active ". (Major-General Sir John Moore—17 January, 1803.)

Present-day light infantry drill is the descendant of the drill taught to the skirmishers, provided by the Light Infantry, to ensure quick thinking and quick movement.

## SECTION : 137.—GENERAL

1. Movements which, in the drill of the Army, start from or end at the position of attention, will in Light Infantry Drill, start from and finish at the position of stand at ease, without further order.

2. Light Infantry standing easy will come to the properly at ease position on being named " **Light Infantry** ".

3. Light Infantry standing properly at ease will come to attention when a unit or sub-unit of which they are part is called by name, *eg*, **Battalion, Company, Platoon, Squad.**

4. *Time of marching*

Quick time—140 paces to the minute.

Double time—180 paces to the minute.

For drill, all movements outside the ranks will be done in double-time except that when markers are moving to a flank to conduct the dressing of a unit or sub-unit they will move out and return in quick time.

5. On the move in quick or double time the rifle is carried at the shoulder by the individual when moving outside the ranks, and by troops in formation when marching in file or single file. It is carried at the trail by troops when marching in line or threes.

The slope is not used nor are bayonets fixed. Rifle exercises are done at 70 movements to the minute.

6. Except as stated in this chapter, the drill of Light Infantry is as laid down elsewhere in this manual.

## SECTION 138 : SQUAD DRILL

1. On all occasions, other than on ceremonial parades, when turning into line at the halt from threes ; file, or single file, and on completion of " open and close order march ", dressing is taken up automatically by all ranks from the directing flank. When individual dressing in the ranks is completed, and when the files or threes are covered off correctly, two distinct movements follow, *ie*, the squad turn head and eyes to the front (pause) and stand at ease. These two

movements are carried out in quick succession from the directing flank, each file or three working together.

**Words of Command**

2. Words of command are given in quick time as follows :—

" **Squad—halt** ".—Right foot leaving the ground.

" **About—turn** ".—Left foot leaving the ground.

" **Right—turn** ".—Right foot passing left.

" **Right in—cline** ".—Right foot passing left.

" **Right—form** ".—Right foot passing left.

" **Left—turn** ".—Left foot passing right.

" **Left in—cline** ".—Left foot passing right.

" **Left—form** ".—Left foot passing right.

" **Mark—time** ".—Left foot coming to the ground.

" **For—ward** " (when marking time).—Left foot being raised.

" **Squad—halt** " (When marking time).—Right foot coming to the ground.

" **Saluting to a flank** ".—Right foot leaving the ground.

### FROM QUICK TO DOUBLE TIME

" **Break into double time—double march** ".—Left foot coming to the ground.

### FROM DOUBLE TO QUICK TIME

" **Break into quick time—quick march** ".—Left foot coming to the ground.

**Dismissing**

3. On the command " **Dismiss** " or on the last bugle note of the " **Disperse** " troops will come to attention, turn to the right, shoulder arms, salute if required, cut their hand away and after a pause march off the parade ground in quick time at the shoulder.

### SECTION 139: RIFLE DRILL

The rifle will be carried at the shoulder on the following occasions :—

(a) When marching in file or single file.

(b) By markers when they are being put out.

(c) By instructors when drilling a squad.

(d) When being " sized " after turning to the right, on the command " **In three ranks—size** "

(e) By NCOs when dressing a squad.

(f) When inspecting a squad.

(g) When being dismissed, after turning to the right.

(h) By individuals moving outside the ranks.

(j) By individual other ranks marching about camp or barracks.

(k) When troops are ordered on parade.

## SECTION 140 : SALUTING WITH THE RIFLE

**At the halt**

1. Light infantrymen will come to attention, shoulder arms and tap the sling with the left hand, left elbow close to the body, forearm horizontal, hand straight, fingers extended, thumb close to the fore-fingers, back of the hand to the front.

**On the move**

2. When a light infantryman, carrying a rifle, passes an officer he will do so at the shoulder and will salute as laid down above, at the same time turning his head and eyes smartly in the direction of the officer, looking him straight in the face.

**Salute to the front or delivering a message**

3. When a light infantryman, carrying a rifle, delivers a written message to or addresses an officer, he will do so at the shoulder unless the officer is on the move ; the soldier will halt two paces from the officer, salute as laid down in para 1 above and deliver the message. If no reply is needed, or when the reply is received, he will salute as before, turn about and march off in quick time.

**The present from stand at ease and stand at ease from the present**

4. " Present arms—one ".—Light infantrymen come to attention.

5. " Light Infantry—two ".—Jerk the rifle up the right side as for the first motion of slope arms.

6. " Light Infantry—three ".—With the right hand force the rifle to the centre of the body, sling to the left, in the position detailed for the second motion of the present from the slope (Sec 55). At the same time strike the rifle with the left hand in the position previously detailed in Sec 55, para 2.

7. " Light Infantry—four ".—As detailed in Sec 55, para 3.

8. " Stand at ease—one ".—Force the rifle to the right side with the left hand, at the same time grasping it with the right hand in the place it is held at the order and forcing it to the position previously detailed for the second motion of the order from the slope (Sec 53) with the left hand just below the nosecap, at the same time *bend the right knee* to close the heels.

9. " Light Infantry—two ".—Lower the butt to the ground and cut the left hand to the side.

10. " Light Infantry—three ".—Stand at ease.

## SECTION 141 : SENTRIES

The drill is as given in Chapter XIII and XIV except the sentries will patrol at the shoulder and salute as laid down for light infantrymen above.

CHAPTER XIX

# DRILL FOR RIFLE REGIMENTS

The drill for rifle regiments is based on the rapid movement and high standard of individual training required by such units in their traditional role.

Movements are done at the double or in quick time as follows :—

| Movement | Rate |
|---|---|
| Double time | 180 to the minute. |
| Quick time | 140 ,, ,, ,, |
| Slow time | 70 ,, ,, ,, |

## SECTION 142 : SQUAD DRILL

### Words of command

1. The word " **Attention** " is not used. Units will come to attention on being named, *ie*, " **Squad** ", " **Section** ", " **Party** ", " **Guard** ", etc.

Units which are standing easy come to the *at ease* position on the cautionary words of command " **Look to your front** ".

### Timing of words of command

2. The time of executive words of command is as follows :—

" Halt ".—Right foot coming to the ground.

" About turn ".—Left foot coming to the ground.

" Right turn ".—Right foot coming to the ground.

" Right in—cline ".—Right foot coming to the ground.

" Right form ".—Right foot coming to the ground.

" Left turn ".—Left foot coming to the ground.

" Left in—cline ".—Left foot coming to the ground.

" Left form ".—Left foot coming to the ground.

" Mark time ".—Left foot coming to the ground.

" For—ward " (When marking time).—Left foot coming to the ground.

" Halt " (when marking time).—Right foot coming to the ground.

" Form squad " (right leading).—Right foot coming to the ground.

" Form squad " (left leading).—Left foot coming to the ground.

" From quick to double time ".—Left foot coming to the ground.

" Break into double time, double march ".—Left foot coming to the ground.

" From double to quick time ".—Left foot coming to the ground.

" **Break into quick time, quick march** ".—Left foot coming to the ground.

Arms drill on the march.—Left foot coming to the ground.

Saluting drill on the march.—Left foot coming to the ground.

Saluting drill when halting.—Right foot coming to the ground.

### The fall in

3. The procedure for falling in on parade is as follows :—

As soon as the command " **Markers** " has been given, the remainder of the parade will stand at ease. On the command " **On parade** " they will come to attention, shoulder arms, march on to parade, halt, face the front, order arms, pick up their dressing on the marker, turn their head to the front and stand at ease in succession from the right.

### Dressing

4. Each man in the squad (except the right hand man of each rank) will turn his head and eyes to the right and, after a pause, the front rank only will extend the left arm, back of the hand upwards, with the knuckles touching the shoulder of the man on the left. After a pause he will take up his dressing in line.

5. On the command " **Eyes front** " the head and eyes will be turned smartly to the front, at the same time the hand will be cut away to the side and the position of attention resumed.

6. Trained soldiers will judge the correct interval without raising the left arm.

### Dismiss

7. The command " **Dismiss** " may be given either from the *attention* or the *squad at ease* position. The flank to which the dismiss will take place will always be named.

## SECTION 143 : RIFLE DRILL

### The shoulder from the trail and vice versa

1. " **Shoulder arms—one** ".—Bring the rifle to a perpendicular position and hold it with the left hand in line with the elbow, then grasp it with the right hand as at the shoulder.

2. " **Two** ".—Cut the left hand to the side.

3. " **Trail arms—one** ".—Grasp the rifle with the left hand in line with the elbow and at the same time with the right hand at the point of balance.

4. " **Two** ".—Bring the rifle down to the trail at the same time cutting the left hand to the side.

**The present from the order and vice versa**

5. " Present arms—one ".—Throw the rifle up the right side catching it simultaneously with both hands the left hand grasping the point of balance, thumb in the hollow of the right shoulder, the right hand grasping the small of the butt, ball of the hand just in front of the right hip, right elbow to the rear; the rifle to be in a vertical position in front of the right shoulder, magazine to the front.

6. " Two ".—Bring the rifle to a perpendicular position in front centre of the body, raising it slightly and turning it with the magazine to the left, butt close to the body; at the same time place the left hand smartly on the stock, wrist on the magazine, fingers pointing upwards, thumb close to the forefinger, point of the thumb in line with the mouth; right hand grasping the small of the butt, with right upper arm close to the body.

7. " Three ".—As in the third motion of the present from the slope, except that the left hand will be inside the sling.   (The hand does not actually quit the rifle.)

8. " Order arms—one ".—Carry the rifle to the right side and seize it with the right hand at the band, and with the left hand round the nose cap, butt just clear of the ground; at the same time bring the right foot smartly up to the left.

9. " Two ".—Lower the butt quietly to the ground as at the order, cutting the left hand away to the side.

**The present from the shoulder, and vice versa**

10. " Present arms—one ".—Using the right hand, cant the rifle up the right side, catching it with both hands as in the first movement of the present from the order.

11. " Two ".—As for the second movement of the present from the order.

12. " Three ".—As for the third movement of the present from the order.

13. " Shoulder arms—one ".—Using both hands, place the rifle over to the right side as in the first movement of the shoulder from the order.

14. " Two ".—As for the second movement of the shoulder.

**The support from the shoulder, and vice versa**

*Note*.—The support is used by sentries when moving on their beat
       and is applicable to the Greenjackets only.

15. " Support—arms ".—To support arms from the shoulder, keep the right hand at the trigger guard, and by bending the right elbow

bring the rifle to a position parallel with the ground, resting along the right forearm, with the magazine to the right. The angle of the rifle will be diagonal to the line of march with the butt leading. (This allows for swinging of the left arm in the normal way.)

16. " Shoulder—arms ".—The converse to the above.

## March at the ease (butts up) from the trail

17. " March at ease—one ".—Bring the rifle up in line with the waist belt, at the same time grasping it with the left hand between the band and the nose-cap, back of the hand uppermost.

18. " Two ".—Carry the rifle smartly across the body and place it on the left shoulder, butt upwards, sling to the left.

19. " Three ".—Cut the right hand smartly away to the side.

*Note*.—When performed on the march, the command is given when the left foot is on the ground. Complete a pace with the right foot and begin the movement on the left, each motion being done as the left foot comes to the ground.

## Trail arms from the march at ease

20. " Trail arms—one ".—Bring the rifle down to a perpendicular position at the left side, at the same time grasping it with the right hand at the point of balance in line with the shoulder, back of the hand towards the body.

21. " Two ".—Carry the rifle over to the right side, in line with the waist belt and parallel to the ground; the grip of the left hand between the band and nose-cap being retained.

22. " Three ".—Lower the rifle to the position of the trail, at the same time cutting the left hand away smartly.

*Note*.— (i) When marching at ease, the command to bring the Squad to *attention* will be " Trail arms ", which will be given as the left foot is on the ground. Complete the pace with the right foot and start the movement on the left, each movement being done as the left foot comes to the ground.

(ii) The *march at ease* and *trail arms* from the *march at ease* is applicable to the Greenjackets only.

## Recover arms from the order

23. " Recover—arms ".—Throw the rifle across the body catching it simultaneously with both hands; rifle vertical in front of left shoulder, magazine to the front; right hand grasping small of the butt, knuckles pressing against the left upper arm near the elbow, right forearm parallel to the ground; left hand grasping the point of balance, thumb in line with the top of the left ear.

**Shoulder arms from the recover**

24. " Shoulder arms—one ".—Bring the rifle to the first position of the *shoulder arms from the order*.

25. " Two ".—Cut the left hand away to the side.

*Note.*—The command " **Order arms** " when at the *recover* is not used.

## SECTION 144 : SQUAD DRILL WITH ARMS

1. The hand will not be made to " tell " on the rifle when carrying out arms drill.   The foot will not be stamped when carrying out drill movements.

2. On the move, rifles will be carried at the trail except on the following occasions when they will be carried at the shoulder :—

   (*a*)  When in file or single file.

   (*b*)  When marching or walking about as individuals.

   (*c*)  When marching on to the parade ground to " form up ".

   (*d*)  When saluting with the rifle.

   (*e*)  By instructors on parade.

   (*f*)  By sentries marching to and from their posts.

   (*g*)  When sizing.

   (*h*)  By NCOs acting as markers or when dressing a squad.

   (*j*)  When dismissing with arms.

3. *Sizing.*—On the executive word of command being given, all personnel will shoulder arms, turn in the direction indicated, move to their appointed place, halt, turn to the front, order arms and remain at attention.

4. On ceremonial parades, if not in the ranks, the commanding officer's orderly and bugler will take station in the supernumerary rank of the leading company.   On moving off they will take station two paces in rear and on either flank of the commanding officer.

5. On commanding officer's or adjutant's parades, on the command " **Rifle exercises** " officers will take three paces forward, turn about, and watch the drill.   On RSM's parades, warrant officers and sergeants will perform these movements when acting as company and platoon commanders.

6. The slope arms position will not be used unless it is necessary to carry bayonets fixed.

*Note.*—The word " sword " will be used instead of " bayonet " in the Green Jackets.

**Turning into file from line**

7. " Right (or left)—turn ".—The rifle is brought from the trail to the shoulder as the right foot (or left) takes the first pace in the new direction, the left hand being cut away to the side as the right (or left) *comes to the ground the second time.*

8. " Right (or left) in—cline ".—On the first incline the rifle remains at the trail.   On the second incline the rifle is brought to the shoulder as above.

**Turning into line from file**

9. " Right (or left)—turn ".—The left hand grasps the rifle in line with the elbow as the right (or left) foot takes the first pace in the new directions ; the rifle is brought to the trail as the right (or left) foot comes to the ground the second time.

10. " Right (or left) in—cline ".—On the first incline the rifle remains at the shoulder.  On the second incline the rifle is brought to the trail as above.

**Turning about—action with the rifle**

11. *When marching in line or threes* : On the first movement of the turn (left foot), bring the rifle to a perpendicular position in front of the right shoulder, magazine to the front, right upper arm close to the body, right forearm parallel with the ground ; retain the rifle in this position until the turn is completed.  Force the rifle down to the trail as the right foot takes the first pace forward in the new direction.

12. *When marching in file* : There is no action with the rifle.

**Dismiss**

13. Come to attention, turn in the direction indicated, shoulder arms, salute for a count of two paces in marching time, and march off in quick time with the rifle at the shoulder.

**Dismiss at the recover.** (Applicable to Green Jackets only.)

14. Come to attention ; turn in the direction indicated ; recover arms ; pause for a count of two paces in marching time ; shoulder arms ; salute (a quick " one-two ") ; pause and march off in quick time with the rifle at the shoulder.


## SECTION 145: SALUTING WITH THE RIFLE

**At the halt**

1. A rifleman, if at the shoulder, will salute by tapping the sling smartly with the left hand, forearm horizontal, back of the hand to the front, fingers straight.  The salute will begin three paces before the officer passes the soldier, and the hand will be cut away on the third pace after he has passed him.

**On the move**

2. A rifleman when passing an officer will do so at the shoulder and will salute as laid down above, at the same time turning the head towards the officer and looking him full in the face. He will salute on the third pace before reaching him and cut the hand away and turn the head to the front on the third pace after passing him.

**When delivering a message or addressing an officer**

3. When a rifleman carrying a rifle delivers a written message to or addresses an officer, he will do so at the shoulder. Unless the officer is on the move, the soldier will halt two paces from the officer, salute as laid down above and deliver the message ; if no reply is needed, or when the reply is received, he will salute as before, turn about and march off in quick time.

## CHAPTER XX

# INSTRUCTORS' INFORMATION

The object of drill and the responsibility of those in authority towards the creating and maintaining of the high standard required is given in the introduction to this manual. Since first impressions are always of paramount importance the responsibility of the drill instructor regarding the recruit cannot be over-emphasized.

This chapter and the next are therefore designed to help individual instructors and at the same time to assist in the training of new instructors.

## SECTION 146 : BEARING OF THE INSTRUCTORS

Since example is usually imitated, the correct bearing of an instructor at all times is of paramount importance.

When drilling a squad he must stand still and correctly to attention. Exaggerated movements of the body, head and hands when shouting are bad.

When he has to move he must turn and march as he would demonstrate. *Wandering* after the squad being drilled is wrong.

Demonstrations must be excellent. When demonstrating movements with a rifle, whip or cane, the demonstration must be given with the article in question. Rifle exercises cannot be demonstrated with a pace stick or cane.

Bad language will not be tolerated.

The dress and turnout of the instructors must always be of the highest order. Frequent inspection of instructors is necessary to maintain the proper standard even in the best unit.

## SECTION 147: HOW TO GET THE MAXIMUM OUT OF A SQUAD

1. Human nature being what it is, two things are necessary : first the good will and skill of the instructor, and second, since drill is not meant to be easy, ability on the part of the instructor to press the squad up to its maximum capacity.

2. The squad will be quick to note your standard and set theirs by yours ; they will be quick to sum up your character. Though a squad can and should laugh with their instructor, there must never be the least taint of familiarity. The squad will work for you and you can press them as long as your skill as an instructor is great and only so long as pressure is necessary. So long as you give praise or credit where credit is due ; so long as you press them only when they deserve it and you know when to let up the pressure ; so long as you continue *Instructing* while you press the squad, such pressure will be useful. There is no excuse for pressing a squad beyond their ability to learn or without continuing instruction ; this is bullying. Your object will be to make your squad drill as well as they can ; to teach them to be as well disciplined as you are.

### Terminology

3. Instructors must bear in mind that the most effective teaching is done through the eye, that is to say, one quick demonstration is worth far more than a lot of talk and no action. The instructor must, therefore, develop a vocabulary of short, incisive words, with which he may impress the squad that there is something positive and definite to be done. For example, in rifle exercises the words *Crack*, *drive*, *force*, *grip*, etc, convey far more to the man under instruction than do, respectively *smack* or *hit*, *carry*, or *hold*. Likewise, in foot drill, *Shoot the foot forward*, *Bend the knee*, mean more than *Carry*, *Pick up* or *Bring the foot in*.

## SECTION 148 : CORRECTION OF FAULTS

1. Faults made by an instructor must be noted by the senior officer or warrant officer on parade and put right before the instructor leaves the parade ground.

If you, as an instructor, are checked by your superior, show your loyalty and discipline by the way you correct yourself.

DISCIPLINE IS THE END—DRILL IS THE MEANS.

## SECTION 149 : SEQUENCE OF INSTRUCTION

1. If desirable, form the squad round you in a half-circle.

2. Tell them in simple language what you are going to teach and give the reason why.

3. Give a complete demonstration judging the time and shouting the word of command.

4. If applicable, give a demonstration by numbers, again shouting the words of command. Deal with one movement at a time, practising it before going on to the next.

5. Point out the common faults as you demonstrate.

6. Reform the squad and practise the movement by numbers and then judging the time. Faults to be corrected all the while.

7. Further practise and supervise the movement whenever and wherever it may occur again. THIS IS THE MOST IMPORTANT ITEM IN THE SEQUENCE. NEVER LET UP.

**Questions**

8. Short rests must be given between exercises, especially in the early stages of recruits' training. When the squad is stood easy for a rest during drill, the instructor should ply the squad with questions. These should cover not only regimental matters and personalities but such things as pay, leave, standing orders, sport and amenities. Officers in charge of drill will ensure that their instructors are prepared in this and that each subject is dealt with in turn.

Drill instructors, themselves undergoing their weekly drilling, should be supervised and practised in this useful art of questioning.

## SECTION 150 : **WORDS OF COMMAND**

1. A good regular word of command will do as much as anything to produce good drill. All officers and instructors must be coached, practised and developed in this by their superiors. Such a word of command does not come of its own, it needs both practice and development before successful drilling of a squad can be achieved.

2. The word of command must be clear and understood by the squad. Words of command are divided into a " cautionary ", which must be clear and explanatory, and an executive, which must be sharp and of a higher pitch than the cautionary.

Throughout this manual words of command are printed in bold type and with inverted commas. A dash separates the cautionary from the executive.

3. Each particular word of command should show the same pause between cautionary and executive, each time it is given. It is not possible to give exactly the same pause in all the different words of command as some are for quick time and some for slow, etc.

4. When it is desired to get back to the last position the command " **As you were** " will be given.

5. The words of command laid down in this manual for drill are *not* intended for use in battle or in the field.

6. Always give a word of command with the full power of your voice. As a senior instructor insist on this particularly with young junior NCOs in the normal daily routine. The reason for this is twofold—every word of command they give is practice for them; a spoken or " confidential " word of command loses authority and leads to bad drill off the parade ground and about barracks.

## SECTION 151 : TIMING OF WORDS OF COMMAND

The following table shows on which foot the executive word should be given.

As a guide, and unless it is otherwise laid down in the table, a cautionary word of command, given on the march, should start as the left foot comes to the ground. It should be drawn out during four paces and should therefore end as the right foot comes to the ground. An interval of about four paces in quick time or three in slow time should be left between the end of the " cautionary " and the " executive ".

| Word of Command | Quick Time. Given as the : | Slow Time. Given as the : | Remarks |
|---|---|---|---|
| (a) | (b) | (c) | (d) |
| " **Halt** " (marching) | Right foot passes the left | The left foot passes the right | From double march : as the left foot reaches the ground |
| " **Quick**—(or **slow**) **march**" in time with the troops already marching | " **Quick** " on the left foot,"**March**" on the right foot, on successive feet | " **Slow** on the leftfoot,"**March**" on the right foot, on successive feet | |
| " **Right**—turn " (incline) | Right foot passes the left | Left foot passes the right | " **Left**—turn " is given on the opposite feet |
| " **About**—turn " | Left foot level with and passing | As the right foot passes the left | |
| " **Mark**—time " | Left foot passes the right | As the right foot passes the left | In double time : As the right foot reaches the ground |
| " **Halt** " (marking time) | Left foot being raised | Right knee fully raised | From double mark time : As the left foot reaches the ground |

| (a) | (b) | (c) | (d) |
|---|---|---|---|
| " For—ward " | Left foot being raised | Right knee fully raised | When double marking time : as the left foot reaches the ground |
| " Change—step " (left foot leading) | " Change " on the left foot, " Step " on the right foot, on successive feet | " Change " on the left foot, " Step " on the right foot, on successive feet | For right foot leading the opposite applies |
| " Break into quick time, quick—march" | — | "Quick" on the left foot, "March" on the right, on successive feet | From double time : " Quick " on the left foot, " March " on the right foot |
| " Break into slow time, slow—march " | Left foot level with and passing the right | | |
| " Break into double time, double—march " | Left foot reaches the ground | | |
| " Open (close)—order " | | As the right foot passes the left | |
| " Right (left)—form " | Left foot level with and passing the right | Right foot level with and passing the left | " Form " is long drawn out, so as NOT to be confused with " Turn " |
| " On the right (left) form—squad " | As for right (or left) turn | | |
| All compliments except : (a) Salute to the front or (b) as on sentry | Left foot reaches the ground / As for halt / As for halt | Right foot reaches the ground / As for halt | |
| On the march ; rifle exercises, sword drill or cane drill | Left foot reaches the ground | Right foot reaches the ground | Except the change at the slope with the rifle on the right shoulder, when opposite applies |

## SECTION 152 : COMMUNICATION DRILL AND MUTUAL DRILL

1. Explain and demonstrate words of command confining them to those given at the halt, including rifle exercises.

2. Place out a supernumerary instructor about 50 yards from the squad. Conduct the squad collectively in giving simple commands to this NCO at the halt, insisting on clear diction and full power from each individual. The instructor must " conduct " to ensure that the class all shout together.

3. Divide the squad into two ranks, placing them out about 30 yards apart, facing one another with about five paces interval between each man. Order one rank to give to their opposite numbers the words of command already practised, independently and without regard to the men on their right and left. After a short time, which should not exceed ten minutes, change over so that the other rank shouts the commands.

4. Form the squad into three ranks and explain, at the halt, the different words of command, *eg*, " Squad will advance ", " Squad will retire ", " Squad will move to the right in threes ". On each occasion point out the relative position of the right-hand man of the front rank.

5. Explain and demonstrate the various positions of the foot on which words of command are given, firstly in slow time, secondly in quick time. With the instructor marching, individual members of the squad should be made to give one word of command to the instructor until the rudiments are understood.

6. Call out two members of the squad, one to command and one to watch, and carry on with members drilling the squad in rotation. The instructor must be patient and encourage continually, remembering that *all members of the squad should hear everything he says*, of an instructional nature, to the member giving the words of command.

7. The position of recruits in a squad should be changed continuously.

## SECTION 153 : CALLING OUT THE TIME

1. In the early stages of training, every member of a squad must be made to call out the time for each movement. This fixes the standard time of 40 movements to the minute in everyone's head, it also makes the individual think what he is doing. Every recruit must be made to shout at the top of his voice, in order to open his lungs and give him confidence.

2. The beat of 40 to the minute is soon learned as " *One* ", " *Two* ", " *Three* " ; movement being made on the count of " *One* ". The squad must remain still in the correct position while the regulation pause of " *Two, Three* " is counted.

Where a quick movement is made " *One, Two* " is counted.

Examples—Turnings at the halt ; the squad shout " *One, Two, Three, One* ", moving each time as they say " *One* ".

Right Dress ; the squad shout " *One, Two* " (for the short pace forward) " *Two, Three* " (for the regulation pause) " *One, Two, Three* " (Turn the head. on " *One* " and count a regulation pause) " *One* " (Start to take up the dressing).

Eyes front ; the squad shout " *One* " as the head and eyes are turned to the front.

## SECTION 154 : TIME AND PACE

1. The times of marching are as follows :—

Quick time—For all units when parading together—116 paces to the minute.

    Light Infantry and Rifle Regiments—140 paces to the minute.

Slow time—65 paces to the minute (all arms).

Double time—180 paces to the minute (all arms).

2. The lengths of pace are as follows :—

| | | | | | |
|---|---|---|---|---|---|
| Normal pace in quick and slow time | | | | — | 30 inches |
| Stepping out | ,, | ,, | ,, | ,, — | 33 inches |
| Stepping short | ,, | ,, | ,, | ,, — | 21 inches |
| Double time | | | | — | 40 inches |
| Side pace | | | | — | 12 inches. |

## SECTION 155 : MECHANICAL AIDS TO DRILL

1. The instruments described below are the mechanical standards for the time and length of pace. The metronome shows the time required ; a drummer beating in time with it can broadcast the cadence ; the pace stick gives the correct length of pace.

Constant checks must be made with these implements in order that a uniform time of drill can be kept as between units. Their frequent use when teaching instructors is of the greatest importance.

### The metronome

2. The metronome gives time both for marching and for rifle exercises. Being a delicate machine it requires frequent checking. This can only be done with a stop watch.

The metronome can be set to any desired number of beats to the minute. Without a constant use of this instrument, it is impossible to maintain a correct and uniform timing for any long period, both in the men under command and among the instructors who are required to call out the time.

### The drum

3. From an instructional point of view, the drum has three main functions. First, to speed up the execution of movements in foot drill at the halt and in rifle exercises when done by numbers.

When used in this way the drummer should stand behind the instructor and with the drum out of view of the troops on parade. The words of command might be " **Rifle exercises by numbers with the drum, slope—arms** ".

4. The drummer is controlled by the instructor, who signals when to beat by extending the fingers of the right hand and immediately re-closing the fist. On this signal the drummer will beat. The squad in this example, would do the first movement of the *slope*. In order to instil the speed of execution into the squad the instructor should vary the pauses between his words of command and the signal.

5. Secondly, to control and beat out the correct time when the squad is judging the time. For this purpose a metronome is used in conjunction with the drum.

Rifle exercises are done at 40 movements to the minute. The metronome will be set at 120. The drummer, with the metronome working at his side, will stand in rear of the squad, and, if possible, far enough away from the men for the ticking of the instrument to be inaudible to them. The instructor's word of command will be, for example, " **Rifle exercises with the drum.—Slope** ". The drummer will, as far as possible, observe a regulation pause before beating the drum for the first time. Thereafter he will beat on every third beat of the metronome until the particular movement is completed, *eg*, for the slope from the order he would beat three times.

6. Thirdly, to beat for the rate of marching, with the metronome set and working at the correct rate, *eg*, 140 paces to the minute for recruits.

The drummer will take up the beating of the drum in time with the metronome with the squad standing still and listening, the instructor at the same time calling out the time. When the instructor is ready to practise his squad, the metronome must be working and the drummer beating before he orders " **Quick—march** ". It is impossible for the drummer to start and pick up the beat if he works on the order " March ".

### The pace stick

7. The pace stick measures exactly the correct length of pace. When it is used in conjunction with the metronome and drum a high standard of marching rhythm and uniformity can be obtained. This is necessary, not only for ceremonial purposes, but also to reduce fatigue on long marches and to set the standard of accuracy required of a drill instructor.

It is the only instrument of the three which the instructor must manipulate himself. To master the swinging of a stick, constant practice is required.

8. The instructor will march alongside the leading man of the squad and, with the pace stick open and swinging, control the length of pace of the squad. The natural tendency for the men is to step

too long, causing bad marching positions and straggling in the squad. As progress is made the instructor should check the length of pace by marching behind the squad with the pace stick swinging. He should repeatedly explain to the squad any faults which occur in the length of pace so that, finally, the correct pace becomes a habit.

## Method of carrying the pace stick

9. When closed, the stick is normally carried either at the trail or under the left arm. When at the trail it is swung with the right arm from front to rear and kept parallel with the ground; when under the left arm it is kept parallel with the ground, the point of balance under the left arm pit, shoes to the rear, the head of the stick held in the left hand, fingers together and on the left, extended and slanting upwards, thumb straight and on the right.

10. When saluting, with the pace stick carried under the arm, the left hand is cut to the side as the right comes up to the salute. As the right hand is cut away the left seizes the head of the stick as detailed above.

11. If the stick is held at the right side in the position of attention the rules for cane drill will apply.

12. When open, the stick is held at the right side as follows :—

(a) When standing at ease the stick is held in the right hand just below the apex, back of the hand to the right, fingers round both shafts, thumb nearest the body round the rear shaft, elbow against the side. The rear shaft is upright with the shoe slightly to the right and to the front of the right toe. The forward leg is extended to the front, point off the ground. The left arm is at the side.

(b) " Squad—attention ".—" *Bend the left knee* " and swing the forward leg of the stick to the rear by rotating the stick to the rear.

(c) " Quick (slow)—march ".—Step off with the left foot. Swing the rear leg of the stick forward by twisting with the fingers and thumb, and rotating the free leg of the stick outwards and forwards. Place the swinging shoe on the ground straight in front of the point already on the ground. Continue this movement until halting or as long as required.

13. When halting, the stick is held in the position of attention detailed above.

14. When ceasing to swing, while still marching, the stick is lifted up so that the forearm is parallel with the ground, hand in front of the right hip, thumb and forefinger round the forward shaft which is upright, other fingers round the rear shaft. This is known as the marching position.

*Note.*—Instructors must be able to swing the stick with either hand.

## NOTES ON INSPECTION

1. *General.*—The following points become second nature with experience and in a good unit, both in their being noticed at inspection and in their observance by the men.

Full wear must be extracted from clothing and as long as it is serviceable it must be worn. There is however no reason why part worn clothing should not be clean, correctly pressed, and in good repair. Clothing worn to the pitch of unserviceability must be noted on inspection.

It is usual to inspect, starting at the right hand man of the front rank, from the head downwards, the front of the rank before the back of it, and the men before their arms.

2. *General Impression.*—Is the soldier clean? Is his uniform clean, well-fitting, pressed, and correctly put on? Are his arms clean? Is he standing at the correct position of attention or slope?

*Note.*—Before starting to inspect, see that any incorrect positions are put right. The inspecting officer, warrant officer or NCO should be accompanied by the next senior on parade who will note anything he is told. The third senior should be posted in front of the squad to see that the men remain steady in the ranks.

3. *Head-dress*

(a) *From the front* :—

  (i) Is the cap clean and free from sweat and hair grease?

  (ii) *Beret.*—Is the cap band square on the head, badge in the correct position, fullness pulled down in the proper way? Is the badge clean and free from the dirty deposit of old metal polish?

  (iii) *Cap SD.*—As above but is the cap properly set up and not worn out at the top in front?

(b) *From the back* :—

  (i) Is the bow at the back of the beret neatly tied with the ends sewn down?

  (ii) Is the cap clean from the back and is the back seam or bow central?

  (iii) Is the hair short? If in doubt tell the soldier to take off his cap so as to see if it is of moderate length on top. Is the hair on the neck shaved?

4. *Face and neck* clean and shaved.

*Note.*—Check that the troops eyes do not follow the inspecting officer.

5. *Battledress jacket*

(a) *From the front :—*

(i) The way this is put on and its fit is vital to a neat appearance. The collar, cuff and jacket must all be carefully fitted. Collars must be scrubbed clean round the neck. The collar fastening must be done up and be well fitting. Buttons must be well sewn on and done up. The jacket belt must be tight and carefully fitted under the belt. The fly of the jacket must be straight and central making a straight line through the belt buckle with the fly of the trousers.

(ii) On parade the jacket pockets must not be stuffed out with papers, etc.

(iii) Designations and badges of rank must be clean and properly sewn on.

(iv) No ends of cotton from the stitching must be allowed to appear.

(v) If worn, ensure that shirt, collar and tie are neat and central.

b) *From the back :—*

(i) Is the collar clean ? Do the collar, waist and cuffs fit well ? There must be no gaping at the cuff, showing shirt or cardigan. The shirt with collar attached must be put on carefully so that the neck of the jacket does not look lumpy.

(ii) The collar, sleeves and body of the jacket only require pressing flat. Additional creases only aggravate the wear of the coat.

(iii) Neither cardigan nor shirt cuffs must show.

6. *Belt*

(a) *From the front :—*

(i) This must be fitted so tight that, during a long parade, the weight of the bayonet cannot pull it down on one side and the battledress jacket cannot ride up underneath.

(ii) The buckle must be central to the front and in line with the clothing buttons.

(iii) When the belt has brass fittings these must be clean both back and front. Any part of the belt turning back underneath must be correctly fastened and squarely under the outer part of the belt.

(b) *From the back* :—

    (i) The frog must be on the left hip—not under the arm or in the small of the back. The bayonet must be inspected for rust and fingermarks on the steel, either by withdrawing from the scabbard or when fixed to the rifle.

7. *Hands.*—Clean, with no tobacco or other stain. Nails clean and trimmed.

*Note.*—Hands should be noted particularly when inspecting at the " *slope* ".

8. *Battledress trousers*

  (a) *From the front* :—

    (i) Trousers must be well braced up. When worn with anklets, the turnover should be no lower than the top buckle of the anklet. Look out for wear on the inside of the leg just at the point of turnover, and at the trouser pockets.

    (ii) When worn without anklets, trousers should just break in the front on the instep and at the back should be level with the top of the heel of the boot.

  (b) *From the back* : Must be flat at the seat, fitting cleanly under the jacket and belt.

9. *Anklets*

  (a) These must be of a large enough size not to wrinkle, gape at the side or bulge, and must be so tightly fitted as to remain straight and not turn round at the ankle.

  (b) The webbing and the straps must not be frayed.

  (c) Buckles, if of brass, will be polished back and front.

10. *Boots*

  (a) *From the front* :—

    (i) These must be in a good state of repair and free from cracks. Laces must be strong and flat, not twisted or knotted. Laces must be done up tight so as to close the lace holes ; this is a matter of fitting and is a service requirement for protection of the instep. Bootlaces will be done up and the ends concealed so that they cannot fall down.

    (ii) Polished boots will be polished on the uppers as well as on the toes and heels.

  (b) *From the back* :—Get some men to lift one foot at a time to see if the soles are in repair and properly studded.

11. *Inspection of Arms.*—Arms should be clean and dry for inspection. Slings should be adjusted to the fitting laid down by the regiment but will be taut.

124

APPENDIX B
## SWORD DRILL

The sword is a traditional badge of rank and honour. In the Army (the mounted squadrons of the Household Cavalry and The King's Troop RHA excepted) the sword indicates a holder of His Majesty's Commission or Warrant.

Sword drill is used for ceremonial purposes only. The main qualities that must be sought after are accuracy and swift but graceful movement.

The drill is divided into three parts—Dismounted, mounted, and funeral exercises.

### PART 1

# DISMOUNTED SWORD DRILL

SAM BROWN BELT
*(a)*

SLING
*(b)*

1. **Position of attention**

Hold the scabbard with the left hand, left arm straight (left arm bent outside the hilt when the sword is *not* drawn), back of the hand to the left, thumb round the front, forefinger pointing down the scabbard, other fingers curled round the back. This position of the left hand is maintained throughout drill except when standing at ease with swords *not* drawn.

The sword (or empty scabbard) is held in the left hand with the left arm straight, hand gripping the scabbard, thumb down the front, back of the hand to the left, finger curled round the back. The sword (or empty scabbard) will be held upright, shoe on the ground close to the foot and just forward of the heel, hilt (or top of the scabbard) close to the side.

2. **" Draw swords—one "**

In one movement carry the right hand across the body, grasp the handle and draw out the blade until the forearm is *horizontal. The back of the* hand is to the rear, fingers and thumb round the handle.

Change the grip of the left hand to hold the scabbard by the rear ring (Officers, upper ring) between the forefinger and thumb, remainder of the fingers curled up in the palm of the hand. Immediately raise the left hand until the forearm is horizontal, elbow close to the side. At the same time carry the right hand across the body, forearm horizontal, grasp the handle and turn the sword, edge to the left ; straighten the left arm to the rear, keeping the right forearm horizontal and the shoulder square to the front.

" Squad—**two** " (Position of the recover)

| | |
|---|---|
| Draw the sword sharply forward and upwards allowing the shoe of the scabbard to move slightly to the rear. Resume the position of attention with the left hand. | Draw the sword sharply from the scabbard. Resume the position of attention with the scabbard and left hand. |

As soon as the point of the sword leaves the mouth of the scabbard, bring it sharply to the position of the recover, *ie*, with the blade perpendicular, edge to the left, upper part of the hilt in line with and opposite the mouth, thumb towards the mouth on the side of the handle.

" Squad—**three** " (Position of the carry)

Force the right arm to the side, elbow close in, forearm horizontal and to the front. Blade perpendicular, edge to the front, the grip held lightly between the forefinger and thumb, other fingers together and slightly curled, hilt resting on the upper part of the hand.

*Note.*— (i) When on parade and the troops fix bayonets, one movement will be done on each word of command.

(ii) When " **Fall in the officers** " is ordered, officers will come to attention and draw swords before stepping off to join their companies.

3. " **Slope—swords** "

Drop the point of the sword to the rear so that the back of the blade rests midway between the neck and the point of the shoulder. Keep the forearm and hand still but release the grip with the last three fingers and put the little finger behind the handle.

4. " **Return swords—one** "

Force the hilt over to the hollow of the left shoulder, blade perpendicular, edge to the left, right forearm horizontal and elbow in line with the shoulder, back of the hand to the front.

| (a) | (b) |
|---|---|
| At the same time push the shoe of the scabbard a little to the rear. | With the left hand change the grip to the ring (forefinger and thumb) and bring the mouth of the scabbard forward about 3 inches and turn its edge to the left. |

Grip the mouth of the scabbard with the left hand and immediately force the point of the sword downwards outside the left shoulder with a quick turn of the right wrist and put it in the scabbard, guiding the blade home with the forefinger. Force the blade home to assume the position of the second motion of *draw swords*. Keep the shoulders square to the front.

" Squad—two "

Force the sword home in the scabbard and resume the position of attention with the left hand and the scabbard. The right hand remains on top of the hilt, back of the hand upwards, fingers and thumb close together and straight, forearm horizontal and close to the body.

" Squad—three "

Cut the right hand to the side.

When on parade and the troops unfix bayonets and the officers are required to return swords, one movement will be made on each word of command.

5. " Stand at—ease " (sword in the scabbard)

| (a) | (b) |
|---|---|
| As previously detailed. | " *Squad—one* "<br>Carry the shoe of the scabbard 12 inches to the left at the same time as the foot. The right hand remains at the side. |
| | " *Squad—two* "<br>Place the palm of the left hand on the top of the hilt. |
| | " *Squad—three* "<br>Force the hilt of the sword straight to the front to the full extent of the left arm. |

6. " Stand at — ease " (sword drawn)

As the left foot is carried off, slope swords.

| (a) | (b) |
|---|---|
| The left hand remains in the position of attention. | The palm of the left hand is put on the mouth of the scabbard instead of the hilt. |

7. Attention from stand at ease

| " Squad—attention "<br>Bring the sword to the carry and come to attention. | " Squad—one "<br>Bring the sword (or empty scabbard) upright to the left side, palm of the hand still on top. |
|---|---|

(If on parade with men equipped with slung swords, this movement will be done on the third motion with the slung sword.)

" Squad—two "
Change the grip of the hand to the position as at attention.

" Squad—three "
Bring the left foot into the right, moving the shoe of the scabbard as well. Carry swords.

8. " Quick—march "

The sword or empty scabbard is kept steady at the side by the left hand.

Jerk up the sword or empty scabbard grasping it at the point of balance. Turn it clockwise edge to the front and grasp it with the thumb on top and pointing down the edge, fingers underneath. The sword will be held at an angle of 45 degrees and at the full extent of the left arm which will be kept still to the side.

9. " Squad—halt "

Lower the sword or empty scabbard to the position of attention.

10. Saluting at the halt

" Salute to the front—on ".—Bring the sword to the recover.

" Squad—two ".—Lower the sword sharply to the right side to the full extent of the right arm edge to the left, point 12 inches from the ground and straight to the front, thumb flat along the handle, fingers gripping it, right hand just behind the thigh.

" Squad—three ".—Bring the sword up to the recover.

" Squad—four ".—Return to the position of the carry.

*Note.*— (i) When the sword is not drawn the normal salute with the hand is given.

(ii) When on parade with troops armed with the rifle and the *present* is ordered, officers with swords will work on the first and third motions of the *present*. On the order " **Slope arms** " they will work with the men .

(iii) When the order " **Fall out the—officers** " is given, they will salute with the sword, form up in rear of the senior officer as already laid down and will return swords before standing at ease.

### Saluting on the march

11. *In slow time.*—The movement starts from the carry, as the left foot comes to the ground and on the word of command " **Eyes— right** ". The movement lasts over four paces, finishing on the right

foot. There is no pause between the movements, which will be carried out as one graceful gesture.

*First motion.*—Shoot the right arm out to the right, arm horizontal, at shoulder height and square off to the right, blade perpendicular, edge to the right. At the same time turn the head and eyes to the right.

*Second motion.*—Carry the sword round in a sweep, keeping the blade perpendicular and the hand and elbow in the same plane as the shoulder, by bending the elbow to bring the hilt to the mouth, with the sword in the position of the recover. The elbow is kept level with the shoulder and the thumb remains round the handle.

*Third motion.*—Continue the sweep to bring the hilt to the point of the right shoulder. At the same time, keeping the edge to the left, change the grip so that the thumb points up the side of the handle. The elbow is still shoulder high with the upper arm square off to the right, forearm horizontal, hand in line with the mouth.

*Fourth motion.*—Lower the sword sharply to the position of the salute.

The timing is as follows :—

Left foot comes to the ground—Shoot the right arm out.
Right foot comes to the ground—Sword at the recover.
Left foot comes to the ground—Sword at the right shoulder.
Right foot comes to the ground—Point lowered.

12. " Eyes—front ".—As the left foot comes to the ground, turn the head and eyes to the front and at the same time bring the sword to the position of the recover, elbow close to the side. As the left foot next comes to the ground bring the sword down to the position of the carry.

13. **In quick time.**—The sword will be retained at the carry. The head and eyes will be turned off on the word of command given to the troops.

If units through regimental custom should wish to salute with the sword in quick time the salute is given working as the left foot strikes the ground.

14. **General notes**

(*a*) At the halt, the sword is normally at the carry when the men are at attention or with arms sloped.

(*b*) On the move the sword is sloped on stepping off and brought to the carry on halting except on the following occasions when the sword will always be at the carry :—

(i) On turning or wheeling on to or reaching the saluting base.

(ii) When falling in or falling out the officers.

(iii) When advancing in review order.

(iv) When guard mounting.

(*c*) When the men march at ease without slinging, the sword will be sloped—*eg*, when marching to a guard.

(*d*) When the men march at ease with rifles slung the sword will be returned. On marching to attention swords will be drawn again, working on the left foot.

PART II

# MOUNTED SWORD DRILL

**" Draw swords—one "**

15. Carry the right arm across the body, over the bridle arm, and draw the sword until the hilt rests on the bridle arm. (If required put the right hand through the sword knot and take two or more turns to secure it.) Grasp the handle, with the forearm and elbow close to the body. Body upright, shoulders square to the front.

" Squad—two ".—Draw the sword sharply and bring it to the position of the recover.

" Squad—three " (Position of the carry).—Force the sword down to the right thigh so that the upper arm is perpendicular, elbow close to the side, wrist resting on the thigh, blade perpendicular, edge to the front, hilt resting on the top of the hand, first three fingers gripping the handle, little finger behind to steady it, pommel pressed against the inside of the thigh.

" Slope—swords "

16. Raise the forearm until it is horizontal, hand in front of the elbow and lower the sword on to the shoulder as already detailed.

" Sit at—ease " (From the slope only)

17. Place both hands on the front of the saddle, right over left, without removing the sword from the shoulder.

18. " Return swords—one ".—As already detailed, passing the right arm over the bridle arm.

" Squad—two ".—As already detailed (if necessary clearing the hand from the sword knot).

" Squad—three ".—Cut the right hand to the side.

**Proving**

19. With the sword at the *slope*, a man ordered to prove will come to the *carry*. On the command **" As you were "** he will *slope swords*.

### Saluting at the halt

20. As already detailed except that on the second motion, the right arm is perpendicular, fully extended and close to the side, blade of the sword touching the leg three inches below the knee.

### Saluting on the march

21. As already detailed but with the position of the salute as in 18 above.

### Approaching a superior

22. An officer or soldier will approach his superior at the *carry* and will salute to the front if the superior is an officer.

## PART III

# FUNERAL EXERCISES WITH THE SWORD

### The reverse from the salute

23. This movement will be done when the men *reverse arms* from the *present*.

" Reverse arms—one ".—Bring the sword to the recover.

" Squad—two ".—Bring the sword to the *carry* as the men with rifles complete the second movement.

" Squad—three ".—Force the sword under the right armpit, edge uppermost, by twisting the wrist and dropping the point to the left front ; hilt on top and in front of the right shoulder, fingers of the right hand together and straight to the right of the handle, thumb to the left, back of the hand to the right, right elbow against the side. At the same time seize the blade with the left hand behind the back, in line with the waist belt, back of the hand underneath. Sword at an angle of 45 degrees.

### The reverse when marching in quick time and vice versa

24. On the command " Break into quick time, quick—march ", from slow time, cut the left hand to the side on the first beat of the left foot. At the same time allow the hilt to drop so that the sword is horizontal. Grasp the scabbard with the left hand as at attention.

25. On the command " Break into slow time, slow—march ", resume the position of reverse arms as the left foot comes to the ground.

### Change swords from the reverse

26. " Change arms—one ".—Bring the sword to the *carry*.

" Two ".—Pass the sword across the body, gripping the hilt with the left hand and cutting the right hand away to the side.

" Three ".—Reverse the sword under the left armpit, edge uppermost, the hilt being grasped with the left hand, the right hand grasping the blade in rear of the body, the forearm parallel to the ground. The blade of the sword to be at an angle of 45 degrees, the left elbow close to the body.

### Rest on your arms reversed from the reverse

27. Working in time with the men release the sword with the left hand, which is cut to the side. Place the point between the feet, hilt central against the body, edge to the right. Grasp the handle with the left hand. Turn the head and eyes to the right and shoot the right arm to the right, at shoulder level, back of the hand uppermost, fingers and thumb together and extended. Bring the arm round in a circular movement until it has traversed 45 degrees, bend the arm and place the right hand on the hilt. Keep the elbow raised as high as possible. Turn the head to the front. Look to the left and do similar movements with the left arm. Place the left hand on top of the right. Look to the front. Drop the chin on the breast and elbows against the body.

" Party—attention ".—Raise the head.

### The reverse from rest on your arms reversed

28. " Reverse arms—one ".—Seize the handle with the right hand in the same grip as at the *reverse*. Hold the hilt steady with the left hand.

" *Squad—two* ".—*Force the sword under the right armpit and seize it with the left hand behind the back in the correct position of the reverse.*

### The salute from rest on your arms reversed

*Note.*—This is preceded by the command " **Party—attention** ".

29. " **Present arms—one** ".—Seize the handle with the right hand, back of the hand to the left. Cut the left hand to the side.

" Squad—two ".—Force the sword to the recover.

" Squad—three ".—Force the sword to the salute.

### To rest on swords reversed from the present

30. " **Rest on your arms reversed—one** ".—Allow the point of the sword to fall forward and downward and place the point on the ground between the feet, edge to the right. The grip of the right hand will change as the sword comes down so that when it rests on the

ground the palm of the hand is resting on top of the hilt. At the same time lower the head on the breast.

" **Two** ".—Place the left hand on top of the right.

*Note*.—The elbows will be kept close to the sides during all movements. The movements will be performed on the first and third motions of the " *Rest on your arms reversed* " with the rifle.

### To present from rest on your arms reversed

31. " **Present arms—one** ".—Raise the head and cut the left hand to the side allowing the right hand to resume its grip on the sword handle.

" **Two** ".—Bring the sword to the " *Salute* ".

*Note*.—The movements will be performed on the first and third motions of the " *Present arms* " with the rifle.

APPENDIX C

# FUNERAL EXERCISES WITH THE PISTOL

1. " **Rest on your arms—reversed** ".—Turn the head and eyes to the right ; at the same time extend the right arm slowly to the right to its full extent in line with the shoulder, palm of the hand open, fingers together, back of the hand upwards. Without pausing, bring the right hand to the butt with a circular motion to the front, fingers remaining straight and not grasping the butt. On completion, allow the right elbow to drop into the right side. Without pause raise the left arm to the left and repeat the movements with the left hand and arm. When the left elbow drops, lower the head on the breast. These movements should be made slowly without jerks and should be continuous.

2. " **Attention** ".—Raise the head and elbows, make a pause, and cut both hands to the side.

3. " **Draw—arms** ".—Draw the pistol and carry it across the body in the *Rest* position.

4. " **Right hand—ready** "

5. " **Present** ".—Without moving the feet, raise the right arm in the air at an angle of 135 degrees, muzzle to be pointing at the same angle as the arm.

6. " **Re-cock** ".—Re-cock without lowering the pistol. Fire and repeat.

7. " **Steady** ".—Assume the *Ready* position.

8. " **Unload** ".—Empty cases will not be collected by the firing party. Men will remain in the unload position and will not *Make* pistols until the NCO in charge of the firing party has inspected them.

# SPECIMEN DRILL PROGRAMMES

Basic drill for National Servicemen

1. Fifty periods spread over ten weeks. The drill for technical arms may be reduced by the exclusion of periods marked * and the number of weeks might be greater.

| Lesson | Subject |
|---|---|
| 1 | Position of attention. Standing at ease. Standing easy and *vice versa*. Formation of three ranks. Dressing, numbering and proving. Open and close order. Turnings and inclinings by numbers. Dismissing. |
| 2 | Turnings and inclinings judging the time. Length of pace and time in marching. Marching and halting in quick time. Eyes right, front and left. Sizing. Saluting at the halt. |
| 3 | Revision Lessons 1 and 2. Saluting on the march. |
| 4 | Marching and halting in slow time. Paces forward and to the rear. Side pace. Wheeling. Breaking into slow and quick time. |
| 5 | Turnings and diagonal march in slow and quick time. Saluting. |
| 6 | Marking time, forward and halt in slow and quick time. Changing step in slow and quick time. |
| 7 | Marching, halting and marking time in double time. Revision Lessons 4, 5 and 6. |
| 8 | General revision of saluting. |
| 9 | General revision of all movements at the halt. |
| 10 | General revision of all movements in slow and quick time. |
| 11 | Marching in line in slow time. Taking open and close order. Eyes right, front, left. |
| 12 | Marching in line in quick time. Eyes right, front and left. Changing direction by wheeling and forming at the halt and in slow time. |
| 13 | Changing direction by wheeling and forming in quick time. Revision saluting. |
| 14 | Saluting fixed and moving points. |
| 15 | Revision all movements at the halt. |
| 16 | Revision all movements in slow time. |
| 17 | Revision all movements in quick time. |
| 18* | Forming squad in slow time, from the halt and on the march. Repetition in quick time. |
| 19 | Revision all saluting. Compliments without head-dress and when in plain clothes. Compliments to the Colours. |

| Lesson | Subject |
|--------|---------|
| 20 | General revision. |
| 21 | General revision. |
| 22 | General revision. |
| 23* | Forming two ranks from three ranks and *vice versa*. |
| 24 | Marching off in single file from threes. Reforming three ranks. |
| 25 | Saluting fixed and moving points. |
| 26 | Position of attention with the rifle. Getting on parade. Short trail. Standing at ease. Standing easy and *vice versa*. Slope from the order and *vice versa*. Dressing with the rifle at the order and the slope. |
| 27 | Marching and saluting in slow and quick time with the rifle. |
| 28 | Revision Lessons 1, 2, 3 and 4. |
| 29* | Revision Lesson 26. |
| 30 | Present from the slope and *vice versa*. Ground arms, take-up arms. |
| 31 | Revision saluting with and without rifles. |
| 32* | Fixing and unfixing bayonets. Revision rifle drill. |
| 33 | Revision lessons 5, 6, 7 and 11. |
| 34 | Port from the order and *vice versa*. Port from the slope and *vice versa*. For inspection port arms, ease springs. |
| 35 | Examine from the port, ease springs. Port from the examine. Order from the examine. |
| 36 | Revision Lessons 12, 13 and 18. |
| 37 | Saluting. |
| 38* | Trail from the order and *vice versa*. Trail from the slope and *vice versa*. Revision Lessons 30, 32, 34 and 35. |
| 39* | Change arms at the slope and at the trail. Revision Lessons 23 and 24. |
| 40 | On guard from the slope and *vice versa*. On guard from the order and *vice versa*. The cant from the order, from the slope and *vice versa*. The high port from the order, slope and on guard. |
| 41 | Revision rifle drill. |
| 42 | Revision foot drill. |
| 43 | Revision saluting. |
| 44* | Secure from the slope and order, and *vice versa*. Change arms at the secure. Shoulder arms from the order and *vice versa*. |
| 45* | Rifle exercises on the march. |
| 46 | Single sentry paying compliments on his post. |
| 47 | Single sentry patrolling and paying compliments on his beat. |
| 48 | Revision Lessons 46 and 47. |
| 49 | General revision. |
| 50 | General revision. |

**Spring Drills**

2. A month's refresher course for junior officers, warrant and non-commissioned officers and trained soldiers. One period a day for 24 working days.

| Period | Subjects |
|---|---|
| 1 | Chapter I. All sections. Squad drill at the halt—without arms. |
| 2 | Chapter II. Marching. Secs 12–17 inclusive. |
| 3 | Chapter II. Marching. Secs 18–23 inclusive. |
| 4 | Chapter III. Marching in line and changing direction. Secs 24-26 inclusive. |
| 5 | Chapter III. Marching in line and changing direction. Secs 27 and 28. |
| 6 | Chapter IV. Forming squad. All sections. |
| 7 | Chapter V. Forming two ranks. All sections. General revision Chapters I and II. |
| 8 | Chapter VI. Marching off in single file. All sections. General revision Chapters III and IV. |
| 9 | Chapter VII. Compliments. Secs 36–38 inclusive. |
| 10 | Chapter VII. Compliments. Secs 39–41 inclusive. |
| 11 | Chapter VII. Compliments. Secs 42 and 43. Also saluting fixed and moving points. |
| 12 | Chapter VIII. Drill with cane or whip. All sections. |
| 13 | Chapter IX. Rifle exercises. Secs 50–56 inclusive. |
| 14 | Chapter IX. Rifle exercises. Secs 57–63 inclusive. |
| 15 | Chapter IX. Rifle exercises. Secs 64–70 inclusive. |
| 16 | Chapter IX. Rifle exercises. Secs 71–76 inclusive. |
| 17 | Chapter X. Rifle exercises on the march. All sections. |
| 18 | Chapter XIII. Sentry drill. Secs 95–97 inclusive. |
| 19 | Chapter XIII. Sentry drill. Secs 98–100 inclusive. |
| 20 | Chapter XIV. Guards and sentries. All sections. |
| 21 | Chapter XV. Platoon drill. All sections Chapter XVI. Company drill. Secs 109–116 inclusive. |
| 22 | Chapter XVI. Company drill. Secs 117–123 inclusive. |
| 23 | Chapter XVI. Company drill. Secs 124–130 inclusive. |
| 24. | Chapter XVI. Company drill. General exercises by setting problems. |

## Casuals Drill

3. A six months' programme based on one period a week for employed men and specialists.

| Lesson | Subjects |
|--------|----------|
| 1 | Revision of foot drill in quick time. |
| 2 | Revision of marching in slow time. |
| 3 | Revision of saluting. |
| 4 | Saluting fixed and moving points. |
| 5 | Revision of arms drill. |
| 6 | *NCOs.* Introduction to words of command. |
| | *Privates.* Revision marching past in column of threes. |
| 7 | *NCOs.* Communication drill and mutual. |
| | *Privates.* Revision marching past in line in slow time. |
| 8 | *NCOs.* Mutual. Stepping a squad off at column distance. Maintaining column distance. Compliments when marching past. |
| | *Privates.* Revision marching past in line in quick time. |
| 9 | Revision. Advance in review order. |
| 10 | Ceremonial parade. Marching past in slow and quick time. Advance in review order. |
| 11 | *NCOs.* How to inspect a squad. Methods of approach and address. |
| | *Privates.* Introduction to words of command. |
| 12 | *NCOs.* Mutual. |
| | *Privates.* Communication drill and revision foot drill. Methods of approach and address to seniors. Entering offices, rooms, etc. |
| 13 | *NCOs.* Mutual. |
| | *Privates.* Mutual. Turnings on the march in quick time. Saluting. |
| 14 | *NCOs.* Introduction to company drill. |
| | *Privates.* Mutual. Commanding squads when marching past. |
| 15 | *NCOs.* Mutual. |
| | *Privates.* Revision saluting and arms drill. |
| 16 | *NCOs.* Any questions by the squad on subjects taught. |
| | *Privates.* Revision marching past in slow and quick time. Advance in review order. |

| Lesson | Subject |
|---|---|
| 17 | Guard mounting. |
| 18 | Guard changing. Posting reliefs. Guards turning out. |
| 19 | Sentry drill. |
| 20 | Sentry drill. |
| 21 | Saluting fixed and moving points. |
| 22 | General revision. |
| 23 | Rehearse ceremonial parade. |
| 24 | Rehearse ceremonial parade. |
| 25 | Dress rehearsal for Commanding Officer's parade. |
| 26 | Commanding Officer's parade. Marching past in slow and quick time. Advance in review order. |

## NCO Drill Cadre Course

4. Based on a squad of corporals and lance-corporals doing a three weeks' intensive course in NCO duties, at 33 periods a week.

The allotment of periods is shown hereunder and is based on six each day, Monday to Friday inclusive, plus three each Saturday, giving a total of 99 periods.

| | | |
|---|---|---|
| Drill | 70 | periods |
| Lectures | 7 | ,, |
| Demonstrations | 5 | ,, |
| Examinations | 8 | ,, |
| Sport | 6 | ,, |
| Pay | 3 | ,, |
| TOTAL | 99 | |

*Lectures*

1. Object of the course and of drill.
2. Discipline and man management.
3. Responsibilities of NCOs.
4. Charge sheets, framing charges, evidence.
5. Minor Offence Reports, Guard Reports, Conduct Sheets.
6. Duty rosters.
7. Duty of Orderly NCOs.

*Demonstrations*

1  Foot and arms drill.
2  Use of drum, metronome and pace stick.
3  Company Commander's and Commanding Officer's Orders.
4  Guard changing, posting reliefs, guards turning out.
5  Colour Drill.

| Lesson | Subjects |
|---|---|
| 1 | Chapter I.   Squad drill at the halt.   Secs 1–6. |
| 2 | Chapter I.   Squad drill at the halt.   Secs 7–11. |
| 3 | Chapter II.   Marching.   Secs 12 and 13. |
| 4 | Revision. |
| 5 | Chapter II.   Marching.   Secs 14–16 inclusive. |
| 6 | Chapter II.   Marching.   Sec 17. |
| 7 | Chapter II.   Marching.   Secs 18 and 19. |
| 8 | Chapter II.   Marching.   Secs 20 and 21. |
| 9 | Chapter II.   Marching.   Secs 22 and 23. |
| 10 | Revision Chapter II.   Marching. |
| 11 | Chapter III.   Marching in line.   Secs 24 and 25, 28–30. |
| 12 | Chapter III.   Marching in line.   Sec 26. |
| 13 | Chapter III.   Marching in line.   Secs 27 and 28. |
| 14 | Revision Chapter III.   Marching in line. |
| 15 | Chapter IV.   Forming squad.   Secs 29 and 30. |
| 16 | Chapter IV.   Forming squad.   Sec. 31. |
| 17 | General revision. |
| 18 | Chapter V.   Forming two ranks.   Secs 32 and 33. |
| 19 | Chapter VI.   Marching off in single file.   Secs 34 and 35. |
| 20 | Chapter VII.   Compliments.   Sec 36. |
| 21 | Chapter VII.   Compliments.   Secs 37 and 38. |
| 22 | Chapter VII.   Compliments.   Secs 39–41 inclusive. |
| 23 | Chapter VII.   Compliments.   Secs 42 and 43.   Saluting fixed and moving points. |
| 24 | Revision saluting. |
| 25 | Chapter VIII.   Drill with cane.   Secs 44–49 inclusive. |
| 26 | Chapter IX.   Rifle exercises.   Secs 50–53 inclusive. |
| 27 | Chapter IX.   Rifle exercises.   Secs 54–57 inclusive. |
| 28 | Chapter IX.   Rifle exercises.   Secs 58–61 inclusive. |
| 29 | Revision Chapter IX.   Rifle exercises. |

| Lesson | Subjects |
|---|---|
| 30 | Revision marching in slow and quick time Chapters II, III and IV. |
| 31 | Chapter IX.   Rifle exercises.   Secs 62–65 inclusive. |
| 32 | Chapter IX.   Rifle exercises.   Secs 66–68 inclusive. |
| 33 | Chapter IX.   Rifle exercises.   Secs 69–72 inclusive. |
| 34 | Chapter IX.   Rifle exercises.   Secs 73–76 inclusive. |
| 35 | Revision rifle exercises. |
| 36 | Chapter X.   Rifle exercises on the march.   Secs 77 and 78. |
| 37 | Chapter X.   Rifle exercises on the march.   Secs 79 and 80. |
| 38 | Revision.   Chapter I.   Squad drill at the halt. |
| 39 | Chapter XI.   Funeral exercises with the rifle.   Secs 81–85 inclusive. |
| 40 | Chapter XI.   Funeral exercises with the rifle.   Secs 86–90 inclusive. |
| 41 | Chapter XIII.   Sentry drill.   Secs 95–97 inclusive. |
| 42 | Chapter XIII.   Sentry drill.   Secs 98–100 inclusive. |
| 43 | Chapter XIV.   Guards and Sentries.   Secs 101–106 inclusive. |
| 44 | Revision. |
| 45 | Mutual Introduction.   Voice production. Chapter XX, Secs 146–149 inclusive. |
| 46 | Mutual.   Chapter XX.   Words of command.   Secs 150 and 151. |
| 47 | Mutual.   Revision Chapter XX.   Communication drill and mutual.   Sec 152. |
| 48 | Revision Chapters II and III.   Marching and changing direction. |
| 49 | Mutual.   Students drill squads. |
| 50 | Mutual.   Students drill squads. |
| 51 | Revision.   Chapter III.   Changing direction. |
| 52 | Mutual. |
| 53 | Mutual. |
| 54 | Revision. Chapters IV, V and VI.  Forming squad, forming two ranks and marching in single file. |
| 55 | Mutual. |
| 56 | Revision.   Chapter VII.   Compliments. |
| 57 | Mutual. |
| 58 | Revision Chapter VIII.   Cane drill.   Chapter IX.   Rifle exercises. |

| Lesson | Subjects |
|--------|----------|
| 59 | Revision Chapter X and XI. Rifle exercises on the march and funeral exercises with the rifle. |
| 60 | Mutual. |
| 61 | Revision. Chapter XIII. Sentry drill. |
| 62 | Mutual. |
| 63 | Chapter XV. Platoon drill. Secs 107 and 108. Chapter XVI Company drill. 109–112 inclusive. |
| 64 | Chapter XVI. Company drill. Secs 113–116 inclusive. |
| 65 | Chapter XVI. Company drill. Secs 117–120 inclusive. |
| 66 | Chapter XVI. Company drill. Secs 121–123 inclusive. |
| 67 | Chapter XVI. Company drill. Secs 124–127 inclusive. |
| 68 | Chapter XVI. Company drill. Secs 128–130 inclusive. |
| 69 | General revision. Students' requests. |
| 70 | General revision. Students' requests. |

Printed in Great Britain under the authority of HIS MAJESTY'S STATIONERY OFFICE by Keliher. Hudson & Kearns. Ltd., Hatfields. London. S.E.1

(24010)  2284/8986  K800  5/51  K.H.K  Gp. 512

*Plate* I

(*a*)
POSITION OF ATTENTION,
WITHOUT RIFLE

(*b*)
POSITION OF ATTENTION,
WITHOUT RIFLE

*Plate* 2

**STAND AT EASE**

*Plate* 3

QUICK MARCH, WITHOUT RIFLE

*Plate* 4

SLOW MARCH, WITH RIFLE

*Plate* 5

*(a)*
SALUTING TO THE FRONT
(WEARING SD CAP)

*(b)*
SALUTING TO THE FRONT
(WEARING BERET)

*Plate* 6

**POSITION OF ATTENTION, WITH RIFLE, BAYONET FIXED**

*Plate* 7

SLOPE ARMS, FIRST POSITION

*Plate* 8

(*a*) **SLOPE ARMS, SECOND POSITION**

(*b*) **SLOPE ARMS, THIRD POSITION**

*Plate* 9

(*a*) ORDER ARMS, FIRST
POSITION

(*b*) ORDER ARMS, SECOND
POSITION

*Plate* 10

(*a*) PRESENT ARMS, SECOND
POSITION

(*b*) PRESENT ARMS, THIRD
POSITION

*Plate* 11

FIX BAYONETS, FIRST POSITION

*Plate* 12

**FIX BAYONETS, SECOND POSITION**

*Plate* 13

(a) UNFIX BAYONETS,
FIRST POSITION

(b) UNFIX BAYONETS,
SECOND POSITION

*Plate* 14

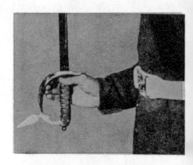

(*b*) POSITION OF THE
RIGHT HAND

(*a*) THE CARRY

Plate 15

(a) THE RECOVER    (b) THE SALUTE

# BASIC AND BATTLE PHYSICAL TRAINING

A series of pamphlets prepared under the direction of the Chief of the Imperial General Staff on aspects of physical training.

| | | |
|---|---|---|
| I, 1944. | General Principles of Basic and Battle Physical Training and Methods of Instruction. | 6d. (7d.) |
| II, 1944. | Basic Physical Training Tables and Basic Physical Efficiency Tests. | 1s. 6d. (1s. 8d.) |
| III, 1946. | Syllabus of Battle Physical Training and Battle Physical Efficiency Tests. | 2s. (2s. 2d.) |
| IV, 1945. | Endurance Training. | 4d. (5d.) |
| V, 1946. | Jumping, Vaulting, Climbing, Scaling and Obstacle Training. | 9d. (11d.) |
| VI, 1946. | Pulling, Pushing, Lifting and Carrying. | 6d. (7d.) |
| VII, 1946. | Throwing, Balancing and Physical Training for Mountain Warfare. | 6d. (7d.) |
| VIII, 1945. | Swimming, Life Saving and Improvised Aids to Crossing Water Obstacles. | 9d. (10d.) |
| IX, 1945. | Boxing and Wrestling. | 6d. (7d.) |
| | Amendments No. 1. January, 1950. | 1d. (2d.) |
| XI, 1948. | Fitness Training for Games and the Organization of Recreational Training. | 9d. (10d.) |
| XII, 1947. | Fitness Training Tables for Boys. (This Training Manual supersedes P.T. Tables for Boys, 1931.) | 6d. (7d.) |
| | Amendments No. 1. March, 1951. | 2d. (3d.) |

*Prices in brackets include postage*

Obtainable from :

## HIS MAJESTY'S STATIONERY OFFICE

York House, Kingsway, London, W.C.2.  429 Oxford Street, London, W.I. (Post Orders : P.O. Box No. 569, London, S.E.1.). 13a Castle Street, Edinburgh 2.  39 King Street, Manchester 2.  2 Edmund Street, Birmingham 3.  1 St. Andrew's Crescent, Cardiff.  Tower Lane, Bristol 1. 80 Chichester Street, Belfast.  Or through any Bookseller.

# RISE AND SHINE!

R.S.M. A. J. BRAND, M.V.O., M.B.E., gives his 7 point recommendation for a parade ground polish.

Known throughout the British Army as "The Voice," R.S.M. Brand, late of the Grenadier Guards and the R.M.A. Sandhurst, has used and recommended Kiwi for twenty-five years. Here is his 7 point method for getting a parade ground polish on a boot

1 *Get a tin of Kiwi Polish.*
2 *Take the lid off the tin.*
3 *Remove dust and dirt from the boot.*
4 *Put a little Kiwi on the boot with a rag or brush.*
5 *Damp a rag with water.*
6 *Moisten the boot with the rag.*
7 *Finish with a dry cloth and "You could shave in it."*

## Deep-shine with KIWI

*It puts life into leather*

WO
Code No.

8903

26 GS Trg Publications 2150

# Infantry   Training

## Volume   I

## Infantry   Platoon   Weapons

## PAMPHLET   No.   3

# No.  4  RIFLE  AND  BAYONET
## (All  Arms)

## 1955

This pamphlet supersedes Infantry Training, Volume I, Pamphlet No. 3,
Rifle and Bayonet (All Arms), 1948, (WO Code No. 8368)

*By Command of the Army Council,*

G. W. Tanner.

THE WAR OFFICE,
5th February, 1955.

## AMENDMENTS

| Amendment number | By whom amended | Date of insertion |
|---|---|---|
| | | |
| | | |
| | | |
| | | |
| | | |
| | | |
| | | |
| | | |
| | | |
| | | |
| | | |
| | | |
| | | |
| | | |
| | | |
| | | |
| | | |
| | | |
| | | |
| | | |

## DISTRIBUTION

*(See Catalogue of War Office Publications, Part II)*

| | |
|---|---|
| Infantry ...  ...  ...  ...  ...  ...  ...  ... | Scale E plus 50% unit pool |
| RE ...  ...  ...  ...  ...  ...  ...  ... | Scale E |
| Other arms  ...  ...  ...  ...  ...  ...  ... | Scale D |
| School of Infantry  ...  ...  ...  ...  ...  ... | 250 copies |

## AMENDMENTS
### No. 1

The photographs appearing in the text of this publication are cancelled. References should be made, as appropriate in the text, to the photographs which follow.

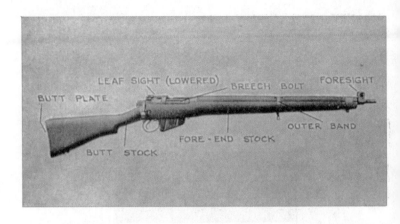

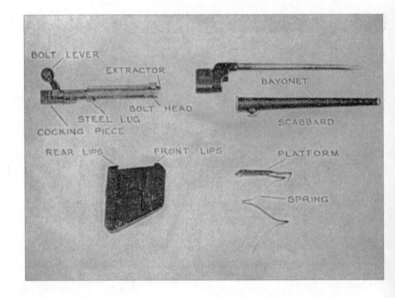

Fig 1.—The No. 4 Rifle

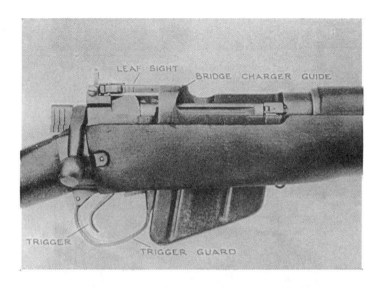

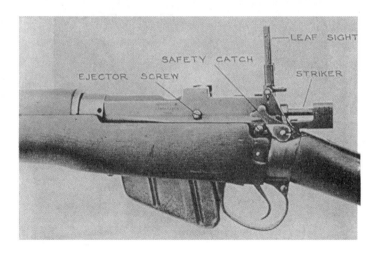

Fig 1 (continued)—The No. 4 Rifle

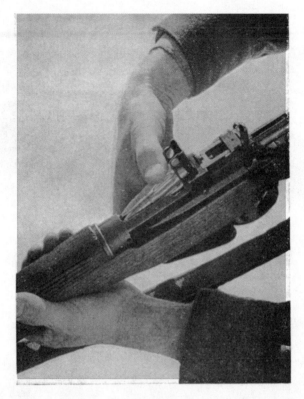

Fig 3.—Loading

Fig 4.—The lying position

Fig 6.—Using a sandbag for steadiness

Fig 7.—The hold

Fig 7.—The hold—continued

Fig 8.—An aim corrector in use

Fig 10.—Loading with a fresh charger, when firing snap shots or rapid

Fig 11.—The high port

Fig 12.—On guard

Fig 13.—The thrust and withdraw—standing enemy

Fig 14.—The thrust and withdraw—enemy on the ground

Fig 15.—Loading and firing positions—kneeling

Fig 16.—Loading and firing positions—sitting

Fig 17.—Loading and firing positions—standing

Fig 18.—Firing from low cover—soft and hard ground

Fig 19.—Firing from cover—kneeling and sitting

Fig 20.—Firing from cover—standing

Fig 21.—Firing round cover

Fig 22.—The butt stroke

Fig 23.—The right shoulder carry

Fig 24.—The alert position

Fig 25.—Firing from the shoulder

Fig 28.—The No. 5 Rifle

Fig 31.—Presenting the ring of the training stick for a thrust on the right

Fig 32.—Presenting the ring of the training stick for a thrust on the left

Fig 33.—Training stick—right parry

Fig 34.—Training stick—butt stroke

Fig 39.—How to use a sling

## CONTENTS

PAGE

INTRODUCTION ... ... ... ... ... ... ... 1

CHAPTER 1.—INSTRUCTIONAL

Introduction ... ... ... ... ... ... ... ... 2
Lesson 1.—Care and cleaning, and filling chargers ... ... ... 2
Lesson 2.—Loading and unloading, and charging magazines ... 8
Lesson 3.—Sightsetting and aiming ... ... ... ... ... 11
Practice 1.—Loading, unloading and aiming ... ... ... ... 13
Lesson 4.—Holding and firing—lying position, 1 ... ... ... 14
Lesson 5.—Holding and firing—lying position, 2 ... ... ... 18
Practice 2.—Elementary firing and aiming ... ... ... ... 19
Live firing 1.—Introductory shoot, grouping and further cleaning ... 20
Lesson 6.—Snapshooting and rapid fire ... ... ... 23
Lesson 7.—Bayonet fighting—" on guard " and thrusting ... ... 25
Practice 3.—Aiming, snapshooting and rapid fire ... ... ... 31
Live firing 2.—Grouping, application and snapshooting ... ... 32
Lesson 8.—Firing from other positions without cover ... ... 33
Lesson 9.—Bayonet fighting—two or more thrusts ... ... ... 38
Practice 4.—Firing from all positions without cover ... ... ... 39
Lesson 10.—Firing from behind cover ... ... ... ... 39
Practice 5.—The use of cover ... ... ... ... ... ... 44
Live firing 3.—Grouping, application, snap and rapid ... ... 45
Lesson 11.—Bayonet fighting—self defence ... ... ... 45
Lesson 12.—Altering the sights ... ... ... ... ... ... 47
Lesson 13.—Aiming off for wind ... ... ... ... ... 48
Practice 6.—Altering sights, and aiming off for wind ... ... 50
Practice 7.—Bayonet fighting ... ... ... ... ... ... 50
Lesson 14.—Close quarter battle ... ... ... ... ... 51
Live firing 4.—Application and rapid at 300 yards ... ... ... 55
Practice 8.—Handling ... ... ... ... ... ... ... 55
Live firing 5.—The assault course ... ... ... ... ... 57


CHAPTER 2.—EXTRA INFORMATION FOR INSTRUCTORS

Introduction ... ... ... ... ... ... ... ... 58
Section 1.—Practice periods ... ... ... ... ... ... 58
Section 2.—Targets and aiming ... ... ... ... ... 59
Section 3.—Sights and the instructor's elevation table ... ... 59
Section 4.—How to examine a rifle ... ... ... ... ... 62
Section 5.—The No. 5 Rifle ... ... ... ... ... ... 63
Section 6.—Holding and firing... ... ... ... ... ... 63
Section 7.—Zeroing ... ... ... ... ... ... ... 64
Section 8.—Coaching ... ... ... ... ... ... ... 65
Section 9.—Firing with harmonized sights in a miniature range ... 71
Section 10.—The training stick ... ... ... ... ... 72

| | | PAGE |
|---|---|---|
| Section 11.—Miniature and 25 yards ranges ... ... ... | | 76 |
| Section 12.—Strengthening, quickening and " shoot to kill " exercises | | 77 |
| Section 13.—Master and pupil ... ... ... ... ... ... | | 79 |
| Section 14.—Mechanism ... ... ... ... ... ... | | 79 |
| Section 15.—Demonstration of weapons ... ... ... ... | | 83 |
| Section 16.—Using a sling ... ... ... ... ... ... | | 84 |
| Section 17.—Training tests ... ... ... ... ... ... | | 85 |

## APPENDIXES

A—Training tests ... ... ... ... ... ... ... 86

## LIST OF FIGURES

| | | |
|---|---|---|
| Figure 1.—The No. 4 Rifle ... ... ... ... ... | 4 and | 5 |
| Figure 2.—Correctly filled charger ... ... ... ... ... | | 7 |
| Figure 3.—Loading ... ... ... ... ... ... ... | | 9 |
| Figure 4.—The lying position ... ... ... ... ... ... | | 10 |
| Figure 5.—Aim picture—range, figure and natural targets ... | | 13 |
| Figure 6.—Using a sandbag for steadiness ... ... ... ... | | 15 |
| Figure 7.—The hold ... ... ... ... ... ... | 16 and | 17 |
| Figure 8.—An aim corrector in use ... ... ... ... ... | | 20 |
| Figure 9.—Wire gauze on a pullthrough ... ... ... ... | | 23 |
| Figure 10.—Loading with a fresh charger when firing snap shots or rapid ... ... ... ... ... ... ... ... ... | | 24 |
| Figure 11.—The high port ... ... ... ... ... ... | | 27 |
| Figure 12.—On guard ... ... ... ... ... ... ... | | 28 |
| Figure 13.—The thrust and withdraw—standing enemy ... ... | | 29 |
| Figure 14.—The thrust and withdraw—enemy on the ground ... | | 30 |
| Figure 15.—Loading and firing positions—kneeling ... ... | | 35 |
| Figure 16.—Loading and firing positions—sitting ... ... | | 36 |
| Figure 17.—Loading and firing positions—standing ... ... | | 37 |
| Figure 18.—Firing from low cover—soft and hard ground ... | | 41 |
| Figure 19.—Firing from cover—kneeling and sitting ... ... | | 42 |
| Figure 20.—Firing from cover—standing ... ... ... ... | | 43 |
| Figure 21.—Firing round cover ... ... ... ... ... | | 44 |
| Figure 22.—The butt stroke ... ... ... ... ... ... | | 46 |
| Figure 23.—The right shoulder carry ... ... ... ... ... | | 52 |
| Figure 24.—The alert position ... ... ... ... ... ... | | 53 |
| Figure 25.—Firing from the shoulder ... ... ... ... ... | | 54 |
| Figure 26.—Bayonet assault course ... ... ... ... ... | | 57 |
| Figure 27.—No. 4 Rifle backsights ... ...... ... ... ... | | 61 |
| Figure 28.—The No. 5 Rifle ... ... ... ... ... ... | | 63 |
| Figure 29.—Harmonized target screen ... ... ... ... | | 72 |
| Figure 30.—The training stick ... ... ... ... ... | | 73 |
| Figure 31.—Presenting the ring of the training stick for a thrust on the right ... ... ... ... ... ... ... ... | | 73 |
| Figure 32.—Presenting the ring of the training stick for a thrust on the left ... ... ... ... ... ... ... ... | | 74 |

PAGE

Figure 33.—Training stick—right parry ... ... ... ... 75

Figure 34.—Training stick—butt stroke ... ... ... ... 75

Figure 35.—The action cocked ... ... ... ... ... 80

Figure 36.—The bolt ... ... ... ... ... ... ... 80

Figure 37.—How the trigger works ... ... ... ... ... 81

Figure 38.—Half cock ... ... ... ... ... ... ... 83

Figure 39.—How to use a sling ... ... ... ... ... 85

## ABBREVIATIONS

The abbreviations used in this pamphlet are:—

LMG ... Light machine gun

MPI ... Mean point of impact

NCO ... Non-commissioned officer

# Infantry Training
## VOLUME I
# Infantry Platoon Weapons
### PAMPHLET No. 3
# No. 4 RIFLE AND BAYONET
### (All Arms)
## 1955

### INTRODUCTION

**Aim of weapon training**

1. The aim of all weapon training is to produce soldiers who can kill the enemy in battle with any platoon weapon.

**Achievement of the aim**

2. To achieve this aim, men must reach a high standard of marksmanship, servicing and fieldcraft with all the weapons, and they must be able to work together as teams under good junior leaders.

**The aim of this pamphlet**

3. This pamphlet contains the material that an instructor needs to teach recruits how to handle rifles and bayonets, and how to shoot accurately.

**Layout**

4. The pamphlet is in two chapters:—

(a) Chapter 1 is divided into (i) lessons, which teach recruits all they need to know (ii) instructions for practice periods, which drive home the skills and techniques and (iii) most important of all, instructions for live firing periods.

(b) Chapter 2 contains more information to help instructors to understand the subject and its presentation better; and tests, which show what standard men have reached.

5. Throughout Chapter 1 two forms of printing are used:—

(a) Portions in ordinary type are notes for instructors.

(b) Portions in *italics* are what instructors should teach recruits.

**Method of instruction**

6. How an instructor teaches a lesson is left to him. It is better to let inexperienced instructors have prepared lesson plans and refer to them during lessons, than to accept wrong or muddled teaching.

7. All instructors should study Successful Instruction, 1951 (WO Code No. 8670).

**Live firing**

8. References to firing practices are in all cases to the current range courses.

## CHAPTER 1.—INSTRUCTIONAL

### INTRODUCTION

1. ·22 rifle firing is a useful introduction to shooting, in that a recruit can concentrate on aiming and trigger pressing without noise and kick to worry him. But, when he goes on to fire ·303, it is important to see that he has not got into bad holding habits, for the kick may make him gun-shy. Boys may not fire ·303 until they are 15½ years old.

2. The first time a man fires ·303, it should be with his own rifle at 100 yards; a 25 yards range may have to do if open ranges are not available, but it is only second best at that stage. Thereafter ·22 shooting is valuable, particularly in bad weather, and can be put into the programme at any time. (*See* Chapter 2, Section 11).

### LESSON 1.—CARE AND CLEANING, AND FILLING CHARGERS

#### AIM

1. To introduce recruits to their rifles, and to teach them how to strip, clean and assemble them, how to clean ammunition, and how to fill chargers.

#### STORES

2. Rifles, bayonets and scabbards, slings, full oil bottles, flannelette, chamber cleaning sticks, drill rounds, cleaning rags and a small brush.

#### NOTES

3. Seat your squad in a semicircle.

4. Always make sure that the men strip their rifles in the right order, use their pull throughs properly, grip the knob of the bolt correctly, open and close the breech sharply, and apply the safety catch correctly; these details are the foundation of good handling.

#### SAFETY PRECAUTIONS

5. Inspect all rifles.

6. Inspect all pouches and drill rounds, and show your own pouches, drill rounds and rifle to the squad.

7. Explain.—*These safety precautions will be carried out at the beginning and end of every lesson or practice.*

8. Explain and, where possible, demonstrate.—*Men can, and too often do, kill or injure a comrade with a loaded weapon by mistake. These rules apply to all weapons, not only rifles, and they will be emphasized in all weapon training:—*

    (a) *In battle or on patrol see that your weapon never points at a comrade. You have to think about this constantly, particularly when you are in file or single file, or when there is a risk of slipping or tripping, or catching anything on branches, undergrowth or rough ground.*

    (b) *If you have to carry a loaded weapon at any other time, make certain that the safety catch is always applied, and that it works properly.*

(c) *If you have to have your weapon loaded in a vehicle, make sure that it cannot fall about or be bumped, and that nothing can interfere with the safety catch. Either hold the weapon in your hand, or lay it on the floor, preferably with something soft under it, and see that it does not move about.*

(d) *Whenever you pick up any weapon, whether your own or someone else's, always look to see if it is loaded.*

(e) *The moment you no longer need to have your weapon loaded, unload it.*

(f) *When you hand a weapon to someone else, either show him first that it is unloaded, or hand it over with the safety catch applied and the muzzle pointing straight up into the air. When anyone hands a weapon to you, insist that he does the same.*

(g) *NEVER point a rifle at anyone in jest.*

(h) *NEVER use drill rounds when aiming at eye discs held to the eyes of other men.*

## APPROACH

9. *The rifle is your personal offensive weapon, and, if you clean it carefully and handle it well, you will find it very accurate and reliable. Do not bang it about, or let it jolt about on the floors of trucks or lie on its side in the sun.*

## STRIPPING

10. Explain and demonstrate; make the squad copy your actions:—

(a) *See that the number on the bolt is the same as the number on the left side of the body. The rifle will not shoot accurately with the wrong bolt in it.*

(b) *Take off the bayonet and sling.*

(c) *To remove the bolt, raise the backsight, push forward the safety catch, press down the bolt catch, pull the bolt as far as back it will go, turn the bolt head upwards, withdraw the bolt, and lower the backsight.*

(d) *Press up the magazine catch, and take the magazine out.*

(e) *Take out the magazine platform; press down the wide end until the narrow end is clear of the front lips, and lift it out narrow end first.*

(f) *Open the butt trap, and take out the oil bottle and pullthrough.*

## CLEANING AND ASSEMBLING

11. Explain and demonstrate paras 12-25; make the squad copy your actions.

12. *The barrel:—*

(a) *Unroll the pullthrough, and pull it out straight.*

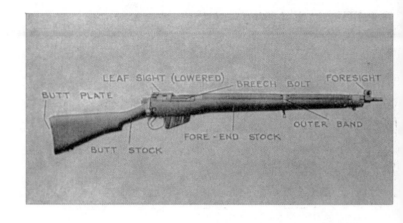

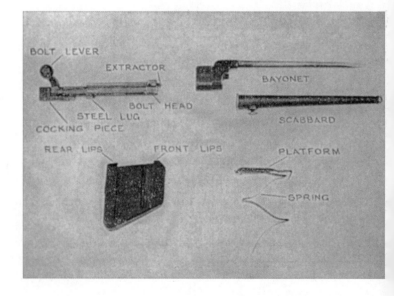

Fig 1.—The No. 4 Rifle

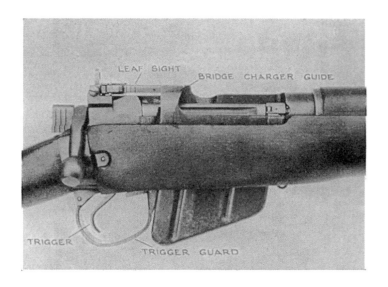

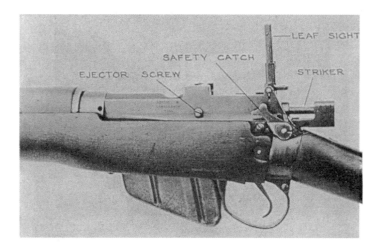

Fig 1 (continued)—The No. 4 Rifle

    *(b) Put a piece of flannelette, four by two inches, in the centre loop, and wrap it round the cord.*

    *(c) Drop the pullthrough weight into the breech behind the bridge charger guide.*

    *(d) Rest the toe of the butt on the ground, and pull the cord through in one movement. Try not to let the cord rub against the muzzle, or it will cause wear, and the rifle will not shoot accurately. Go on pulling through until the barrel is clean; when the flannelette gets dirty, refold it so as to get as much use out of it as you can.*

    *(e) Examine the bore; hold the muzzle close to your eye; look into the grooves for dirt, and move your head back from the muzzle at the same time; do the same from the breech end.*

13. *The chamber.—Put a piece of dry flannelette in the slot of the chamber cleaning stick, and wrap it round the stick. Turn the flannelette in the chamber several times. Then oil both chamber and bore with a piece of flannelette four by one and a half inches.*

14. *The outside of the rifle.—Clean off all dirt with an oily rag. Use a small brush for the crevices.*

15. *The bolt:—*

    *(a) Remove all dirt, and oil the bolt slightly; but, if the climate is dry and dusty, leave it dry.*

    *(b) NEVER use abrasives like sandpaper or grit.*

16. *To put back the bolt:—*

    *(a) Make sure that:—*

        (i) *The number on the bolt and the number on the rifle are the same.*

        (ii) *The bolt head is screwed up.*

        (iii) *The lug and cocking piece are in line.*

        (iv) *The safety catch is forward, and the back sight up.*

    *(b) Put the bolt in, press down the bolt catch, turn the bolt head down, and push the bolt forward; push its knob sharply forwards and then downwards to close the breech.*

    *(c) Press the trigger; to do this, hold the small of the butt firmly with your right hand, with the forefinger on the lower part of the trigger; press gently, and you will feel a check, which is the end of the first pressure; go on pressing (the second pressure) until the cocking piece goes forward.*

    *(d) Apply the safety catch by turning it to the rear, keeping the bolt lever down with your fingers.*

    *(e) Lower the backsight.*

    *(f) If the cocking piece stays half way forward (the " half cock "), pull it back, open the breech, see that the chamber and magazine are clear, close the breech, and, keeping the muzzle up, press the trigger. If you get " half cock " when shooting, pull the cocking piece back, and go on firing.*

17. *Practise the squad at removing and replacing the bolt.*

18. *The magazine:*—
    *(a) Clean it inside and out, and the platform and spring, with an oily rag.*
    *(b) To put back the platform, put the wide end in first, and tilt it slightly. Test to make sure that it works freely.*
    *(c) To replace the magazine, put the front end in first, and press the magazine home; test that it is secure.*

19. *Oil bottle.—Put it back in the butt trap, head first.*

20. *Pullthrough.—Loop the cord loosely once round your hand, leaving about an inch of cord free; slip the loop off your hand, and twist the rest of the cord tightly round it, leaving enough free to allow the weight to go into the special compartment in the butt trap.*

21. *Bayonet.—Remove all dirt, and clean it with a slightly oily rag.*

22. *Sling.—Put it back on the rifle.*

23. Practise the squad at stripping and cleaning their rifles.

## AMMUNITION AND CHARGERS

24. *Dirty ammunition and chargers cause jams and inaccurate shooting. Clean and inspect each round, especially the base half, and discard any damaged rounds. Wrap flannelette round the base of a round, and run it backwards and forwards through the charger until the charger is clean.*

25. *Fill chargers as shown* (Fig 2). Pass a correctly filled charger round the squad.

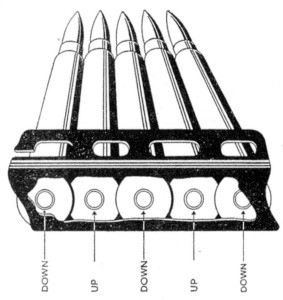

Fig. 2.—Correctly filled charger

## CONCLUSION

26. Questions from and to the squad.

27. Sum up, stressing the need for safety precautions, the accuracy and reliability of the rifle, and how important it is to strip, clean and handle it correctly.

## LESSON 2.—LOADING AND UNLOADING, AND CHARGING MAGAZINES

### AIM

1. To teach recruits how to load and unload their rifles, and how to charge magazines.

### STORES

2. Rifles, drill rounds, chargers and flannelette.

### NOTES

3. Let the men practise in their own time first, and criticize each of them in turn; then exercise them by word of command; insist on smart, correct actions.

### PRELIMINARIES

4. Safety precautions.

5. Revise the cleaning of ammunition and chargers (Lesson 1).

### APPROACH

6. *In battle your life may depend on loading fast. You must practise loading until it becomes automatic; then your mind is free to concentrate on actions that cannot be automatic, such as aiming and firing.*

### LOADING (See Fig 3)

7. Explain and demonstrate paras 8–10. Make the men copy your actions in any comfortable position.

8. *To load:—*

    *(a) Push forward the safety catch, and open the breech.*

    *(b) Put a full charger in the charger guide.*

    *(c) Put your right thumb on the top round just in front of the charger.*

    *(d) Press the rounds into the magazine in one movement, until .he top round is under the magazine lips. To get extra pressure, put your fingers under the woodwork or the magazine.*

    *(e) Flick out the empty charger, and load with a second one.*

    *(f) Close the breech, apply the safety catch, button up your pouch, and grip the small of the butt, with your trigger finger outside the trigger guard.*

Fig 3.—Loading

9. *If a jam occurs:—*

 (a) *Open the breech.*

 (b) *Adjust or take out the jammed round; press the rounds down into the magazine, and let them spring up again; tap the bottom of the magazine sharply.*

 (c) *If the rounds jam in the charger, use another charger.*

10. *Once you have been given the order "Load", it is your job to see that your rifle is always loaded.*

## UNLOADING

11. Explain and demonstrate; make the men copy your actions.—*To unload:*—

    *(a) Push the safety catch forward.*

    *(b) Move the bolt quickly backwards and forwards, without lowering the bolt lever, until the rifle is empty.*

    *(c) Press the trigger, and apply the safety catch.*

12. Practise the men at loading and unloading.

## LOADING IN THE LYING POSITION (See Fig 4)

13. Explain and demonstrate; make the men copy your actions. *To load lying down:*—

    *(a) Take a long pace forward with your left foot, move your rifle into your left hand and get down, breaking your fall with your right hand, with your body at an angle to the direction in which you are going to aim.*

    *(b) Keep your legs well apart, and your heels on the ground if you can.*

    *(c) Keep your left arm stretched right out, and your right hand on the small of the butt, with the forefinger outside the trigger guard.*

    *(d) Load as before.*

Fig 4.—The lying position

## UNLOADING IN THE LYING POSITION

14. Explain and demonstrate; make the men copy your actions.—*On the command " Unload ", unload as before, hold your rifle with your left hand, put your right hand on the ground, draw up one knee and stand up.*

15. Practise the men at loading and unloading in the lying position.

## CHARGING MAGAZINES AND LOADING

16. Explain and demonstrate; make the men copy your actions:—

    *(a) To charge magazines:*—

        *(i) Load the magazine with two chargers.*

        *(ii) Take off the magazine.*

        *(iii) Close the breech, press the trigger, apply the safety catch, put back the magazine and button up the pouch.*

*(b) To load, push forward the safety catch, open and close the breech, and apply the safety catch.*

17. Practise the men at charging magazines, loading when their magazines are already charged, and charging magazines again. See that they pick up the unloaded rounds.

## UNLOADING (ALTERNATIVE METHOD)

18. Explain. —*If you unload in the ordinary way, the rounds are scattered on the ground; in the dark you may lose them, and if it is muddy they get dirty. At night or on muddy ground, use the alternative method of unloading.*

19. Explain and demonstrate; make the men copy your actions: —*To unload by the alternative method:—*

    *(a) Take out the magazine, open the breech slowly, and take the round out of the chamber; close the breech, press the trigger, and apply the safety catch.*

    *(b) Empty the magazine and put it back in the rifle; put the rounds into chargers.*

20. Practise the men at unloading by the alternative method.

## PRACTICE

21. Give the men practice in the whole lesson.

## CONCLUSION

22. Questions from and to the squad.

23. Sum up; emphasize the need for constant practice.

## LESSON 3.—**SIGHT SETTING AND AIMING**

### AIM

1. To teach recruits to set their sights and aim.

### STORES

2. Rifles, aiming rests for half the squad, range and figure targets, and diagrams.

### NOTES

3. No two people see the same aim picture. So long as a man's aim is consistently the same, accept it, even if you do not think that it is exactly right; his rifle will be zeroed to allow for it.

4. Always make sure that sights are upright and correctly set.

5. When a recruit lays a wrong aim, this is a good way of showing him what his mistake is:—

    *(a)* Hold something white in front of the muzzle of his rifle.

    *(b)* Tell him to make sure that his foresight is in the middle of the aperture.

    *(c)* Take the white thing away, and put it back at once.

    *(d)* Get him to say what was wrong with his aim.

6. When men are aiming at figure targets, you should consider an aim correct if the point of aim is nearly in the centre of the target.

7. Put out range targets up to 500 yards, and figure targets up to 300 yards.

8. Divide the squad into details, so that each man of a detail has an aiming rest.

9. See Chapter 2, Section 2 for more about aiming.

## PRELIMINARIES

10. Safety precautions.

11. Examine sights to see that there is no play in the backsight, the aperture is not deformed, and the foresight blade is firm and not deformed. Always do this before any aiming instruction.

## APPROACH

12. *A shot cannot be accurate unless the aim is correct. Aiming is not automatic; you must concentrate on seeing the same aim picture every time you fire a shot.*

## SIGHT SETTING

13. Explain and demonstrate; make the men copy your actions:—

    *(a) The back sight is marked with numbers; it is set for a given range when the line on the slide is opposite the appropriate line on the leaf.*

    *(b) To set the sights, press the catch on the slide, or turn the adjusting screw, according to the sort of sight fitted.*

14. Practise the men at setting their sights at ranges up to 600 yards.

## THE BATTLE SIGHT

15. Explain.—*As well as the adjustable backsight, there is a fixed aperture sight, or battle sight; if you aim through it at the middle of a standing man at any range up to 400 yards, you will hit him.*

## THE AIMING REST

16. Show the men how to set up the rest with one leg towards the target, and how to put the rifle in it, with the magazine above the curved piece, and the sling to the right.

## AIMING

17. Use diagrams (Fig 5) to explain the aim picture men must see each time, and how to get it:—

    *(a) Shut the left eye (right eye for a left-handed shot).*

13

*(b)* *Look through the middle of the aperture at the target, and choose your point of aim.*

*(c)* *Keep the sights upright, and put the tip of the foresight on the point of aim. (If you are shooting at a range target, put the tip of the foresight immediately under the middle of the black aiming mark).*

*(d)* *Make sure that the point of aim is still in the middle of the aperture.*

Fig 5.—Aim picture, range, figure and natural targets

18. Lay correct aims at range and figure targets at 100 yards.

19. Explain.—*You can lay a steadier aim if you rest your left elbow on top of the tripod, with your chin in your left hand. Keep your eye where it would be if you were firing.*

20. Get the men to look at your aims, and then try laying aims themselves at range targets up to 500 yards and figure targets up to 300 yards.

CONCLUSION

21. Questions from and to the squad.

22. Sum up; emphasize that the thing to remember is the right aim picture for each sort of target, not the detail of para 17.

### PRACTICE 1.—LOADING, UNLOADING AND AIMING

AIM

1. To practise loading, unloading and aiming.

STORES

2. Rifles, drill rounds, chargers, flannelette, aiming rests, range and figure targets.

NOTES

3. Skill comes by practice only. To keep men interested, introduce competitions, and make them criticize each other, whenever you can.

PRELIMINARIES

4. Safety precautions.

APPROACH

5. *You cannot shoot fast for long unless you are good at loading; that is why everyone has to pass a test in loading, unloading, and loading again with a fresh charger* (Chapter 2, Section 17, Tests 1-3).

PRACTICE

6. Practise the men at loading and unloading, aiming at all sorts of targets, charging magazines, and unloading by the alternative method.

CONCLUSION

7. Questions from and to the squad.

8. Sum up; tell them how they have progressed.

### LESSON 4.—HOLDING AND FIRING—LYING POSITION, 1

AIM

1. To teach recruits how to hold and fire their rifles.

STORES

2. Rifles, drill rounds, targets, half-full sandbags.

NOTES

3. Use an eye disc to check steadiness and rough alignment, when the men are practising aiming and firing. The disc should be about a yard from the muzzle, and at a height to suit the firer.

4. Give half the men eye discs, and get them to criticize the firers as masters and pupils. *(See* Chapter 2, Section 13).

5. **Do not have eye discs and drill rounds in use together.**

6. Give the order " Rest " occasionally; the men should apply their safety catches, lay their rifles down bolt uppermost, and rest. When you are ready to go on, order " Position ".

7. For more about holding see Chapter 2, Section 6.

8. Give the men half-full sandbags, or even their small packs, to help them to keep steady. Place them so that they support the lower part of the forearm only, not the wrist, hand or rifle. (See Fig 6).

Fig 6.—Using a sandbag for steadiness

PRELIMINARIES

9. Safety precautions.

10. Test trigger pressures, and explain.—*The pressure should be smooth; if it feels rough, it needs an armourer to adjust it.*

11. Revise the cleaning of rifles, ammunition and chargers (Lesson 1).

APPROACH

12. *The basic firing position is lying down; the important points are:—*

   *(a) To get into a comfortable, firm position.*

   *(b) To hold the rifle firmly with both hands.*

   *(c) To fire without disturbing your aim.*

13. *Practise all the "automatic" actions, until they really are automatic; then your mind is free to concentrate on aiming and firing.*

THE HOLD (See Fig 7)

14. Demonstrate the firing position; let the men test how firm your hold is. Order " Without drill cartridges—load—200 ".

15. Explain and demonstrate; make the men copy your actions:—

   *(a) Look at the target, push forward the safety catch, bring your rifle up to your shoulder, keep both elbows on the ground, take the first pressure, lower your cheek onto the butt, and aim.*

   *(b) The things to remember about the hold are:—*

      (i) *Keep your body well round to the left, legs well apart, and heels on the ground if you can.*

(ii) *Make your elbows and the base of your chest into a tripod to support the rifle.*

(iii) *With your right hand grip the small of the butt firmly, and pull the rifle back into your shoulder.*

(iv) *With your left hand grip the rifle as far forward as you comfortably can.*

(v) *Lock the position by pressing your chin against the butt. Your head must be far enough back not to have to move when you reload.*

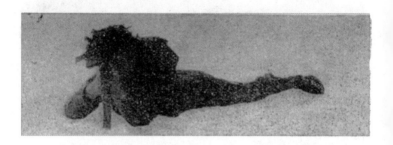

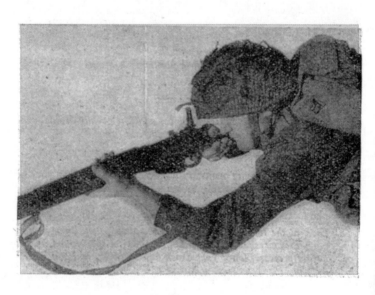

Fig 7.—The hold

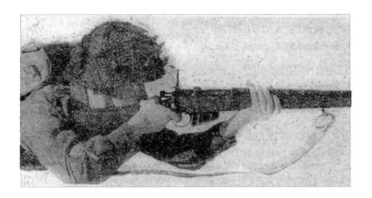

Fig 7.—The hold—continued

16. Practise the men at holding; check the points from para 15 *(b)* and try the " bolt test " (Chapter 2, Section 6) on each man.

## TESTING AND ADJUSTING POSITIONS

17. Explain and demonstrate:—*To shoot well, you must be in a position in which your rifle points naturally at the target. To test whether your position is right:—*

   *(a) Lie down in a position that you think will suit your target, bring your rifle up into a comfortable aiming position, and see where the sights are pointing; if they are pointing at, or very near to, your target, your position is all right; if they are not, it is wrong.*

   *(b) To move the muzzle sideways, shift your body round without moving your left elbow; to move it up or down, keep both elbows still, and ease your body forwards or backwards; keep your hold the same in either case.*

   *(c) Go on testing and adjusting until you get the position right; with practice you will get it right first time.*

   *(d) Always test your position, and fire two or three shots (without ammunition), before you fire any range practice.*

18. Get the men to practise testing and adjusting their positions; use an eye disc to make certain that they have understood.

## CONCLUSION

19. Questions from and to the squad.

20. Sum up.

## LESSON 5.—HOLDING AND FIRING—LYING POSITION, 2

### AIM, STORES AND NOTES

1. See Lesson 4, paras 1-8.

### PRELIMINARIES

2. Safety precautions.

3. Revise holding, and testing positions (Lesson 4).

### TRIGGER CONTROL

4. Explain.—*You must take the second pressure without disturbing your aim; you will not succeed unless your grip on the small of the butt is really tight, and your whole position firm and steady.*

5. Show the squad how to fire; point out that your rifle does not move when you take the second pressure.

6. Make the men take up correct firing positions, practise taking the first and second pressures, and watch their foresights. Stress the fact that they must practise until they can take the second pressure without the foresight moving.

### BREATHING

7. Explain and demonstrate.—*At the moment you fire a shot, your lungs should be half empty, and your breathing controlled. The procedure is:—*
    *(a) Aim, breathe in, and let the muzzle drop a little.*
    *(b) Breathe out, and bring the muzzle up; as the foresight reaches the aiming mark, fire the shot, if you are satisfied that the aim is good.*
    *(c) If you do not get a good aim in four or five seconds, breathe in, and try again.*

8. Practise the squad at controlled breathing.

### FIRING

9. Explain and demonstrate; make the men copy your actions.—*The normal rate of fire is five rounds a minute. You must be determined to shoot well, and concentrate on aiming accurately and taking the second pressure smoothly. The sequence of action is:—*
    *(a) Test your position, and load.*
    *(b) When a range is ordered, set your sights, and push forward the safety catch.*
    *(c) On the command "Fire":—*
        *(i) Aim, and take the first pressure; control your breathing, and take the second pressure when the aim is correct; go on aiming for a moment.*
        *(ii) Declare your aim—correct, high left, etc.*

(iii) *Keep your head still and firm on the butt, and reload at once; aim again, and then go back to the loading position. Count the rounds you fire, and go on firing at the normal rate until you are given the order "Stop"; apply your safety catch.*

10. Make the men practise firing; coach each of them in turn, and check the points listed in para 9.

## RAPID RELOADING

11. Explain and demonstrate with drill rounds:—
   (a) *Grip firmly with your left hand, to keep control.*
   (b) *Grip the knob of the bolt firmly, and move it backwards and forwards again so fast that the two movements look like one.*
   (c) *Keep your head still, and your cheek pressed hard against the butt; tilt the rifle a little to the right, and try to keep your right elbow down.*
   (d) *Get a firm grip of the small of the butt again quickly, and take the first pressure.*

12. Make the men practise with drill rounds; coach each man in turn, and let them coach each other in pairs.

## PRACTICE

13. Make the men practise everything they have learnt in Lessons 4 and 5.

## CONCLUSION

14. Questions from and to the squad.

15. Sum up; remind the men.—*Always think about aiming and firing: none of the other firing actions should require any conscious thought; they must become automatic.*

## PRACTICE 2.—ELEMENTARY FIRING AND AIMING

### AIM

1. To practise firing at the normal rate, and aiming.

### STORES

2. Rifles, drill rounds, eye discs, targets; aim corrector No. 2, Mark 3 for the instructor.

### NOTES

3. With an aim corrector you can see exactly how the firer aims and fires.

4. Hold the aim corrector above the raised backsight, with " TOP " uppermost, the clamping screw undone, and the arrow pointing towards the muzzle; lower it down the backsight onto the slide, until the reflector is opposite the aperture, and tighten the clamping screw. Put the coloured glass in the slot that runs from front to rear. See Fig 8.

Fig 8.—An aim corrector in use

PRELIMINARIES

5. Safety precautions.

6. Remind the men how to test their positions, how to aim, what is the sequence of firing, and how important it is to declare aims truthfully.

7. Order " Test position—load—200—fire "; check each man in turn. Order " Unload "; comment on their performance, good and bad.

PRACTICE

8. Practise the men, as masters and pupils, at aiming at all sorts of targets, firing, and declaring their aims.

CONCLUSION

9. Questions from and to the squad.
10. Sum up.

LIVE FIRING 1.—INTRODUCTORY SHOOT, GROUPING AND FURTHER CLEANING

AIM

1. To consolidate the teaching of Lessons 1-5, to practise grouping, and to teach the men more about cleaning.

STORES

2. Rifles, cleaning materials, boiling out kit, gauzes, chamber cleaning sticks, sandbags, targets, ammunition, binoculars, zeroing equipment, coaches' notebooks, AB 142 for every man.

NOTES

3. Live Firing 1 is written primarily for instructors whose men are firing ·303 for the first time. However, it may be a help for them to fire Practice 1 of the Miniature Range Rifle Practices first; if they do, only para 5 below applies, and you can forget about the rest until the men fire it with ·303, which they must in any case do before going on to Live Firing 2.

4. If an open range is not available, a 25 yards range and 200/25 representative targets are the next best thing.

5. Recruits must have their ABs 142 with them; and the score, size, pattern and position of each group, and anything else of interest to coaches must be recorded. Each man should have a coach.

6. Recruits should not fire more than five shots without a break, nor more than 25 in a day; nor should they fire in shirt sleeves. Coaches must see that men do not hold their rifles loosely, and consequently grow gun shy.

7. Have an armourer on the range, so that, if anyone consistently gets good groups in the same place, his rifle can be zeroed; he should also inspect all rifles before they are fired.

8. Repeat the introductory shoot (paras 12-15) until results are satisfactory, before going on to Live Firing 2.

## PRELIMINARIES

9. Safety precautions; preparation of the range.

## APPROACH

10. *You are going to fire live ammunition, to put into practice what you have already learnt; and you are going to learn how to clean your rifles before and after firing.*

## CLEANING BEFORE FIRING

11. Explain and demonstrate; make the men copy your actions.—*Clean the rifle as you do every day, and also see that:*—

(a) *The bore, chamber, face of the bolt, magazine platform and inside of the magazine, cocking piece and woodwork are dry.*

(b) *The sights are black and the aperture free from dirt.*

(c) *The gas escapes are clear.*

(d) *Ammunition and chargers are clean and dry.*

## INTRODUCTORY SHOOT

12. Use an AB 142 to describe the targets to the men.

13. Explain range procedure, safety precautions and butt duties (Infantry Training, Volume III, Pamphlet No. 31, 1948 (WO Code No. 8399).

14. Explain:—

(a) *A man who can put his shots into a small group can become a good shot. You will not group well unless:*—

(i) *You always use the same point of aim—in this case the bottom of the white patch.*

(ii) *Your position, hold, aim and trigger work are correct and the same for each shot.*

      (iii) *You take great care over each shot.*

   *(b) Your coach cannot help you unless you declare honestly where you were aiming at the moment of firing each shot.*

15. Each man should fire the grouping practice of the Rifle Course at least twice, but not consecutively. After each pair of details has fired, take the men forward to look at their targets; discuss his group with each man:—

   *(a)* Compare his declarations with the positions of shots on the target.

   *(b)* Tell him the size of his group for scoring and coaching purposes, and explain any error in the zeroing of his rifle.

   *(c)* Explain what his scoring area would have been at longer ranges.

   *(d)* Tell him whether the pattern of the group shows that he is doing anything wrong, or that his rifle is faulty, or both.

   *(e)* Record results in his AB 142, and give him encouragement.

## CLEANING AFTER FIRING

16. Explain and demonstrate; make the men copy your actions:—

   *(a) Strip the rifle for cleaning.*

   *(b) Use a funnel, and pour five or six pints of boiling water through the barrel from the breech end; take care not to spill any water between the woodwork and the barrel. If boiling water is not available, use warm or cold water. If no water is available, clean the bore thoroughly, and oil it; use boiling water at the first opportunity.*

   *(c) Clean the bore with dry flannelette until there is no sign of dirt or fouling, and the rest of the rifle as you do every day.*

   *(d) Inspect and oil the bore, and assemble the rifle.*

   *(e) The bore sweats for several days after firing; clean, inspect and oil it every day.*

   *(f) You may use a wire gauze to clean fouling from a worn barrel, if an officer gives permission; on active service you keep the gauze on your pullthrough, and it is the normal thing to clean the bore with. To fit the gauze* (see Fig 9):—

      (i) *Fold it into an "S", and put it through the loop nearest the weight.*

      (ii) *Coil the two halves of the "S" tightly round the loop until the two rolls meet. Remove any loose strands, and oil the gauze.*

      (ili) *Pack it with flannelette if you want it to fit tighter in the bore,*

 SECTION

Fig 9.—Wire gauze on a pullthrough

## CONCLUSION

17. Questions from and to the squad.

18. Sum up.

### LESSON 6.—SNAPSHOOTING AND RAPID FIRE

#### AIM

1. To teach recruits how to fire snapshots and rapid.

#### STORES

2. Rifles, drill rounds, eye discs or representative targets, aim corrector, cleaning materials.

#### NOTES

3. Make the men count out loud the number of rounds as they fire them; this helps them to learn to count instinctively as they fire.

#### PRELIMINARIES

4. Safety precautions; inspect bolts to see that they are clean and oiled.

5. Revise rapid reloading (Lesson 2).

#### APPROACH

6. *Snapshooting is firing one or two shots quickly; rapid fire is a series of quick shots. With practice you can fire a snap shot in three seconds, and 15 or more rapid shots in a minute.*

7. *To achieve these rates, you must speed up all the automatic actions, especially loading with a fresh charger, so that you still have time to concentrate on aiming and firing.* Stress this point all the way through.

#### FIRING A SNAP SHOT

8. Explain and demonstrate; make the men copy your actions:—

   (a) *When the target appears, bring your rifle quickly into the shoulder, aim, fire, and declare the point of aim.*

*(b) Reload instantly, aim, and take the first pressure. If there is no need to fire a second shot, go back to the loading position.*

9. Divide the squad into masters and pupils, and make them practise with eye discs but no drill rounds. Start with a time limit of seven seconds, and gradually cut it down to four. Check each man in turn.

## RAPID FIRING

10. Explain and demonstrate with drill rounds; stress these points:—

*(a) On the command "Rapid", take aim.*

*(b) To control the rifle, your left hand must grip like a vice and pull the rifle back into your shoulder.*

*(c) On the command "Fire", fire as fast as you can accurately.*

*(d) When you reload, keep the butt in the shoulder, and your cheek pressed firmly against it.*

*(e) Count the rounds you fire; do not declare your aim.*

*(f) Load quickly with a fresh charger; keep your left hand and elbow still, and lower only the butt to the ground (see Fig 10); do not button up your pouch until you next stop firing.*

*(g) In battle, on the order "Rapid fire", go on firing until you get the order "Stop", or until there is no longer any need to fire.*

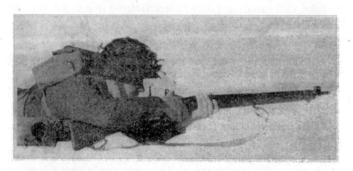

Fig 10.—Loading with a fresh charger, when firing snap shots or rapid

11. Make the men practise; first in their own time; then as masters and pupils, with eye discs but no drill cartridges; and finally with drill rounds, by word of command, at figure targets.

## CONCLUSION

12. Questions from and to the squad.

13. Sum up.

## LESSON 7.—BAYONET FIGHTING—"ON GUARD" AND THRUSTING

### AIM

1. To teach recruits the " on guard " position and the thrust.

### STORES

2. Rifles, bayonets, dummy enemy, training stick, string.

### NOTES

3. The aim of bayonet training is to make men confident that they can kill with the bayonet, and to train them to work together in teams.

4. Encourage the men to develop individual styles to suit their size and build.

5. Try to instil a spirit of vigour and determination into your squad. Make them do everything at the double, except where it is otherwise stated. The keynote is speed and vigour; if a man is quick and vigorous, do not penalize him for small technical faults.

6. Chapter 2, Section 10 describes how to use a training stick.

### PRELIMINARIES

7. Safety precautions; fix bayonets, loosen slings, cock actions, apply safety catches.

### APPROACH

8. *Sometimes, usually during an assault, or when fighting in woods, villages and other confined spaces, or at night, the use or threat of the bayonet has a decisive effect.*

### THE HIGH PORT

9. Explain and demonstrate; make the men copy your actions:—
   *(a) This is the normal, and safest, way to carry a rifle with a fixed bayonet.*
   *(b) Hold the rifle diagonally across your body, far enough forward so that you can come instantly into the firing or " on guard " position (see Fig 11).*

10. Practice the " high port " from the " order ".

### ON GUARD

11. Put the men in two ranks eight paces apart, with five paces between men in the ranks.

12. Explain and demonstrate; make the men copy your actions:—
   *(a) You come into the " on guard " position when you are nearing the enemy in an assault, or when you are about to attack an enemy with the bayonet.*

(b) On the command " On guard ", take a full pace forward with your left foot; at the same time move your rifle into the " on guard " position (see Fig 12).

(c) On the command " Rest ", put the butt between your feet.

13. Practise the men at " on guard " and " high port ", standing still and on the move.

## THE THRUST—STANDING ENEMY

14. Explain and demonstrate (see Fig 13):—

(a) You deliver a thrust from about five feet from your enemy, from the " on guard " position.

(b) Deliver the thrust. Grasp the rifle firmly, bring your right foot forward, and thrust the bayonet into the enemy with the whole weight of your body behind it.

(c) Withdraw. Pull the rifle straight back till the bayonet is clear.

(d) Punch forward " on guard ", and advance.

15. Practise the thrust.

16. Explain and demonstrate. You usually make your thrust on the move, and you can do it with either foot leading, or jump in with both feet; see that you always keep the bayonet pointing at the enemy.

17. Practise the thrust at a walk and at the double.

## THE THRUST—ENEMY ON THE GROUND

18. Explain and demonstrate (see Fig 14):—

(a) Make the thrust as before, but with the rifle aimed downwards; to avoid accidents, keep your feet clear of the enemy.

(b) Stamp one foot on the enemy near the bayonet, slide your left hand forward, pull out the bayonet, come " on guard ", and advance.

19. Practise the thrust at a ground enemy, standing still, at a walk, and at the double.

## PRACTICE

20. Organize the squad into details ten yards from the dummy enemy; the words of command to give, and the action on them, are:—

(a) At the halt:—

(i) " Front (next) rank—on guard—ready ". The men place themselves in front of the dummy enemy; see that they are the right distance away.

(ii) " At the dummy enemy—thrust ". They thrust, withdraw and advance.

(b) At the walk or double.—" Front (next) rank—on guard—one thrust—at the walk (double)—thrust ". The men advance, thrust and withdraw, and advance again.

21. Always make the men pass the dummy right shoulder to right shoulder.

22. Finally, exercise the men with a training stick, but first make them tie their scabbards onto their bayonets with string; for details see Chapter 2, Section 10.

CONCLUSION

23. Questions from and to the squad.

24.—Sum up; stress the importance of speed, vigour and an offensive spirit.

Fig 11.—The high port

Fig 12.—On guard

Fig 13.—The thrust and withdraw—standing enemy

Fig 14.—The thrust and withdraw—enemy on the ground

## PRACTICE 3.—AIMING, SNAPSHOOTING AND RAPID FIRE

**AIM**

1. To give men more practice at aiming, snapshooting and firing rapid.

**STORES**

2. Rifles, drill rounds, cleaning materials, eye discs (or small targets with a pin hole in the middle), range and figure targets, aiming rests.

**NOTES**

3. Recruits need all the practice you can give them at handling their rifles quickly and accurately, and particularly at reloading, and loading with a fresh charger; and they need individual attention when doing it.

**PRELIMINARIES**

4. Put out the targets at ranges up to 300 yards.

5. Safety precautions.

**AIMING**

6. Practise aiming at the range and figure targets.

**SNAPSHOOTING**

7. Test each man at firing a snapshot in five seconds; point out any faults they make.

8. Practise snapshooting, first as masters and pupils, then at figure targets, gradually reducing the time limit from five to three seconds. Watch for these faults, and correct them if you see them:—

(a) Bad positions; apply the bolt test if necessary.

(b) A weak grip with the left hand.

(c) An incorrect grip with the right hand after reloading.

(d) Slovenly reloading, and movement of the head.

**RAPID FIRE**

9. Test each man at firing rapid for a minute; point out any faults they make.

10. Practise rapid fire, first as masters and pupils, then at range and figure targets, gradually working up to ten rounds in 40 seconds. Watch for these faults, and correct them if you see them:—

(a) Aiming and firing too quickly.

(b) Bad positions and holds.

(c) Slovenly reloading, and movement of the head.

(d) Failure to count the rounds and load with a fresh charger at the right moment.

(e) Poor clearing of jams.

**CONCLUSION**

11. Questions from and to the squad.

12. Sum up the progress made.

## LIVE FIRING 2.—GROUPING, APPLICATION AND SNAPSHOOTING

### AIM

1. To practise grouping again, to teach recruits to apply their groups to a target, and to practise snapshooting.

### STORES

2. Rifles, ammunition, cleaning and boiling out equipment, four foot and large snap targets, binoculars, zeroing equipment, coaches' notebooks, ABs 142.

### NOTES

3. See Chapter 2, Section 8. If you want a man to change his point of aim, show him on a representative target where it should be.

### PRELIMINARIES

4. Safety precautions, and cleaning before firing.

### SHOOTING

5. **Grouping.**—Fire the grouping practice of the Rifle Course. Discuss results and repeat if necessary.

6. **Application.**—
   - *(a)* Explain.—*Once you know how small a group you can fire at 100 yards, you also know how big it should be at other ranges; double the range and you double the size of the group, halve the range, and you halve it, and so on. For instance, if your normal group at 100 yards is 8 inches, at 200 it should be 16, at 300 24, and at 25 yards 2 inches. In an application practice, you try to put your group on the target with the middle of it (the mean point of impact or MPI) in the middle of the target.*
   - *(b)* Fire the application practice of the Rifle Course. Repeat it as often as time and ammunition allow.

7. **Snapshooting.**—Fire the snapshooting practice of the Rifle Course, but do not set a time limit for a man's first try; arrange for the targets to disappear immediately after he has fired each shot. By the end of the period, try to get them firing an accurate snapshot from the loading position in four seconds.

### CONCLUSION

8. Cleaning after firing.

9. Sum up results, and see that they are recorded.

## LESSON 8.—FIRING FROM OTHER POSITIONS WITHOUT COVER

AIM

1. To teach recruits to shoot kneeling, sitting and standing, without cover.

STORES

2. Rifles, drill rounds, target, eye discs.

NOTES

3. Use an eye disc to check aiming and firing in all positions.

4. Indicate the position by ordering " Standing, etc—load ".

PRELIMINARIES

5. Safety precautions.

6. Revise the lying position (Lessons 4 and 5).

APPROACH

7. *If you cannot see your target lying down, you have to shoot from other positions, even in the open.*

8. *Whatever the position, you load, set the sights, fire, and act on the commands " Stop " and " Go on " as you learnt to lying down; the hold is the same too, except in the standing position.*

THE KNEELING POSITION (See Fig 15)

9. Explain and demonstrate; make the men copy your actions:
   - *(a) Kneel on your right knee, keeping it well out to the right, and sit on your right heel; rest your left elbow behind your left knee and the butt on your right thigh; that is the loading position in which you load, and set your sights.*
   - *(b) Slide your left elbow forward to rest in front of your left knee cap, or behind it; bring the butt into the shoulder; keep your right elbow well up: that is the firing position.*

10. Practise the squad.

THE SITTING POSITION (See Fig 16)

11. Explain.—*The sitting position is useful for firing downhill or across a valley.*

12. Explain and demonstrate; make the men copy your actions:—
   - *(a) Sit down with your legs crossed or apart, and your feet wherever they are comfortable; hold the rifle as you did kneeling: that is the loading position, in which you load and set your sights.*
   - *(b) Rest your elbows behind, in front of, or just inside your knees, and bring the butt up into the shoulder: that is the firing position.*

13. Practise the squad.

THE STANDING POSITION (See Fig 17)

14. Explain.—*You stand up to fire over high cover, or to fire a snapshot in the move.*

15. Explain and demonstrate; make the men copy your actions:—

   (a) *Face the target; turn half right; balance your body evenly on both feet, with the muzzle of the rifle up, and the butt just in front of your hip: that is the loading position, in which you load and set your sights.*

   (b) *Lean forward a little, and bring the butt into the shoulder; hold with your right hand in the ordinary way, but as far forward as you can reach with your left hand; pull the rifle hard back into the shoulder: that is the firing position.*

   (c) *Aim at the bottom of the target, and take the first pressure; bring the rifle up, and fire as the foresight reaches the centre of the target.*

16. Practise the squad.

PRACTICE

17. Practise the squad at using all positions as they advance; do not use drill rounds, or they will get lost.

CONCLUSION

18. Questions from and to the squad.

19. Sum up.

Fig 15.—Loading and firing positions—kneeling

Fig 16.—Loading and firing positions—sitting

Fig 17.—Loading and firing positions—standing

## LESSON 9.—BAYONET FIGHTING—TWO OR MORE THRUSTS

### AIM

1. To teach recruits how to kill enemies with the bayonet one after another.

### STORES

2. Rifles, bayonets, standing and ground dummies, training stick, string.

### PREPARATIONS

3. Put out the dummies in pairs, with one dummy of each pair one yard behind and to the left of the other.

### PRELIMINARIES

4. Safety precautions; make the men cock their rifles, push their safety catches forward, loosen their slings, and fix bayonets.

5. Revise " on guard " and one thrust (Lesson 7).

### APPROACH

6. *You may have to kill two or more enemies with the bayonet, one after another.*

### TWO THRUSTS

7. Explain and demonstrate:—

*(a) Make the first thrust in the ordinary way.*

*(b) If your second opponent is out of range, punch forward " on guard ", advance on him, and thrust again. If he is so close that you have no room or time to come " on guard ", withdraw from the first thrust, point your bayonet at him, make another thrust, and advance. If there are more enemy, kill them in the same way.*

8. Practise the squad at making two thrusts at the dummies, at a walk and at the double. Give the order " Front (next) rank—on guard—two thrusts —at the walk (double)—thrust ".

9. Move the dummies so that one of each pair is about five yards behind and to the left of the other. Repeat para 8.

10. Move the dummies to irregular intervals, and repeat the practice; but order " Advance ", and let the men kill the enemy in their own way.

11. Make the men tie their scabbards onto their bayonets, and practise them with the training stick.

## CONCLUSION

12. Questions from and to the squad.

13. Sum up.

## PRACTICE 4.—FIRING FROM ALL POSITIONS WITHOUT COVER

### AIM

1. To give men more practice at handling their rifles in all positions.

### STORES

2. Rifles, drill rounds, targets, eye disc.

### PRELIMINARIES

3. Safety precautions.

### PRACTICE

4. Practise the men, first at the halt and then on the move, at using all firing positions and types of fire. Use the eye disc to see how steady they are.

5. For variety, divide the men into masters and pupils, and run competitions in getting into position, loading, and loading with a fresh charger.

### CONCLUSION

6. Questions from and to the squad.

7. Sum up.

## LESSON 10.—FIRING FROM BEHIND COVER

### AIM

1. To teach recruits how to fire from behind cover.

### STORES

2. Rifles, drill cartridges, figure targets.

### NOTES

3. Choose a piece of ground with all types of cover on it.

4. Avoid drill movements, and do not expect each man's actions to be exactly the same.

5. Criticize and correct, as far as possible, by asking questions.

### PRELIMINARIES

6. Safety precautions.

7. Revise the standing position (Lesson 8). Leave rifles loaded.

### APPROACH

8. *In battle you must be able to shoot accurately from any sort of cover.*

### FIRING POSITIONS

9. Explain and demonstrate:—

    *(a) If your fire position is a good one, you will:—*

        (i) *Have cover from fire and view.*

        (ii) *Have a good view of your arc of fire or target.*

        (iii) *Have room to use your weapon freely, and shoot accurately.*

        (iv) *Be able to approach it under cover, and advance from it easily.*

    *(b) Do not move or expose yourself in your firing position more than you have to, and always rest your weapon correctly.*

    *(c) When firing over soft cover, rest your hand and forearm; if the cover is hard, rest your rifle on it as near your left hand as you can.*

### TAKING COVER AND FIRING

10. **Low cover.**—Explain and demonstrate. (See Fig 18).

11. **Orders and actions.**—*The section commander's orders, and your action on them are:—*

    *(a)* "*Down* "              *Get down, crawl to cover, keep your rifle out of sight, and observe; if no other order follows, try to spot the enemy and shoot him, until the section commander takes control again. Remember the sequence "Down, crawl, observe, fire ".*

    *(b) Range*              *Set your sights, get into a firing position, and push forward your safety catch; that is the position of readiness.*

    *(c)* "*Fire* ", "*Stop* ", *and* " *Go on* ".    *Usual action.*

41

*(d) "Prepare to advance (move)", or "Behind cover".*  Apply the safety catch, get behind cover, lower you sights, and get ready to move.

*(e) "Advance (move)".*  Move.

12. Kneeling and sitting (see Fig 19).—Explain and demonstrate.—*Kneel on one or both knees, or sit down, whichever suits the cover best.*

13. Standing (see Fig 20).—Explain and demonstrate.—*Lean against the cover, if you can, to steady yourself.*

14. Firing round cover (see Fig 21).—Explain and demonstrate.—*Fire round the right-hand side of the cover, if you can; steady your rifle against the cover as near your left hand as possible.*

15. Narrow cover.—Explain and demonstrate.—*Lie, kneel, sit or stand straight behind it, with your legs together.*

16. Practise the men with all types of cover.

CONCLUSION

17. Questions from and to the squad.

18. Sum up.

Fig 18.—Firing from low cover—soft and hard ground

Fig 19.—Firing from cover—kneeling and sitting

Fig 20.—Firing from cover—standing

Fig 21.—Firing round cover

## PRACTICE 5.—THE USE OF COVER

AIM

1. To practise handling with all types of cover.

DRESS AND STORES

2. Battle order, rifles, drill cartridges, figure targets.

NOTES

3. Choose ground with all types of cover, and put out targets to suit the cover available.

PRELIMINARIES

4. Safety precautions. Order " Standing load ".

PRACTICE

5. Practise the men at firing from low cover like banks, folds in the ground and low walls, and kneeling, sitting and standing behind ordinary and narrow cover; point out the target area, and give orders like " Down ", " Take cover " or " Advance ", and fire control order.

6. Check all points of elementary training. It is a help to get half the men to criticize the rest.

CONCLUSION

7. Questions from and to the squad.

8. Sum up.

## LIVE FIRING 3.—GROUPING, APPLICATION, SNAP AND RAPID

If time and ammunition allow, now is the time for the men to do Live Firing 2 again, and to fire another application practice of the Rifle Course. It is important that men should be given every opportunity to practice firing with fixed bayonets.

## LESSON 11.—BAYONET FIGHTING—SELF DEFENCE

### AIM

1. To teach recruits self defence.

### STORES

2. Rifles, bayonets, training stick, string.

### NOTES

3. It is usually best to have the men in one rank for demonstrations and for practice without the training stick; and in one or two ranks, or a circle, for practice with the training stick; but it depends on the size of the squad.

4. Chapter 2, Section 10 describes how to use a training stick.

### PRELIMINARIES

5. Safety precautions; make the men fix bayonets, cock their rifles, and loosen their slings.

6. Revise two or more thrusts (Lesson 9), and then make the men tie their scabbards to their bayonets.

### APPROACH

7. *You must know how to defend yourselves against a bayonet attack, but, once you have succeeded in that, your one aim must be to attack and kill.*

### RIGHT PARRY AND THRUST (See Fig 33)

8. Explain and demonstrate; make the men copy your actions.—*If an enemy attacks you on the right, parry his thrust by straightening your left arm vigorously, point your bayonet at him, thrust, withdraw, come " on guard ", and advance.*

9. Practise the men against an imaginary enemy until they get the actions right; then exercise each man in turn with the training stick.

### LEFT PARRY, BUTT STROKE AND KILL (See Fig 22)

10. Explain and demonstrate; make the men copy your actions.—*If an enemy attacks you on the left, punch your rifle far enough to the left to beat off his thrust; bring your right foot forward and swing your rifle round to hit his head with the butt; point your bayonet at him as he lies on the ground, thrust, withdraw, and advance.*

11. Practise the men against an imaginary enemy until they get the actions right; then exercise each man in turn with the training stick.

12. Explain.—*If you attack an enemy on his left, and he parries, he will instantly follow up with a butt stroke; you must act quickly and violently first to avoid the butt stroke, and then to kill him; what you do depends on the openings he gives you.*

PRACTICE

13. Practise the whole lesson, except para 12, again.

CONCLUSION

14. Questions from and to the squad.

15. More practice with the training stick.

16. Sum up; emphasize again that you defend yourself first, and then go in and kill your enemy.

Fig 22.—The butt stroke

## LESSON 12.—ALTERING THE SIGHTS

AIM

1. To teach recruits the elevation table, and how to aim up or down.

STORES

2. Rifles, aiming rests, range and figure targets, auxiliary aiming marks, ABs 142.

NOTES

3. You must know the appropriate coach's elevation table (Chapter 2, Section 3). The recruits' table is simple, easy to remember, and only approximate; give them a copy to stick in their ABs 142 for use on the range.

4. It is best to teach the lesson with targets at proper distances, but you can get almost the same value out of it indoors with small targets (see Chapter 2, Section 2, paras 1 and 2).

5. Put out the range targets between 200 and 500 yards, and the figure targets at 200 and 300 yards.

6. Prepare auxiliary aiming marks; for a range target this is a cut out aiming mark to hang in the appropriate position on the target; for a figure target it is another figure target to put up by its side the right distance away.

7. Rehearse your assistants.

PRELIMINARIES

8. Safety precautions. Examine sights.

9. Use your AB 142 to make sure the men know the dimensions of targets.

ALTERATION OF SIGHTS

10. Explain.—*If you find your shots going too high or too low, you must alter the setting of your backsight, if there is time. This table shows how much higher or lower the shots will go at various ranges, for each hundred yards by which you alter the backsight; an alteration of fifty produces half the effect:*—

| Range to target | Rise or fall for alteration of 100 yards |
|---|---|
| 200 | ½ foot |
| 300 | 1 foot |
| 400 | 1½ feet |
| 500 | 2 feet |
| 600 | 2½ feet |

11. Question the men, and set them practice problems at range and figure targets; get an assistant at the target to signal the value and position of an imaginary shot, or mark shots on a target in your AB 142, and show the men that; tell the men to adjust their sights; discuss results.

## AIMING UP OR DOWN

12. Explain.—*If your shots are going too high or too low when you are firing rapid or snapshooting, or too high when your sights are set at 200, all you do is aim up or down enough to correct the error.*

13. To give the men practice at aiming up or down:—
   (a) Get an assistant to show where shots are striking.
   (b) Tell the men to aim so as to correct the error, with their rifles in aiming rests; then get the assistant to put auxiliary aiming marks in position.
   (c) Discuss results. Tell the men to aim at the auxiliary aiming marks; have the auxiliary marks removed, and the men will see how they should have aimed in the first place.

## CONCLUSION

14. Questions from and to the squad.

15. Sum up.

## LESSON 13.—AIMING OFF FOR WIND

AIM

1. To teach men how to aim off for wind.

STORES

2. Rifles, aiming rests, range and figure targets, auxiliary aiming marks, ABs 142.

NOTES

3. See Lesson 12, paras 3-7.

PRELIMINARIES

4. Safety precautions. Examine sights.

5. Revise altering sights (Lesson 12) and dimensions of targets (AB 142).

## AIMING OFF FOR WIND

6. Explain.—*The wind blows a bullet off its course. It is always the firer's responsibility to aim off into the wind, without changing his elevation.*

7. Amounts to allow for wind.—Explain:—
   (a) *A fresh wind has a noticeable effect on grass, smoke, flags, dust, the side of your face, etc. If a fresh wind is blowing straight across the line of fire, multiply by itself the first figure of the range in yards to the target, and aim off that number of inches. For example, if the range is 300 yards, aim off 3 × 3 = 9 inches.* Practise the squad.

*(b)* *If the wind is strong, double the allowance; if it is gentle, halve it.
For example, if the range is 400 yards, and a strong wind is
blowing straight across the line of fire, aim off* 4 × 4 × 2 = 32
*inches; but if the wind is gentle, aim* 4 × 4 ÷ 2 = 8 *inches.*
Practise the squad.

*(c)* *If the wind is blowing at an oblique angle to the line of fire, halve
the allowance. For example, if the range is 300 yards:—*
(i) *For a strong wind aim off* 3 × 3 × 2 ÷ 2 = 9 *inches.*
(ii) *For a fresh wind aim off* 3 × 3 ÷ 2 = 4½ *inches.*
(iii) *For a gentle wind aim off* 3 × 3 ÷ 2 ÷ 2 = 2¼ *inches.*

8. Use your AB 142 to explain and demonstrate.—*You will find aiming
off on the range easier, if you remember these tips:—*

*(a)* *On a 4-foot target, the edge of the black aiming mark is 6 inches
the edge of the target 24 inches, and a point half way between the
edge of the aiming mark and the edge of the target 15 inches
from the middle of the target.*

*(b)* *On a 6-foot target, the edge of the black aiming mark is 12 inches
the edge of the target 36 inches, and a point half way between
the edge of the black aiming mark and the edge of the target 24
inches, from the middle of the target.*

*(c)* *The average width of a man or a figure target is 18 inches.*

9. Practise the squad.

## AIMING UP OR DOWN, AS WELL AS OFF

10. Explain.—*You may have to aim off, and aim up or down at the same
time. For example, if you are firing rapid at 300 yards, and see that your shots
are going a foot high and a foot to the right, you must aim a foot below and
a foot left of your original point of aim.*

11. Practise the squad.

## PRACTICE

12. To practise the squad:—
*(a)* Give them a problem and tell them to aim, with their rifles in
aiming rests.
*(b)* Get an assistant to put the auxiliary aiming mark in position;
criticize the men's aims. So long as its elevation is right, accept
as correct any aim that is near the middle of the auxiliary
aiming mark.
*(c)* Make the men aim at the auxiliary aiming mark; then have it
removed, and the men will see how they should have aimed
in the first place.

## CONCLUSION

13. Questions from and to the squad.

14. Sum up.

## PRACTICE 6.—ALTERING SIGHTS, AND AIMING OFF FOR WIND

**AIM**

1. To practise men at using the elevation table, and aiming off for wind.

**STORES**

2. Rifles, aiming rests, range and figure targets, auxiliary aiming marks, ABs 142.

**NOTES**

3. If there are more men than aiming rests, while part of the squad uses the rests, the others should work out the problems on targets in their ABs 142.

**PRELIMINARIES**

4. Safety precautions. Examine sights.

**PRACTICE**

5. Question the men on the elevation table (Lesson 12).

6. Give them practical problems involving altering their sights, and aiming up and down.

7. Question them on the wind allowance table (Lesson 13).

8. Give them practical problems involving aiming off, and aiming off and up or down together, at range and figure targets.

**CONCLUSION**

10. Questions from and to the squad.

11. Sum up.


## PRACTICE 7.—BAYONET FIGHTING

**AIM**

1. To give men more bayonet fighting practice.

**STORES**

2. Rifles, bayonets, standing and ground dummies, training stick, string.

**NOTES**

3. Repeat this practice whenever there is time. Exercise a man with a training stick, whenever you think that his movements want speeding up.

**PRELIMINARIES**

4. Safety precautions. Make the men fix bayonets, cock their rifles, and loosen their slings.

PRACTICE

5. Practise these actions in any order, with standing and ground dummies in all positions:—

(a) One thrust, at a walk and at the double.

(b) Two or more thrusts, with time to come " on guard " between them.

(c) Two or more thrusts, with no time to come " on guard " between them.

(d) A combination of (b) and (c).

6. Get the men to tie their scabbards to their bayonets. Exercise them with the training stick in thrusting and self defence standing in a circle, at any time during the period.

CONCLUSION

7. Questions from and to the squad.

8. Sum up.


LESSON 14.—CLOSE QUARTER BATTLE

AIM

1. To teach recruits how to fight at close quarters.

STORES

2. Rifles, bayonets, figure targets.

NOTES

3. Put out various targets within a radius of 100 yards.

PRELIMINARIES

4. Safety precautions. Fix bayonets.

APPROACH

5. *In built up areas, jungle and woods, and during an assault, you will find yourself face to face with the enemy at short range; you must be able to get in the first shot at lightning speed, and kill. That is what is meant by close quarter l..tle.*

THE WALK-UP POSITIONS

6. Explain and demonstrate; make the men copy your actions.—*When you are likely to meet the enemy at short range, you must carry your rifle in such a way that you can bring it instantly into a firing position. There are three walk-up positions; use whichever is best in the circumstances:—*

(a) The high port (see Lesson 7).

(b) The right shoulder carry (see Fig 23).—*Hold the rifle by the small of the butt, and carry it over your right shoulder, magazine up, with the safety catch applied. The position leaves your left hand free.*

Fig 23.—The right shoulder carry

*(c) The alert position* (see Fig 24).—*Use it when you think danger is near. Hold the rifle with your left hand on the small of the butt, and your right hand as far forward as you can reach, the butt under your arm or on your hip, and the muzzle pointing to the left and a bit down with the safety catch forward.*

Fig 24.—The alert position

7. Make the men practise all the positions.

FIRING

8. Explain.—*When you see a target, you must shoot fast, without having to pause to think.*

9. Firing from the shoulder.—Explain and demonstrate:—

(a) *Bring the rifle up to your shoulder quickly, keep your right elbow well up, your left arm straight and your left foot forward, and*

*take aim roughly, along the barrel or over the sights* (see Fig 25).
*Drop down on one knee or dodge to cover as you fire, if you need
to.*

(*b*) *Fire (both pressures together), and reload at once. If you want a
really high rate of fire, keep your forefinger and thumb on the bolt
knob, and fire with your middle finger.*

Fig 25.—Firing from the shoulder

(*c*) Practise the squad,

10. Firing from the hip.—Explain and demonstrate:—

(a) *You can fire very quickly from the hip at anyone not more than ten yards away; this should only be used at very close quarters.*

(b) *Come " on guard" push the safety catch forward, press the butt into your side, look at the enemy, straighten your left arm, fire at him (both pressures at once), and reload instantly.*

(c) Practise the squad.

11. Make the men practise the whole lesson.

## CONCLUSION

12. Questions from and to the squad.

13. Sum up.


LIVE FIRING 4.—APPLICATION AND RAPID AT 300 YARDS

## AIM

1. To give men practice at shooting at 300 yards.

## STORES

2. Rifles, ammunition, 4-foot targets, cleaning materials and ABs 142.

## PRELIMINARIES

3. Safety precautions.

## PRACTICES

4. Fire the rapid and application practices of the Rifle Course.

## CONCLUSION

5. Questions from and to the squad.

6. Talk about results and see that they are recorded. Tell the men the grouping capacity they have achieved.

### PRACTICE 8.—HANDLING

1. To train men to obey orders quickly and accurately, and to use their ifles intelligently and correctly whatever happens.

## DRESS

2. Battle order.

## NOTES

3. The practice is primarily for squads, but it is suitable for sections oo. Put your men through it frequently.

4. Give all fire control orders from where the fire unit commander would be in battle.

5. Do not practise the standing, kneeling or sitting positions except in circumstances in which they would be right in battle; and never allow or order rapid fire unless the target justifies it.

6. Within 300 yards of the enemy, bayonets are usually fixed.

7. To start with, do the practices at the halt in the open; later do them on the move, and make the men use cover.

8. Always show the men where the enemy is supposed to be.

## PRELIMINARIES

9. Safety precautions; put the men in a line two paces apart.

## APPROACH

10. *In battle, it is vitally important to obey orders instantly and accurately.*

## EXERCISE 1.—AT THE HALT

11. Order " Load ", with drill cartridges, and give a fire control order onto an easy target; make sure the range is about correct.

12. To assess the men's work, ask yourself:—
   *(a)* Are their fire positions good?
   *(b)* Do they load and reload well?
   *(c)* Is their bolt work quick enough?
   *(d)* Do they use their safety catches properly?
   *(e)* Do they adjust their sights quickly and accurately?
   *(f)* Do they recognize their targets quickly?
   *(g)* Do they know the difference between slow and rapid fire and snapshooting?
   *(h)* Do they know what to do on the orders " Stop ", " Go on " and " Unload "?
   *(j)* Are they " on their toes " to hear fresh orders?

## EXERCISE 2

13. As Exercise 1, but on the move, first at a walk and at the double in the open, then with various types of cover.

14. To assess the men's work, ask yourself the same questions (para 12), and also these:—

   *(a)* Are their movements cautious enough when you order " Prepare to advance "?
   *(b)* Do they get up and down quickly?
   *(c)* Do they make good use of cover?
   *(d)* Do they think of moving between shots?
   *(e)* Do they open fire from just where they went to cover?

CONCLUSION

15. Questions from and to the squad.

16. Sum up.

## LIVE FIRING 5.—THE ASSAULT COURSE

AIM

1. To practise an assault with ball ammunition.

STORES

2. Weapons, ammunition, targets and cleaning materials.

NOTES

3. Run the practice on a bayonet assault course (Fig 26), ending on a firing point from which the men can fire live ammunition. Use representative range targets to start with, so that you can see how exertion affects the men's grouping. Repeat this period constantly.

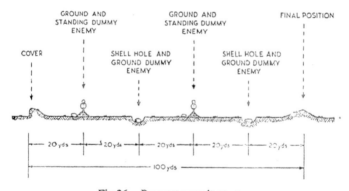

Fig 26.—Bayonet assault course

4. The instructor acts as commander, and controls the advance.

5. Unless the men are already well trained, it may be best to put them over the course by stages, and correct their faults at each stage.

6. If they are going to fire live ammunition, put it on the firing point; never let them load till they get there.

PRELIMINARIES

7. Safety precautions.

APPROACH

8. *A controlled advance shakes the enemy's morale, and gets you to the objective not too exhausted; if the final charge gets out of control, the effect is reduced, and the enemy may have time to deal with you one by one.*

## THE CONTROLLED CHARGE

9. Explain.—*In a controlled charge, these are the principles to follow:—*

(a) *Everyone breaks cover at the same moment.*

(b) *Advance at a steady double, each man keeping touch with the man on his left at least two paces apart.*

(c) *Carry your rifles at the high port over obstacles.*

(d) *Make the final charge with dash and determination.*

(e) *As you advance, each of you decides which enemy to kill, and then goes flat out to kill him.*

(f) *The moment the assault is over, find a good fire position, and be prepared to open fire.*

10. Practise the men first without, then with, live ammunition.

## CONCLUSION

11. Questions from and to the squad.

12. Sum up what has been achieved.

## CHAPTER 2.—EXTRA INFORMATION FOR INSTRUCTORS

### INTRODUCTION

1. This chapter contains extra information for instructors, to help them to understand the subject more thoroughly, and make training more varied.

2. Do not teach it to recruits. You will find it useful, however, when it comes to answering questions on things that the lessons do not cover; and it is suitable to teach to a NCOs' cadre.

## SECTION 1.—PRACTICE PERIODS

1. All training must be progressive; unnecessary repetition is boring. A recruit learns skills and facts in the lessons, and he should be taught them once only during his service; he then needs a lot of time and practice to speed up his actions, and get the facts fixed in his mind.

2. During practice periods it may be obvious that the men have failed to grasp a particular skill or fact, and you may have to teach them part of a lesson again.

3. The practices in this pamphlet are a guide to the best way of exercising recruits, but you must watch their weak points, and plan practices accordingly.

4. Spot and check faults immediately, or recruits will go on making the same mistakes, and make no progress.

5. Put a practice into the programme whenever there is time, but keep varying the method.

## SECTION 2.—TARGETS AND AIMING

### Small scale targets

1. If you want to use a representative target at short range, you can work out how big it should be; multiply each dimension (in inches) of the full sized target, aiming mark or scoring circle by the range in yards at which you are going to use the small target, and divide by the range in yards that the practice is to represent; the answer is the dimension of the small target, aiming mark or scoring circle in inches.

2. For example, if you want to know how big a target to use at 100 yards, to represent a 6-foot target at 600 yards, the sum is $\dfrac{72 \times 100}{600} = 12$, and the target should be 12 inches square.

### Principles of aiming

3. An aim cannot be accurate unless the aim picture—the alignment of the eye, backsight, foresight and point of aim—is correct. The target does not look distinct unless you look exactly through the centre of the aperture.

4. You can focus your eye on only one thing at a time; you cannot focus it exactly on the foresight and target together; you must concentrate on one or the other. In battle a target is usually moving or camouflaged, and you cannot see to aim at it without focussing your eye on it; with practice you learn to focus your eye on the foresight, just to check its position in the aim picture, a fraction of a second before you fire.

5. With a distinct, stationery target, like a range target, some men find it better to concentrate on the foresight than on the target. Do not explain this to anyone, or let him practise it, until he has finished his recruit training, or you may confuse him; it is useful mainly in competition shooting.

## SECTION 3.—SIGHTS AND THE INSTRUCTOR'S ELEVATION TABLE

1. The elevation table that recruits learn must be simple; it is therefore only approximate. Coaches need something more accurate.

2. Fig 27 shows the different backsights fitted to No. 4 Rifles.

**The Mark 1 backsight**

3. You adjust it in clicks, and one click moves the MPI up or down about as many inches as the first figure of the range in yards to the target.

For example:—

(a) One click at 300 yards raises or lowers the MPI three inches.

(b) Two clicks at 400 yards raise or lower the MPI eight inches.

4. As a coach, you may have to advise recruits what range to set on their sights for a first shot; remember that a rifle fires the same number of clicks high or low at all ranges.

**The Mark 2 backsight**

5. It has two apertures, marked 300 and 600, and no other settings are possible. The only way to make a correction is to aim up or down.

6. At 200 and 300 yards the MPI is about a foot lower with the bayonet fixed than without it.

7. The rules for accurate shooting are:—

| Range | Aperture | Bayonet | Remarks |
|-------|----------|---------|---------|
| 200 | 300 | Fixed | *Aim down eight inches* |
| 300 | 300 | Fixed | |
| 400 | 300 | Not fixed | |
| 500 | 600 | Not fixed | Aim down 2½ feet |
| 600 | 600 | Not fixed | |

**The Mark 3 backsight**

8. It is like the Mark 1, but it is not adjusted in clicks, and you can set it only at whole hundreds of yards. It is better to set the sights too high and aim down, than too low and aim up.

9. Use the recruits' elevation table, which is accurate enough for all practical purposes. For more detailed information see Infantry Training, Volume I, Pamphlet No. 10, 1951 (WO Code No. 8697), Lesson 12.

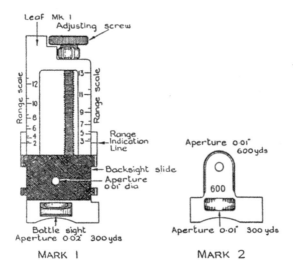

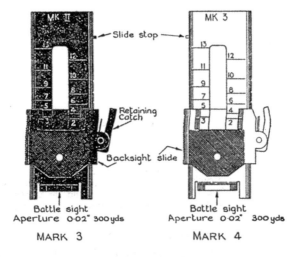

Fig 27.—No. 4 Rifle backsights

## SECTION 4.—HOW TO EXAMINE A RIFLE

1. Officers and NCOs must know how to examine a rifle to see that it is being kept fit for battle.

**How to examine a rifle**

2. **The barrel.**—Look for rust, cuts, bulging or fouling:—

(a) Pull the rifle through; rust shows on the flannelette, or as dark patches in the barrel.

(b) A cut looks like a short hair.

(c) A bulge shows as a dark circle.

(d) Metallic fouling shows as streaks or patches on the lands, or in the grooves near the muzzle.

3. **The sights.**—See that:—

(a) The foresight blade is firm, and not deformed.

(b) There is no play in the leaf of the backsight, and that the slide stays firm wherever you set it.

(c) Neither sight lacks browning.

**The magazine:**—

(a) See that the numbers on the magazine and rifle are the same, there are no dents, and the platform moves up and down freely.

(b) Examine the magazine catch, and see that the auxiliary spring is in position.

5. **The bolt.**—See that:—

(a) The numbers on it and the rifle are the same.

(b) The extractor is not worn, nor the extractor spring weak.

(c) The striker sticks out the right amount through the face of the bolt.

(d) The cocking piece is firm on the striker, and the bents are not burred.

(e) There is not too much play in the bolt way.

6. See that the sear holds the cocking piece back securely as you close the breech, and that there are two distinct trigger pressures, with no roughness on the second.

7. **The safety catch:**—

(a) See that it is not too easy to move.

(b) Apply it: the cocking piece should move back a little; it should be impossible to raise the bolt lever; and the trigger should move easily to and fro without letting the cocking piece go forward.

8. See that the butt is not loose.

9. The muzzle should not fit tightly to the woodwork. If there is no play in the muzzle the rifle needs adjustment by an armourer.

**Preservation of the woodwork**

10. Once a month, the storeman or some other suitable person should wipe the woodwork clean with a dry rag, put on a little linseed oil with a clean rag without getting any onto the metal parts, stand the rifle in the shade for three hours, and then wipe off the oil thoroughly.

## SECTION 5.—THE No. 5 RIFLE

1. The No. 5 Rifle is a lightened version of the No. 4, and weighs just over seven pounds; the mechanism is the same. To save weight, the barrel is 6½ inches shorter, and six inches of it have no woodwork covering. (See Fig 28).

2. The muzzle has a flash hider, and takes a No. 5 bayonet with an eight-inch blade. There is a rubber pad instead of a butt plate, and you carry cleaning materials separately in a cleaning compact, a small, flat tin box with compartments for oil bottle, pullthrough, gauze, flannelette and bristle brush.

3. The backsight goes up to 800 yards, and is like the No. 4 Rifle backsight, Mark 1.

Fig 28.—The No. 5 Rifle

## SECTION 6.—HOLDING AND FIRING

1. A good firing position is neither strained nor uncomfortable. The firer's body should be as far round to the left as it can be without the bolt touching his cheek as he reloads.

2. Rifles have long, normal or short butts, and a man cannot get into a good firing position unless his rifle has the right length of butt for him; there are two ways to test this:—

(a) If a man has difficulty in bringing the butt into his shoulder, it is too long; if his nose and mouth are too close to his right hand in the firing position, it is too short.

(b) The bolt test:—

(i) When a man is in what he thinks is a comfortable firing position, tell him to keep his head still; and draw the bolt slowly back; if it does not touch his cheek, move it quickly backwards and forwards to show him that he need not move his head as he reloads, which means that his rifle fits him and his position is good.

(ii) If the bolt does touch his cheek, get him to move his body farther round to the right; if the bolt still touches his cheek, he needs a longer butt.

3. Always try to get men to shoot right-handed, as rapid reloading is difficult for a left-handed shot. Occasionally you may have to let a man shoot left-handed; the firing position is the same as for a right-hander (Lesson 4), except that you read " right " for " left ", and " left " for " right ", all through.

4. A man should grip his rifle with the whole of both hands; do not let him grip with his fingers and thumbs only.


## SECTION 7.—ZEROING

1. Before a man fires his annual course, and at other times if necessary, his rifle must be zeroed; and before that is done, an armourer must examine it to see that it is serviceable, and that all screws are tight.

2. Men who consistently fire eight-inch or smaller groups zero their own rifles; expert shots should zero other men's rifles for them.

3. The proper range is 100 yards; 25 yards is a poor substitute.

4. Targets:—

(a) At 100 yards.—A four-foot target with a four-inch by three-inch white patch on the centre of the bottom of the aiming mark.

(b) At 25 yards.—A 200/25 representative target with a three eighths-inch by half-inch white patch, or a white screen with one-inch square black aiming marks

5. The men fire lying down, with their forearms rested (see Fig 6). Each man fires two warmers into the stop butt, and then a five round group; if he has to fire another group, he needs no warmers.

6. Choose a day when there is good light and little wind.

7. If the MPI is left, move the foresight to the left; if right, to the right. If the MPI is high, fit a higher foresight; if low, a lower one: foresights available are:— ·03, —·015, ·0, ·015, ·03, ·045, ·06 and ·075; foresights for No. 4 and No. 5 rifles are not interchangeable.

8. After any alteration a man must fire another group; which may show that the sights need altering again.

9. Always record the fact that a rifle has been zeroed; and any error that it still has.

10. These tables provide the necessary information for zeroing:—

(a) Table 1—elevation:—

| Rifle | Bayonet | Sights set at | Inches that MPI should be above the point of aim | | Permissible vertical error in inches | | Inches (approximate) by which the MPI rises or drops when you fit the next smaller or larger foresight | |
|---|---|---|---|---|---|---|---|---|
| | | | 100 yards | 25 yards | 100 yards | 25 yards | 100 yards | 25 yards |
| No. 4 (a) | Not fixed | 200 | 3 | ¾ | 2 | ½ | 2 | ½ |
| No. 4 (b) | Fixed | 300 | 6 | 1½ | 2 | ½ | 2 | ½ |
| No. 5 | Not fixed | 200 | 3½ | 1 | 2¼ | ½ | 2¼ | ½ |

(a) = with leaf backsight.  (b) = with Mark 2 backsight.

(b) Table 2—lateral adjustment.:—

| Rifle | Cramp | Inches that one turn moves the MPI | | Inches that a move of one blade's width moves the MPI | |
|---|---|---|---|---|---|
| | | 100 yards | 25 yards | 100 yards | 25 yards |
| No. 4 | No. 3 | 4 | 1 | 6 | 1½ |
| No. 5 | No. 4 | 6 | 1½ | 8 | 2 |

## SECTION 8.—COACHING

**General**

1. A soldier is entitled to expert coaching during his recruit training, and whenever else the conditions of the practice he is firing allow it.

2. The aim of classification range practices is to train men to shoot under comparatively easy conditions, so that they have a chance to get good results, which they can see on the target and in their ABs 142. Good results give them confidence, make them feel masters of their weapons, and prepare them for more advanced shooting.

3. All officers, warrant officers and NCOs must know how to coach on the range, and should be instructed in the art.

4. Good coaches make the most of their time on the range by intelligent coaching, and by doing their job systematically, quietly and efficiently. Bad coaches waste time, and do endless harm to their men. Supervising officers must be able to put a stop to bad coaching at once.

## What a successful coach must know

5. To be a successful coach, you must know everything in this pamphlet, particularly the instructor's elevation table (Chapter 2, Section 3) and all about zeroing (Chapter 2, Section 7).

6. You must be able to spot why a man is shooting badly, and put him right; these are some of the common causes:—

    (a) These are the firer's fault:—

        (i) Bad aiming; for instance, he may not see the correct aim picture every time, or he may stay in the aim too long, or aim too high or too low when aiming off for wind.

        (ii) Bad trigger work; for instance, he may snatch the trigger.

        (iii) He may move his body as he fires.

        (iv) Bad position and hold; for instance, he may not be comfortable, or he may hold loosely with either hand.

        (v) He may breathe wrongly; he may be gun-shy, too anxious to do well, or not determined enough; or he may not declare his aim honestly.

        (vi) He may not have cleaned his rifle properly; he may have tampered with it and damaged it in some way; or it may have the wrong bolt.

    (b) These are outside the firer's control:—

        (i) Bad light or bad weather.

        (ii) His rifle may be badly zeroed or in bad condition, or the butt may be the wrong length for him.

        (iii) Bad eyes, bad health and so on.

        (iv) Bad coaching or bad range organization.

7. You must know what the rifle and ammunition are designed to do; these are the facts:—

    (a) Before the Army gets them:—

        (i) All rifles are fired from a mechanical rest—the most accurate method possible—and four out of five shots must hit a rectangle $1\frac{1}{2}$ inches by 1 inch at 100 feet.

        (ii) One rifle in every ten, and any that are doubtful as a result of the first test, are tested again at 600 yards; and ten shots out of ten must hit an 18-inch square.

(b) Even from a mechanical rest a rifle cannot put all its shot through the same hole; they form a pattern, which is called a group; the capacity of the rifle and ammunition determine the size of the group.

(c) When a man fires from the shoulder, his group is bound to be larger; how big it is depends on how well he aims, holds and fires. This size of the group is the capacity of a combination of the rifle, ammunition and firer.

8. You must understand grouping, which is the foundation of good shooting:—

(a) A group is a series of shots (usually five) fired at the same aiming mark, with the same aim and hold. The middle of the group is called the mean point of impact (MPI). The smaller the group, the better the shot. The main aim of all shooting training is to get men to aim, hold, fire, and control their nerves so as to achieve as small a group as possible.

(b) Standard grouping rings have diameters of 4, 8, and 12 inches for groups fired at 100 yards, or 1, 2 and 3 inches at 25 yards; you can use them to classify men as:—
   (i) Above average     if they achieve a 4-inch group at 100 yards, or a 1-inch group at 25 yards.
   (ii) Average     if they achieve an 8-inch (2-inch) group.
   (iii) Below average     if they achieve a 12-inch (3-inch) group

(c) Anyone who cannot achieve at least a 12-inch (3-inch) group needs more training before firing his course, or he will fail, and loose confidence.

(d) For coaching (but not scoring) purposes you can also use rings with diameters of 5, 6, 7, 9 ,10 and 11 inches.

(e) A man's grouping capacity at any stage of his training is the average size of group that he can achieve at that time. Since the foundation of coaching is to know exactly what a man's grouping capacity is, the more groups he fires, the better; and every one must be recorded.

9. You must understand the theory of the group:—

(a) Once you know a man's grouping capacity at 100 yards, you also know the smallest area that, in theory, should contain all his well fired shots at any other range; for the size of his group varies in direct proportion to the range at which he is firing; for instance, at 200 yards it is twice, at 300 yards three times, and at 25 yards a quarter, what it is at 100 yards. In an application practice he applies his group to the centre of the target, and his grouping capacity determines his expected scoring area. For example, if his grouping capacity is eight inches (at 100 yards), his expected scoring area at 200 yards is a 16-inch circle with its centre in the middle of the target; if all his shots are as good as he can make them, they should all be well inside the inner ring.

*(b)* This theory is the basis of coaching, but you must apply it sensibly. For instance, a 4-inch grouper is not likely to put all his shots into the 12-inch bull at 300 yards, although that is his " expected scoring area "; such things as wind, light and the sighting of his rifle will affect his shooting, and the aiming mark may be harder to see than it was at 100 yards; nor will he shoot as accurately when he is firing rapid or at a moving target.

*(c)* A good coach can tell whether a shot is a good one or not, except for one thing—the aim. Coaching is a waste of time unless the firer tells you what aim picture he was seeing at the moment of firing each shot, whether it was " correct ", " high left ", " right ", " low ", etc. See that your men know how to declare their aims, and realize how important it is to do it honestly.

*(d)* Remember his declarations when you look at a man's group. For instance, if he declared one shot to be high left, and you find that it was high left of the others, you can ignore it when you judge his grouping capacity; but you would be unwise to ignore more than one such shot in a group; for scoring purposes, all five shots must count.

*(e)* A man's rifle may be wrongly sighted, for direction or elevation, or both; unless you know this (his MPI at 100 yards should be recorded in his AB 142), you are liable to advise him badly. For instance, his rifle may fire six inches low at 100 yards; the instructor's elevation table (Section 3) tells you that it will be six clicks low at all ranges; so, before he fires his first shot in an application practice, you should advise him to put his sights six clicks higher than the range to the target.

*(f)* You must know how to get the best out of a firer. Nothing is more fatal to good shooting than a coach for whom nothing is ever right. To get the best results, you must understand your man and be in perfect harmony with him; and the range organization must be good, so that there is no air of hustle, and the man arrives on the firing point ready to shoot, with a rifle that fits him, is clean and in good condition, and has been inspected and had its sights blackened; with ammunition that is clean and has been inspected; and understanding the practice and knowing which is his target.

## Coaching procedure—grouping practices—The Foundation of Good Shooting

10. Before firing:—

*(a)* Take a notebook, pencil and binoculars onto any range; and a representative target onto a 25 yards or miniature range.

(b) Take the firers' AB 142, study his old grouping records, and decide how well he ought to shoot. He should understand the practice already, and know which target to shoot at; but just make sure.

(c) See that he tests his position properly, and sets his sights right.

(d) Lie down on his right (or left, if he shoots left-handed), near enough to see everything he does, but not so close as to get in his way.

11. **During the practice:—**

(a) Watch the man, not the target, so that you notice anything he does wrong.

(b) After each shot, note down his declaration and anything that you noticed.

(c) Be careful not to coach too much; if you want to talk, do it between shots, or tell him to rest and apply his safety catch.

(d) If his rifle has the wrong length of butt, or if he does any of these things, you should be able to spot them and put them right:—

   (i) Stays in the aim too long.

   (ii) Moves his left elbow between shots.

   (iii) Holds too loosely.

   (iv) Fails to have his head in the same position for each shot.

   (v) Snatches the trigger, flinches, breathes wrongly, or comes off aim too quickly after firing.

12. **After firing.**—After every second detail has fired, go up to the targets with the men; examine each man's group, and explain it to him, in this sequence:—

(a) Compare his declarations with the shots in the order in which they arrived.

(b) See how big the group is for both coaching and scoring purposes, and where the MPI is; and enter them all in his AB 142.

(c) See whether the pattern of the group suggests anything wrong with the rifle; if there is the slightest doubt, fire a group yourself to test it.

Then tell the man what he did well or badly, and give him advice for the future.

### Coaching procedure—application practices

13. " Application " means that a man tries to fire a group with the MPI in the middle of the target, so that all the shots go into his expected scoring area and he gets the best score that he is capable of getting.

14. Before the practice, the man should be allowed to fire two sighting shots, which do not count in his score; their purpose is to let him find the right sighting and point of aim, without wasting scoring shots; if they are used intelligently, he is more likely to get a good score.

15. Before he fires his first sighter, decide what range he should set his sights at, and what his point of aim should be; consider where the MPI of his group was at 100 yards, how he did in any previous application practices, and what the wind and light are like.

16. See that he fires both sighters carefully, and without altering his sights or point of aim, or you cannot judge where the MPI is forming. Provided that both shots are good ones, take the MPI as half way between them, and decide whether to advise the man to alter his sights or point of aim in order to get the MPI into the middle of the target. The real position of the MPI becomes clearer as he fires each scoring shot; watch its movement carefully, and advise him accordingly. Do not advise any alteration:—

> (a) From a shot that the firer declared to be a bad one, or that you noticed anything wrong with.

> (b) From the MPI of his sighters, or from a scoring shot, if it is inside his expected scoring area.

> (c) From one shot only; except that, if one sighter is a miss, it is usually sound to halve the distance between the other shot, if it is outside his expected scoring area, and the middle of the target, and advise the man to alter his sights or point of aim to correct that amount.

17. Otherwise coaching is the same as for a grouping practice, except that you record in the firer's AB 142, or on a representative target, the position of each shot as the marker signals it, and you do not go forward to look at the targets. At the end of the shoot, discuss the man's shooting with him, and prepare him for the time when he has to shoot without a coach.

## Coaching procedure—snap and rapid practices

18. Snap and rapid practices usually follow an application practice, so that you know how a man should set his sights and where he should aim. If a snap or rapid practice is the first of the day, two sighting shots should be allowed first.

19. Most men fire low when firing quickly, and it is as well to advise them to put their sights up an extra 50 yards.

20. Kneel behind the man's right shoulder; watch the strike, and give quick advice, such as " Go right one foot " or " Steady—don't rush it " It is in the discussion afterwards that you can help the man most.

## Shortage of coaches

21. If there are not enough coaches, divide the men into pairs, as masters and pupils; one experienced coach can supervise several pairs. See that the masters know the firers' expected scoring areas, and tell them their duties, which are:—

> (a) To make a note of the firers' declarations, and to plot the shots on their score cards.

*(b)* To watch the strike and give corrections in snap and rapid practices.

*(c)* To let the coach know whenever a shot falls outside the expected scoring area.

*(d)* To watch for possible causes of bad shooting, and tell the coach anything they notice.

Keep a general eye on things yourself, and give advice when called. Under this system, men take more interest in shooting, and gradually learn the finer points of marksmanship.

### Conclusion

22. Coaching is an art; there are no fixed rules, but certain guiding principles. To be a good coach, you must first master the weapon yourself, and then get plenty of practice in range coaching.

23. No book can give you the answers to all the problems you will meet; you master the art by knowing the principles and by actual coaching experience. You must be persevering, patient and enthusiastic; and it is a help to be a good shot. Grouping is the foundation of all good shooting.

## SECTION 9.—FIRING WITH HARMONIZED SIGHTS

### Aim

1. To give NCOs practice at giving fire control orders, and men at recognizing targets and shooting at them.

### Stores

2. Rifles, ammunition, landscape target and screen (Fig 29), small replica of landscape target, binoculars, measuring rod 27 inches long, plumb line consisting of a small weight on a piece of string, scoring rectangles 5 inches by 4 inches and 2½ inches by 2 inches, patching materials, blackboard and chalk.

### Preparation of the rifles

3. Set the sights for harmonized firing (1,400 for No. 2 Rifles, " H " for No. 8 Rifles), and get skilled shots to fire at the aiming marks at the bottom of the sky screen, and go on altering the sights until they put at least two consecutive shots between the horizontal lines at the top; record the rifle numbers and sight settings on a board to be kept in the range, and do not allow any further adjustment of the sights.

4. Harmonized firing is also possible with No. 4, but not No. 5, Rifles on a 25 yards range; set the sights at 1,300; have your horizontal lines 23 and 25 inches above the bottom of the aiming mark; and use a measuring rod 24 inches long.

5. The reason for harmonized firing is to avoid damage to landscape targets.

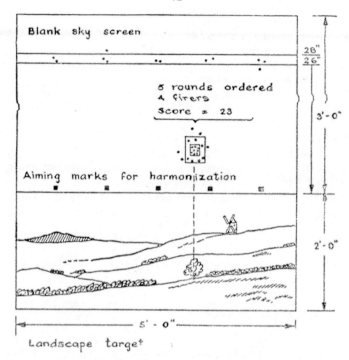

Fig 29.—Harmonized target screen

### Conduct of a shoot

6. Put the section in position, and get the section commander to *organize an arc of fire*. With a pin, point out the target to the section commander on the replica; he goes back to the section, and gives a fire control order; the section fires (two or three rounds are enough). Cover the sky screen, and get each man to show you where he aimed.

7. To assess fire effect, hold the measuring rod vertically (check with the plumb line), with the bottom on the target. Make a mark on the screen at the top of the rod, and put the centre of the scoring rectangle on the mark; shots in the small rectangle count two, in the large rectangle one.

### SECTION 10.—THE TRAINING STICK

#### Introduction

1. Use the training stick (Fig 30) to speed up men's actions during bayonet training. Its value depends entirely on the instructor's speed and vigour.

2. When you are using a training stick, scabbards must always be on bayonets, and tied on with string.

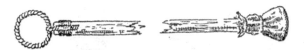

Fig 30.—The training stick

3. The pad represents the point of an enemy bayonet; when you come " on guard " with it, the recruit also comes " on guard ".

4. The ring represents any part of the enemy's body; when you present it, the recruit thrusts at it.

5. When you put the pad on the ground, the recruit advances past you.

**Thrusts**

6. Figs 31 and 32 show how to present the ring for a man to make a thrust on the left and on the right.

7. To make him do two thrusts, jump away from him as he withdraws after the first.

Fig 31.—Presenting the ring of the training stick for a thrust on the right

Fig 32.—Presenting the ring of the training stick for a thrust on the left

**Parries**

8. To exercise a man in self defence:—

   *(a)* Come " on guard ", with your pad just in front of the point of his bayonet.

   *(b)* When he is new to it, tell him which side the pad is coming in.

   *(c)* Thrust the stick forward hard with your right arm, but do not step in.

   *(d)* If the pad comes in on his right, the man parries, points his bayonet at you, thrusts without moving his feet, withdraws, and comes " on guard " again (see Fig 33).

   *(e)* If the pad comes in on his left, the man parries, and makes a butt stroke at an imaginary enemy (see Fig 34); then put the ring where the enemy would have fallen, and he makes a thrust at it, withdraws, comes " on guard " again, and advances. Do not put the pad where the man could hit it with his butt stroke.

   *(f)* Check and repeat as necessary.

Fig 33.—Training stick—right parry

Fig 34.—Training stick—butt stroke

## SECTION 11.—MINIATURE AND 25 YARDS RANGES

**General**

1. Miniature and 25 yards ranges are substitutes for the open range; they cannot replace it.

2. Infantry Training, Volume III, Pamphlet No. 33, 1952, WO Code No. 8713 contains details of targets and apparatus.

3. Infantry Training, Volume III, Pamphlet No. 31, 1948, WO Code No. 8399 contains details of safety precautions.

**Miniature ranges**

4. The chief advantages of a miniature range are:—
   *(a)* You can use it after dark and in all weathers.
   *(b)* It is easy to make, and most permanent barracks have one.
   *(c)* Recruits can practise shooting without using up ·303 ammunition, or growing gun-shy.

5. Its chief disadvantages are:—
   *(a)* Men do not fire their own rifles, nor get used to the " kick ".
   *(b)* They do not have to consider wind or light.

6. These are some of the things you can do on a miniature range:—
   *(a)* Rehearse practices before annual classification.
   *(b)* Shoot with harmonized sights (see Section 9).
   *(c)* Fire miniature range battle practices (see Infantry Training, Volume III, Pamphlet No. 33, 1952, WO Code No. 8713, Chapter 6).
   *(d)* Run competitions.
   *(e)* Practise men at holding, aiming and firing.

7. These practices are suitable for a miniature range:—
   *(a)* Grouping at a 200/25 representative target, with scores of 20, 18, 16 and 14 for one-, two- and three-inch, and three-inch and one wide, groups.
   *(b)* Application at a 200/25 representative target, with scores of 4, 3, 2 and 1 for bulls, inners, magpies and outers.
   *(c)* Snapshooting at figure targets, with exposures starting at seven seconds and gradually coming down to four. Allow two sighting shots at a representative target first. Give three points for each hit.
   *(d)* Aiming off, up and down at 200/25 representative targets, or figure targets against a white screen. Set the sights for a direct hit on the point of aim, and make the men fire two sighters to compare with their other shoots; to get a more accurate comparison, engrave the outlines of targets on talc, and put the centre of the talc target where the MPI should be if the firer has solved the problem correctly.

8. Coaches must spot with binoculars or telescopes from the firing point.

9. One click of the backsight moves the shot up or down $\frac{1}{4}$ inch.

10. Keep a board in the range with these figures recorded against each rifle number:—

(a) Sighting for a hit on the point of aim.

(b) Sighting for a hit ¾ inch above the point of aim.

(c) Sighting for harmonized shooting.

11. The No. 8 Rifle handbook (WO Code No. 10141) gives detailed information about the rifle.

**25 yards ranges**

12. A 25 yards range is usually available near barracks, and it has the advantage over a miniature range that men use their own rifles, and get used to them.

13. You can fire all miniature range practices, and it may be possible to have a bayonet assault course finishing on the firing point.

### SECTION 12.—STRENGTHENING, QUICKENING AND "SHOOT TO KILL" EXERCISES

1. This section gives examples, but you can vary the exercises as much as you like. *See* also Basic and Battle Physical Training, Part X, 1944, Shoot to Kill (WO Code No. 7209).

**Strengthening exercises**

2. Introduce them for the last five minutes of any lesson.

3. Exercise 1.—Holding

(a) The aim is to strengthen the muscles that men use to hold their rifles in the aim; practise it in all positions without cover.

(b) Start the exercise with the men in the aim, with actions cocked and safety catches forward. Words of command, and the men's actions on them, are:—

(i) " Right hand off "—they hold their right hands clear of their rifles.

(ii) " Change "—they take a normal two-handed hold of the rifle, and then hold the left hand clear.

(iii) " Both hands on "—they hold the rifle with both hands again. Do not repeat " Change " more than three times to start with. Give the orders slowly, to show that the movements should be slow and steady.

## 4. Exercise 2.—Handling

*(a)* The aim is to exercise men in coming quickly into the aiming position; practice it in all positions without cover.

*(b)* Words of command, and the men's actions on them are:—

   (i) " Without drill cartridges—load "—the men go through the action of loading, and test their positions.

   (ii) " 300 "—they set their sights.

   (iii) " Up "—they come smartly into the aiming position, take the first pressure, and aim.

   (iv) " Down "—they return to the loading position, with their forefingers along the trigger guard.

   Give the orders crisply, to show that the movements should be quick. Pause for about three seconds between " up " and " down ", and do not repeat more than six times to start with.

### Quickening exercises

5. Introduce them for the last five minutes of any lesson, or during a lesson, particularly a static one, when the men are getting sleepy.

## 6. Exercise 3.—Loader versus filler

*(a)* The aim is to exercise men in loading, reloading and filling chargers.

*(b)* Divide the men into pairs, one loader to one filler. Give the filler drill rounds and three chargers; he fills the chargers and hands them one at a time to the loader, who loads and re-loads as fast as he can. If the filler cannot keep the loader supplied, the loader shouts " Waiting ", and wins.

*(c)* Set a time limit of 90 seconds to start with, and gradually increase it to three minutes. See that the filler fills the chargers correctly.

## 7. Exercise 4.—Loading, taking cover and reloading in the shoulder

*(a)* The aim is to speed up men's movements.

*(b)* Line the men up ten yards from cover (a wall, bank, etc).

*(c)* Words of command, and the men's actions on them are:—

   (i) " Load "—they load with ten drill cartridges; the last man to finish loses a point.

   (ii) " Down "—the men double to cover, and get into proper positions to observe; the last man in a correct position loses a point.

   (iii) " 300 "—they set their sights, and shout " Set "; check their sights; the last man to finish loses a point, and anyone who sets his sights wrong loses two.

(iv) Indicate a target.

(v) " Fire "—they aim, try not to give their positions away,
and fire; no scoring.

(vi) " Reload "—they reload in the shoulder; take off one
point for a misload or slow movement.

(vii) Repeat " Fire " and " Reload " seven times; then order
" Unload ", or, if you mean to do the exercise again,
" Load "; and add up the scores.


## SECTION 13.—MASTER AND PUPIL

1. The master and pupil method of practice in its simplest form is for
one man (the pupil) to work under the supervision of another (the master);
the instructor keeps an eye on both.

2. At all stages of training it stimulates interest, keenness and attention
to detail, and is particularly useful with large squads and in competitions.
Used regularly, it also develops initiative and leadership, and you can spot
potential leaders by watching the masters at work.


## SECTION 14.—MECHANISM

**How the bolt works**

1. **Primary extraction.**—When you raise the bolt lever, the bolt turns,
and the stud on the cocking piece moves from the long cam groove at the
back of the bolt to the short, pulling the striker back about ⅛ inch; the lug
under the bolt moves down a sloped slot in the left side of the body of the
rifle, pulling back the bolt and the cartridge case about ⅛ inch.

2. **Extraction and ejection.**—When you pull back the bolt, the extractor
draws the cartridge case out of the chamber, pressing the other side of the
rim of the case against the body, and ejecting it. There is an ejector screw
in the left-hand side of the bolt way that helps to eject the case, if it has not
gone already. To eject the case cleanly, pull the bolt back sharply.

3. **The magazine spring.**—When the bolt head is clear of the rim of the
*top round in the magazine*, the magazine spring raises the round a little;
an auxiliary spring in the front of the magazine keeps the platform at the
right angle.

4. **Feeding the round.**—As you push the bolt forward again, the bottom
of the head catches the base of the top round, and pushes it into the chamber.

5. **The cocking piece.**—As the bolt goes forward, the full bent of the cocking piece meets the nose of the sear, which stops the cocking piece and striker from going any further forward; the bolt goes on forward, and compresses the main spring inside it (see Fig 35).

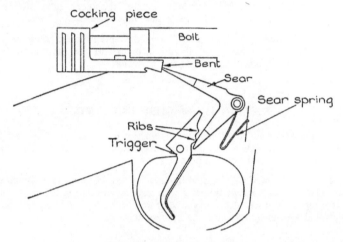

Fig 35.—The action cocked

6. **The locking action.**—When you turn the bolt lever down, the rib on the bolt slides over the resisting shoulder on the right of the body, and the lug on the bolt slides into the sloped slot in the left of the body; this finally closes and locks the breech (see Fig 36).

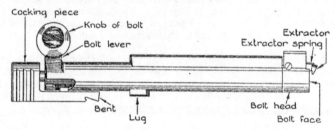

Fig 36.—The bolt

7. **The trigger.**—When you fire, the two ribs of the trigger bear one after the other on the lower arm of the sear, producing two pressures; the first brings the nose of the sear to the bottom of the full bent of the cocking piece; the second releases the cocking piece (see Fig 37).

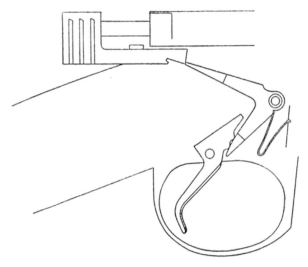

First Pressure

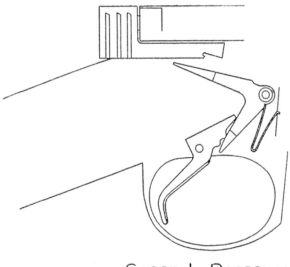

Second Pressure

Fig 37.—How the trigger works

8. The shock of discharge goes equally to both sides of the body, on the right through the rib of the bolt to the resisting shoulder, on the left through the bolt lug to the back wall of the sloped slot.

9. The safety catch:—

(a) When the action is cocked, and you apply the safety catch, the locking bolt rotates, slips into the forward recess of the cocking piece, and moves the bent back from the nose of the sear; and the locking pin slips into the short cam groove.

(b) When you apply the safety catch with the action forward, the locking bolt slips into the back recess, and the locking pin into the short cam groove.

(c) When the safety catch is applied, you cannot move the cocking piece or the bolt at all.

(d) Before you apply the safety catch, make sure the bolt lever is right down.

10. Half cock (see Fig 38).—You can get half cock in two ways:—

(a) If you fire when the bolt lever is not right down, the stud on the cocking piece may hit the rounded corner of the stud between the two grooves of the bolt, turn the bolt to the right, and close the breech: or it may hit the stud square, and hold back the striker; if you then turn the bolt lever right down, the nose of the sear slips into the half bent, the cocking piece stud slides half way down the long groove, and you cannot fire or open the breech until you have pulled the cocking piece right back again.

(b) If the action is cocked, and the safety catch not right forward, the locking bolt partly engages the forward locking recess, and the cocking piece is forced back a little; if you fire, the nose of the sear pushes back the cocking piece and slips under the full bent, and the mainspring sends the cocking piece a little forward; if you then push the safety catch forward, the cocking piece goes forward, and the half bent catches the nose of the sear. If you apply the safety catch properly before pushing it forward, you do not get a half cock. The remedy is to pull the cocking piece right back again.

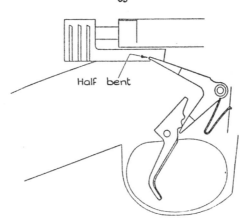

Fig 38.—Half cock

11. Safety devices:—

(a) If a blow back or burst case causes too much pressure in the barrel, the gas gets away through the gas escapes.

(b) The two studs on the bolt and cocking piece, and half cock, make it impossible to fire a shot when the breech is not properly closed.

SECTION 15.—DEMONSTRATION OF WEAPONS

1. Early in their training, to give them confidence in their weapons and to set them a standard to aim at, it is a good thing to show recruits what the weapons can do in the hands of trained men.

2. To save time, demonstrate the rifle, LMG and sub-machine gun, and a bit of theory, on a classification range. As a last resort you can demonstrate the weapons, but not theory, on a 25-yards range.

3. Arrange the demonstration with great care, so that everything goes like clockwork, and the men are impressed; the main things to remember are:—

(a) Layout.—The spectators must be able to see everything.

(b) Rehearsals must be thorough, or the demonstration may fail to give the men confidence in the weapons.

(c) The demonstrators should sight their weapons just before the demonstration.

(d) Safety precautions must be in accordance with the regulations.

4. The things to demonstrate, with suitable commentaries, are:—

(a) Rifle (at 200 yards):

(i) Five rounds at the slow rate.

    (ii) Five rounds snap, with four-second exposures.

    (iii) Fifteen rounds rapid in a minute.

    (iv) The most skilful instructor firing as fast as he can; it must be at least 20 rounds in a minute.

*b)* **LMG** (at 200 yards):—

    (i) Single rounds, two magazines in a minute.

    (ii) Bursts at the slow rate, one magazine in a minute.

    (iii) Rapid fire, four magazines in a minute.

*(c)* A section firing rapid for 30 seconds at a group of falling plates.

*(d)* Sub-machine gun:—

    (i) Five single rounds from the shoulder at 25 yards at different targets.

    (ii) 10 rounds fired in bursts from the waist at two Figure 11 targets, as the firer advances from 10 to 5 yards.

*(e)* **Theory** (with tracer):—

    (i) Trajectory at 600 and 400 yards.

    (ii) Fire a full LMG magazine from a tripod in one burst at a six-foot target at 300 yards, to show the cone of fire.

    (iii) To show the effect of sight elevation, get a man to fire at a target 600 yards away and then at one 300 yards away, both with sights set at 600, and then at the 300 yards target again with his sights at 300.

    (iv) Get someone to fire at a target 600 yards away, first not making, then making, allowance for the wind.

    (v) Get a LMG to engage a piece of flat ground, and then a piece of sloping ground, to show the difference in the size of the beaten zones, and why you have to make bold alterations in elevation when firing at targets on slopes.

    (vi) Get a LMG to fire from its tripod at a target at 600 yards, with flat, level ground between gun and target, to demonstrate the dangerous space and dangerous zone. Put figure targets at intervals along the dangerous zone.

5. At the end of the demonstration, answer questions, if there are not too many spectators, or split the spectators into syndicates to discuss the demonstration under NCOs.

6. For details about how to organize a demonstration see Training for War, WO Code No. 8508, Appendix C.


## SECTION 16.—USING A SLING

1. After his recruit training a soldier is allowed to use a sling to help him to hold his rifle steady. The sling must be the normal one, and attached to the rifle at the normal sling swivels.

2. Leave the sling as long as possible; hold the rifle with your right hand, and put your left hand through the loop; pass your left hand back under the front of the sling, and grip the rifle about the point of balance; pull the rifle back a bit with your left hand, hitch the sling well up your left upper arm, and aim (see Fig 39). Adjust the sling, until it is comfortable.

Fig 39.—How to use a sling

## SECTION 17.—TRAINING TESTS

**Aim**

1. To find out what standard of training men have reached.

**Dress**

2. Battle order.

**Notes**

3. Grade men as follows:—

| | |
|---|---|
| Skilled ... ... | 90-100 marks |
| Above average ... | 80- 89 marks |
| Average ... | 60- 79 marks |
| Below average ... | 50- 59 marks |
| Failed ... ... | Less than 50 marks. |

4. Recruits should achieve at least " average " at the end of their basic training; trained men who cannot do better than " average " need more instruction. When a man is transferred, always tell his new unit his grading.

5. Before testing a man, explain the test to him, and let him ask questions if he does not understand; once the test begins, do not help him any more. Always tell him the result of the test, and where he went wrong.

6. Appendix A gives the tests in detail.

## TRAINING TESTS—Appendix A

| Test No. | Subject | Stores | Conditions | Marking |
|----------|---------|--------|------------|---------|
| (a) | (b) | (c) | (d) | (e) |
| 1 | Loading | Drill rounds. in chargers. Watch. | On the command "Load", the man loads with ten rounds. Take the time from "load", until he has loaded, applied his safety catch, done up his pouch, and got his right hand back on the small of the butt. | 18 seconds—10<br>20 seconds— 8<br>24 seconds— 5<br>Over 24 seconds—NIL<br>Take off a mark for every mistake.    HPS—10 |
| 2 | Charging magazines | Drill rounds. Watch. | On the command "Standing—charge magazines", the man charges his magazine with ten rounds. Take the time from "magazines", until he has charged his magazine, applied his safety catch, done up his pouch, and got his right hand back onto the small of the butt. | 16 seconds—10<br>18 seconds— 8<br>22 seconds— 5<br>Over 22 seconds—NIL<br>Take off a mark for every mistake.    HPS—10 |
| 3 | Wind and elevation tables | Targets to suit the problems. | Set the man four problems on the practical use of the tables; one must be on aiming off and up or down together. Make the man point out on the target where he would have aimed. | Each correct answer—2½<br>Take off something for every mistake.    HPS—10 |

| | | | | |
|---|---|---|---|---|
| 4 | Loading with a fresh charger | Drill rounds in chargers. Watch. | The man lies down, in the aim, with rifle cocked, and a charger of five rounds in his pouch. On the command "Fire", he fires, loads with five rounds, and fires again. Take the time from "fire", until he has the butt back in the shoulder, and has taken the first pressure. | 6 seconds—10<br>8 seconds— 8<br>12 seconds— 5<br>Over 12 seconds—NIL<br>Take off a mark for every mistake.     HPS—10 |
| 5 | Firing | Watch. Aim corrector. Drill rounds. 200/25 representative targets. | The man tests his position, limbers up and sets his sights. On the command "Fire", he fires five rounds at the target. Time limit one minute from "Fire". | For each well aimed shot, correctly declared—1.<br>Take off ½ mark for every mistake.     HPS—10 |
| 6 | Snapshooting | Watch. Eye disc. | The man lies down, with sights set and rifle cocked (NO drill cartridges). Put the eye disc to your eye for four seconds, five times; he fires a shot each time. If his foresight remains steady, assume that the shot is a good one. | For each good shot—2.<br>Take off a mark for every mistake.     HPS—10 |
| 7 | Rapid fire | As for Test 5. | The man tests his position, limbers up, loads with five rounds, sets his sights, and aims. On the command "Rapid—fire", he fires five rounds at the target, reloads with a charger of five rounds from his pouch, and fires five more rounds. Time limit 40 seconds from "Fire". | For each good shot—1.<br>Take off one mark for every mistake, and for each round unfired at the end of 40 seconds.     HPS—10 |

## TRAINING TESTS—Appendix A—*continued*

| Test No. | Subject | Stores | Conditions | Marking |
|---|---|---|---|---|
| (a) | (b) | (c) | (d) | (e) |
| 8 | Firing from cover | Drill rounds. | Choose suitable ground, and test the man with two sorts of cover. Order "Advance—down", give a fire control order, and order "Fire—stop—prepare to advance—advance". | Take off one mark for every mistake.<br><br>HPS—10 |
| 9 | Grouping | 5 rounds ·303 ball. Cover (for recruits only). | To be fired at 100 yards, if possible, or, failing that, 25 yards. Recruits only may rest their fore-arms. | 4-inch/1-inch group—20<br>8-inch/2-inch group—18<br>12-inch/3-inch group—16<br>12-inch/3-inch group with one shot wide—14<br>HPS—20 |

4225  Wt 49277/8361  180M 4/55  B&M Ltd.  Gp 531

WO
CODE No.

8890

26/GS Trg Publications/2111

# Infantry Training

## Volume I

### INFANTRY PLATOON WEAPONS

### PAMPHLET No. 2

## FIELDCRAFT

### (ALL ARMS)

## 1954

(This pamphlet supersedes Infantry Training, Volume I, Infantry Platoon
Weapons, Pamphlet No. 2, Fieldcraft (All Arms) 1948 (WO Code No. 8382)).

*By Command of the Army Council.*

*G. W. Turner.*

THE WAR OFFICE,
1st November, 1954.

## AMENDMENTS

| Amendment Number | By whom amended | Date of insertion |
|---|---|---|
| *1* | *[signature]* | *15·11·61.* |
| *3* | *W Gibbs* | *Feb 62* |
| *2* | *H. Gloom* | *12 Mar 62* |
| | | |
| | | |
| | | |

### Distribution
*(See Catalogue of War Office Publications, Part II)*

| | | | | | | | | |
|---|---|---|---|---|---|---|---|---|
| Infantry | ... | ... | ... | ... | ... | ... | ... | Scale F |
| RASC | ... | ... | ... | ... | ... | ... | ... | Scale D |
| Other arms... | ... | ... | ... | | | | | Scale C |
| School of Infantry | | | | – | | | | 250 copies |

### Films

Visual Training, Part I — C 984 " Why things are seen ".
"   "   Part II — C 985 " How to see ".
"   "   Part III — C 986 " How to observe ".
"   "   Part IV — C 987 " What does the enemy see? " (Ground View).
"   "   Part V — C 988 " What does the enemy see? " (Air View).

C 1009 " Dangerous journey ".
C 475 " Movement ".
C 476 " Fieldcraft ".
C 444 " Use of fire ".

### Film strips

FS No. 807 " Map reading ", Part VII.
FS No. 581 " Scanning, searching and visual memory ".

### Posters

WO Code No. 7107, No. 2, " Cut out aids to visual training ".

,,   ,,   ,,   7108, No. 3, " Points of view (ground) ".

,,   ,,   ,,   7109, No. 4, " Methods of scanning ".

,,   ,,   ,,   7111, No. 6, " Points of view (air) ".

## CONTENTS

|  |  | *Page* |
|---|---|---|
| INTRODUCTION | ... ... ... ... ... ... ... | 1 |

### CHAPTER 1.—INSTRUCTIONAL LESSONS

| | | |
|---|---|---|
| Lesson 1. | —Visual training—introduction ... ... ... ... | 3 |
| Lesson 2. | —Judging distance—unit of measure ... ... ... | 4 |
| Lesson 3. | —Judging distance—appearance method ... ... | 5 |
| Lesson 4. | —Elementary observation ... ... ... ... | 7 |
| Lesson 5. | —Recognition of targets ... ... ... ... ... | 8 |
| Practice 1. | —Indication of targets ... ... ... ... ... | 10 |
| Lesson 6. | —Personal camouflage and concealment ... ... | 11 |
| Practice 2. | —Concealment and camouflage ... ... ... ... | 19 |
| Lesson 7. | —Moving with and without rifles ... ... ... | 19 |
| Lesson 8. | —Moving with LMGs ... ... ... ... ... | 24 |
| Lesson 9. | —Aids to judging distance ... ... ... ... | 29 |
| Practice 3. | —Movement and observation ... ... ... ... | 30 |
| Lesson 10. | —Locating the enemy ... ... ... ... ... | 30 |

(iv)

## LIST OF FIGURES

Figure  1.   —The direct method   ...   ...   ...   ...   ...   9
Figure  2.   —Example of the clock ray method in use   ...   ...   10
Figure  3.   —Personal camouflage   ...   ...   ...   ...   ...   13
Figure  4.   —Camouflaging the steel helmet ...   ...   ...   ...   14
Figure  5.   —Looking through or round, not over cover   ...   ...   14
Figure  6.   —Looking over cover, without breaking a straight line...   15
Figure  7.   —Avoiding a skyline   ...   ...   ...   ...   ...   15
Figure  8.   —Use of shadow   ...   ...   ...   ...   ...   ...   16
Figure  9.   —Background   ...   ...   ...   ...   ...   ...   17
Figure 10.   —Avoiding isolated cover   ...   ...   ...   ...   18
Figure 11.   —The monkey run, with and without a rifle   ...   ...   21
Figure 12.   —The leopard crawl, with and without a rifle ...   ...   22
Figure 13.   —The roll, with and without a rifle   ...   ...   ...   23
Figure 14.   —The walk   ...   ...   ...   ...   ...   ...   24
Figure 15.   —The leopard crawl with a LMG   ...   ...   ...   25
Figure 16.   —The side crawl with a LMG   ...   ...   ...   ...   26
Figure 17.   —The knee crawl with a LMG   ...   ...   ...   ...   27
Figure 18.   —The combined leopard crawl with a LMG   ...   ...   28
Figure 19.   —The combined leopard crawl (second method)   ...   28

## ABBREVIATIONS

LMG  = Light machine gun
NCO  = Non commissioned officer
OP   = Observation post
SAA  = Small arms ammunition

# INFANTRY TRAINING

Volume I

INFANTRY PLATOON WEAPONS

PAMPHLET No. 2

# FIELDCRAFT

(All Arms)

## 1954

### INTRODUCTION

Aim of weapon training

1. The aim of all weapon training is to produce soldiers who can kill the enemy in battle with any platoon weapon.

Achievement of the aim

2. To achieve this aim, men must reach a high standard of markmanship, servicing and fieldcraft with all the weapons, and they must be able to work together as teams under good junior leaders.

3. Markmanship and servicing are no good by themselves; a man must also be expert at fieldcraft; he must be able to:—

   (a) Use his eyes and ears to find the enemy, without being seen himself.

   (b) Make the best use of ground and cover.

   (c) Judge distances accurately.

   (d) Indicate and recognize targets, obey fire control orders, and understand fire discipline.

   (e) Act as a sentry in a forward area, and know exactly what he is responsible for.

   (f) Move silently, with or without weapons, stores or equipment.

   (g) Act aggressively on his own, out of sight and earshot of his comrades.

   (h) Be alert, confident and cunning whatever happens.

4. A skilled man without the " guts " to do his job in battle is useless. Soldiers need to be tough, physically and morally; but the training—assault courses, route marches, long exercises and so on—must work up gradually; the men will reach the required standard quicker, if they come successfully through a series of tests that are easy to start with, and gradually get harder, than if they are suddenly made to try something that is too much for them.

5. Individual fieldcraft training is an excellent way of developing character; and if promising soldiers are allowed to lead teams in fieldcraft exercises, and act as assistant instructors and umpires, they will learn a lot about leadership. Instructors can do more in peace time for morale in war, by developing men's characters and training them to lead, than in any other way.

## The place of fieldcraft in the training syllabus

6. *Fieldcraft is an integral part of weapon training.* Unless a man learns markmanship and servicing (technical handling), and fieldcraft (battle handling), at the same time, his progress towards becoming a fighting soldier suffers.

7. The first lesson in fieldcraft, Visual Training—Introduction, should come soon after a man has started on the rifle; and thereafter he should learn weapon and fieldcraft lessons side by side.

## The aim of the pamphlet

8. This pamphlet contains the material that an instructor needs to teach recruits individual fieldcraft.

## Layout

9. The pamphlet is in two chapters:—

(a) Chapter 1 contains the lessons that recruits must learn, and practice periods to drive home the skills and techniques that they have learnt.

(b) Chapter 2 contains more information, to help instructors to understand the subject and its presentation better.

10. Two forms of printing are used:—

(a) Portions in ordinary *type are notes* for instructors.

(b) Portions in *italics* are what instructors should teach recruits.

## Method of instruction

11. The way *to teach* fieldcraft is to give the recruits demonstrations, including films, and explain to them what they are seeing, and then as soon as possible make them practice what they have seen.

## Lesson plans

12. For the benefit of instructors who lack the experience or the time to devise their own lessons, most of the lessons are fairly detailed.

13. The lessons are designed for average recruits introduced to the subject for the first time; they may prove unsuitable for many reasons, of which the most important are the intelligence and knowledge of the recruits, and the time and training facilities available.

14. Instructors should study Successful Instruction, 1951 (WO Code No. 8670), and deviate from the exact form of the lessons as much as circumstances dictate. Best of all, they should produce their own lesson plans, and be allowed to refer to them during the lessons.

**Demonstrations**

15. Demonstrations must be carefully prepared and rehearsed, whether they are on a big scale, or just the instructor showing his squad how to crawl. Poor demonstrations are of little value.

**Length of periods**

16. Fieldcraft does not lend itself to strict 40 minute periods. Some lessons and practices need far longer, and others are best combined into a day and night exercise.

## CHAPTER 1.—INSTRUCTIONAL LESSONS

### LESSON 1.—VISUAL TRAINING—INTRODUCTION

AIM

1. To introduce visual training, and to teach why things are seen.

STORES

2. Visual Training Film, Part I, " Why things are seen ", B/C 984 (10 minutes).

3. If the film is not available, give an indoor or outdoor demonstration.

APPROACH

4. Explain:—
   (a) *Visual training is training in observation and concealment.*
   (b) *To OBSERVE is to see through the enemy's CONCEALMENT; to CONCEAL yourself is to defeat his OBSERVATION. Once you are trained in both, you can find and kill the enemy without being seen.*
   (c) *You can find out a lot about the enemy by watching him; by concealing yourself you can deceive him, and, if he attacks, you can meet him with short range fire from where he least expects it.*
   (d) *The important things are:—*
   *See without being seen.*
   *Notice details.*
   *Learn to understand the meaning of what you see, and make the right deductions.*

DEMONSTRATION

5. Introduce the film or demonstration.

6. Explain, as a commentary on the film or demonstration.—*These are the things that make any object visible:*—

(a) *Shape.*—*You can recognize some things instantly by their shape, particularly if it contrasts with the surroundings. If you want to hide, three of the distinctive shapes to disguise are the smooth, round top of your steel helmet, the hard line of its brim, and the square outline of your pack.*

(b) *Shadow.*—*In sunlight an object may cast a shadow that gives it away. Always keep in shade, if you can; the shade itself affords cover, and there is no tell-tale shadow. Remember that as the sun moves, so do the shadows.*

(c) *Silhouette.*—*Anything silhouetted against a contrasting background is conspicuous. Any smooth, flat background, like water, a field or worst of all, the sky, is dangerous. Always try to put yourself against an uneven background, such as a hedge, trees, a bush, or broken ground. A thing may be silhouetted if it is against a background of another colour.*

(d) *Surface.*—*If anything has a surface that contrasts with its surroundings, it is conspicuous. Shiny helmets and white skin contrast violently with most backgrounds, and need disguising.*

(e) *Spacing.*—*In nature things are never regularly spaced. Regular spacing means man-made objects.*

(f) *Movement.*—*Nothing catches the eye quicker than sudden movement. However well you are concealed, you will give yourself away when you move, unless you are careful.*

CONCLUSION

7. Questions from and to the class about the demonstration or film.

8. Repeat the things that make objects easy to see (para 6).

### LESSON 2.—JUDGING DISTANCE—UNIT OF MEASURE

AIM

1. To teach recruits how to judge by unit of measure.

STORES

2. Four large and twelve small flags, signal flag, whistle and rangecards.

NOTES

3. Put out the large flags 100 yards from a central view point, so that they can be seen across different types of ground, rising, falling or flat, and open or broken.

4. Choose a number of objects up to 400 yards from the view point, and lay a small flag every 100 yards between view point and objects, but so that the men cannot see them from the view point. Distances must be accurate.

5. When the men have judged a range, always make them set their sights at it; they get practice in sight setting, and they are not influenced by other men's answers.

## APPROACH

6. *It is important to be able to judge distances right, so that fire may be fully effective, and observers' reports accurate on this point.*

7. *There are several ways to judge distance; this lesson deals with a way known as the " unit of measure ".*

## THE UNIT OF MEASURE

8. Explain:—
- *(a) Take 100 yards as your unit, and see how many units you can fit in between yourself and the object.*
- *(b) This method is no good unless you can see all the ground between yourself and the object, nor for distances over 400 yards.*

9. Get the men to look at the large flags from all firing positions, and try to remember what 100 yards looks like. Show them how difficult it is, if there is any dead ground between them and the object.

10. For practice, make the men put themselves 100 yards from a given object. Discuss each man's error with him, and go on until the men get consistent results. Some men may consistently over-estimate or under-estimate; they must remember this when fitting in their 100 yard units.

11. Get the men to judge the distance to the objects that you chose before the lesson, and to show you how they fitted in their units. Then get someone to put up the small, 100 yards flags, and discuss the men's results with them.

## CONCLUSION

12. Questions from and to the squad.

13. Sum up.

## LESSON 3.—JUDGING DISTANCE—APPEARANCE METHOD

### AIM

1. To teach recruits how to judge distances by the appearance method.

### STORES

2. Rifles, signal flags, a̶l̶i̶g̶n̶i̶n̶g̶ ̶p̶o̶s̶t̶s, range cards.

*POINTER STAFFS*

NOTES

3. Before the lesson starts, station men (or Figure 10 targets) up to 600 yards away, and choose or put out other things—trees, bushes, vehicles, etc—up to 1,000 yards; and measure the distance to each.

4. If a classification range is available, put the objects on, or in line with, the firing points.

PRELIMINARIES

5. Safety precautions.

6. Revise ' Unit of measure ' (Lesson 2).

APPROACH

7. *Another way to judge the distance to an object is to study what it looks like compared with its surroundings; this is called the appearance method. It takes a lot of practice, under varying conditions, to become good at it.*

CONDITIONS THAT AFFECT APPEARANCE

8. *Things seem closer than they are, when:—*
   *(a) The light is bright, or the sun is shining from behind you.*
   *(b) They are bigger than other things around them.*
   *(c) There is dead ground between them and you.*
   *(d) They are higher up than you are.*

9. *Things seem farther away than they are, when:—*
   *(a) The light is bad, or the sun is in your eyes.*
   *(b) They are smaller than other things around them.*
   *(c) You are looking across a valley, or down a street, or a ride in a wood.*
   *(d) You are lying down.*

10. Question the squad.

DEMONSTRATION

11. Show the squad what men look like up to 600 yards away, and what other things look like up to 1,000 yards away; point out how the prevailing conditions affect their appearance.

PRACTICE

12. Make the squad judge the range to various men and objects. Set a time limit for each problem, and tell the men to set their sights at the estimated range.

CONCLUSION

13. Questions from and to the squad.

14. Sum up.

## LESSON 4.—ELEMENTARY OBSERVATION

AIM

1. To teach elementary observation.

STORES

2. Visual Training film, Part III, " How to observe ", B/C 986.

3. Bits of military equipment—boots, weapons, etc.

4. Visual Training Poster No. 4, " Methods of scanning " (WO Code No. 7109).

5. Rifles and ~~aiming tests~~. *POINTER STAFFS.*

NOTES

6. Choose a piece of ground with folds, bushes, trees, banks, hedges, etc. Make sure it can be divided into foreground, middle distance and distance.

7. Put out the bits of equipment (para 3), so that some are fairly easy to see, and some more difficult, and so that they provide varying degrees of contrast of colour, tone, surface, shape and shadow.

PRELIMINARIES

8. Question the men on why things are seen (Lesson 1).

HOW TO SEARCH

9. Explain the aim of the lesson. Show the film.

10. If the film is not available, explain.—*The normal way to search ground is to divide it into foreground, middle distance and distance, and search each of them, in that order, from right to left. In that way you are sure that you do not leave out any of the ground; but there are other ways of dividing the ground up, which may sometimes be better, particularly if the ground is very broken.*

PRACTICE

11. Get the men to divide the ground into foreground, middle distance and distance. Discuss their answers with them.

12. Tell the men to search the area, and write down the bits of military equipment that they see.

13. Ask the men what they have seen, why some things were easier to see than others, and how they identified things of which they could only see part. If you are not sure that a man has seen the right thing, make him aim at it with ~~his rifle aiming instrument~~. *A POINTER STAFF*

CONCLUSION

14. Questions from and to the squad.

15. Show Visual Training Poster No. 4.

16. Sum up, and point out how observation and concealment are related.

## LESSON 5.—RECOGNITION OF TARGETS

AIM

1. To teach recruits how to recognize targets.

STORES   *POINTER STAFF*

2. Rifles and ~~aiming rests~~, range card, landscape targets, diagrams and blackboard.

NOTES

3. Recruits get false impressions about direction from landscape targets; so teach the lesson in the open if you can. If you have to use landscape targets, remember that:—

*(a)* It is impossible to judge distances.

*(b)* The landscape is so narrow that no target on it can be more than slightly left or right. Three adjoining landscape panels give better results, if the men are not more than ten yards away from them.

4. Choose your ground carefully, and pick the sort of target that men might have to recognize in battle, and at realistic ranges.

5. Have a diagram of the clock ray to use on the landscape target; the best sort of diagram is black figures on talc.

6. The sequence for instruction in recognition is:—

*(a)* Indicate the target.

*(b)* Order " Aim ".

*(c)* Check the aims, and discuss them.

7. Examples are given, but is it always better to choose your own examples on the ground.

PRELIMINARIES

8. Safety precautions. ~~Rifles in aiming rests~~. *ISSUE POINTER STAFF*

APPROACH

9. *When your section commander indicates a target, you must be able to recognize it, so that you can shoot at it. To make it easier, there are certain methods of indication that everyone uses.*

ARCS OF FIRE

10. Explain and demonstrate.—*It is easier to recognize a target if you know the area in which it is likely to be; such an area is known as an arc of fire. When your section commander shows you the arc of fire, he:—*

*(a)* *Points out the axis, or middle, of the arc.*

*(b)* *Shows you its left and right boundaries.*

*(c)* *Points out a number of prominent objects, or reference points, which must be easy to identify and a reasonable distance apart, gives each one a name, and tells you the range to it; and if any object is large, like a copse, tells you what bit of it he is using as the reference point.*

## METHODS OF INDICATION

11. *Direct method.*—Explain and demonstrate:—
   (*a*) *Obvious targets are indicated by what is known as the direct method.*
   (*b*) *The section commander tells you the range and where to look, and describes the target; the terms he uses are:*—
      (i) " *Axis of the arc* ", *for targets on or very near the axis.*
      (ii) " *Left* " *or* " *right* ", *for targets 90 degrees from the axis.*
      (iii) " *Slightly* ", " *quarter* ", " *half* " *or* " *three quarters* ", *and* " *left* " *or* " *right* ", *for targets between the axis and* " *left* " *or* " *right* ".*

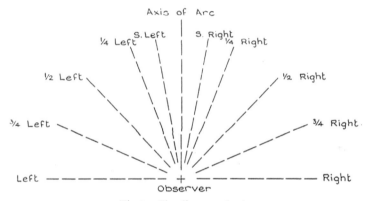

Fig 1.—The direct method.

   (*c*) *An example might be* " 300—*half right*—*lone bush* ".
12. *Reference points.*—Explain and demonstrate:—
   (*a*) *For less obvious targets, the section commander may use reference points and the direct method together, and perhaps* " *above* " *or* " *below* " *as well.*
   (*b*) *Examples are:*—
      (i) " 300—*bushy topped tree (the reference point)—slightly right—small bush (the target)* ".
      (ii) " 200—*corner of copse—slightly right and below—small bush*".

13. For practice, indicate some targets to the squad by the direct and reference point methods.

14. *Clock ray.*—Explain and demonstrate:—
   (*a*) *For more difficult targets, the section commander may use a reference point and a clock ray.*
   (*b*) *Imagine a clock face standing up on the landscape with its centre on the reference point.* If you have a talc clock face, put it against the landscape target.

*(c) To indicate a target, the section commander tells you the range, the reference point, and whether the target is to the right or left of it, and the appropriate hour on the clock face, to give you the direction to look in from the reference point.*

*(d) An example is " 300—windmill—right—4 o'clock—small bush ". (See Fig 2.)*

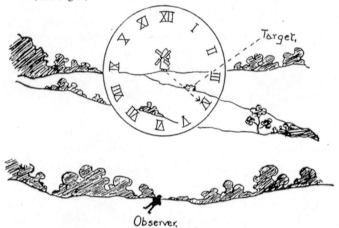

Fig 2.—Example of the clock ray method in use.

15. Give the squad some clock ray indications for practice.

16. Further practice in all methods, if there is time.

CONCLUSION

17. Questions from and to the squad.

18. Sum up.

## PRACTICE 1.—INDICATION OF TARGETS

AIM

1. To exercise recruits and, if necessary, NCOs and trained men in indicating and recognizing targets by the methods taught in Lesson 5.

STORES

2. Rifles, ~~aiming rests~~, range cards.
POINTER STAFF
NOTES

3. Keep to the indication of ·realistic targets; do not get involved in fire control orders.

4. Later periods give more practice in indicating targets.

PRELIMINARIES

5. Safety precautions. R̶i̶f̶l̶e̶ ̶a̶i̶m̶i̶n̶g̶-rests. *ISSUE POINTER STAFF*

6. Organize an arc of fire.

PRACTICE

7. Tell the men what method of indication they are to use, and give them an example. *AIM A POINTER STAFF AT*

8. Make the men turn their backs; l̶a̶y̶ ̶a̶ ̶r̶i̶f̶l̶e̶ ̶i̶n̶ ̶i̶t̶s̶ ̶a̶i̶m̶i̶n̶g̶ ̶r̶e̶s̶t̶ ̶o̶n̶ a suitable target; pick a man, and make him look along the sights and identify the target; k̶n̶o̶c̶k̶ ̶t̶h̶e̶ ̶r̶i̶f̶l̶e̶ ̶o̶f̶f̶ ̶a̶i̶m̶; and turn the men about. *POINTER STAF*

9. The chosen man indicates the target to the others, who aim their r̶i̶f̶l̶e̶s at it; check their aims.

10 Criticize the indication under these headings:—

    *(a)* Was the range about right?

    *(b)* Was the indication clear, sufficient, and as short as possible?

11. Repeat as often as is necessary for everyone to get practice. As time goes on, leave it to the men to decide what methods to use.

CONCLUSION

12. Questions from and to the squad.

13. Sum up, and comment on the standard reached.

## LESSON 6.—PERSONAL CAMOUFLAGE AND CONCEALMENT

AIM

1. To demonstrate and practise personal camouflage and concealment.

DRESS AND STORES

2. Battle order, helmet nets, scrim, camouflage cream, burnt cork and water. Improvised camouflage materials such as sacking, foliage and grass. Signal flag and whistle.

NOTES

3. Group several squads together for the demonstration, and use their NCOs as demonstrators.

4. Choose ground with all types of cover on it—hedgerow, wall, bushes, folds, banks, etc.

5. The demonstration will be most effective, if you can rehearse it immediately before you give it.

6. Figs 3—10 illustrate the sort of situations to demonstrate; show the wrong way and the right in each case, and get the men to search the area where the demonstrators are.

7. It is possible to demonstrate and practise personal camouflage indoors, but not the rest of the lesson.

PRELIMINARIES

8. Safety precautions.

APPROACH

9. *You must know how to camouflage and conceal yourself in battle, or you will be an easy target for the enemy.*

DEMONSTRATION

10. Explain and demonstrate.—*The tone and colour of your hand, neck and face, and the shape, surface and silhouette of your helmet and pack, must not contrast with their backgrounds. To avoid these contrasts:—*
- (a) *Put camouflage cream, mud, burnt cork, or something similar on your face, neck and hands: put on more for night work than for day* (Fig 3).
- (b) *Put a hessian cover on your helmet to dull the shine, a net on top of that to hold scrim, etc, and garnishing in the net to disguise the helmet's distinctive shape, particularly the shadow under the brim* (Fig 4).
- (c) *Tie string across your pack, and use it to hold foliage, etc, to break up the pack's outline* (Fig 3).
- (d) *You may have to camouflage your weapon by binding scrim or hessian round shiny metal or wood parts; but be careful that none of it blocks your view over the sights.*

11. Divide the men into pairs, and make each pair practise personal camouflage as master and pupil, while the NCOs move to their places for the next part of the demonstration.

12. Explain and demonstrate:—
- (a) *Look round or through cover, rather than over it* (Fig 5); *if you have to look over it, try not to break a straight line* (Fig 6).
- (b) *Avoid skylines* (Fig 7).
- (c) *Use shadow, and remember that when you are in the sun, your own shadow is very conspicuous, and that shadows move with the sun* (Fig 8).
- (d) *Choose a background to match your clothes* (Fig 9).
- (e) *Avoid isolated cover; the enemy is likely to watch it, and it is easy to give a fire order onto* (Fig 10).
- (f) *Try not to be seen going into or leaving cover.*
- (g) *Move carefully.*

CONCLUSION

13. Sum up the demonstration.

14. Questions from and to the squad.

15. Stress these points again:—
- (a) *The aim of camouflage and concealment is to escape observation by the enemy.*
- (b) *If you want to kill without being killed, learn to see without being seen.*

Too much                    Too little                    Just right

For  daylight

Fig 3.—Personal camouflage.

Fig 4.—Camouflaging the steel helmet.

Fig 5.—Looking through or round, not over cover.

Fig 6.—Looking over cover, without breaking a straight line.

Fig 7.—Avoiding a skyline.

Fig 8.—Use of shadow.

Fig 9.—Background.

Fig 10.—Avoiding isolated cover.

## PRACTICE 2.— CONCEALMENT AND CAMOUFLAGE

AIM

1. To practise personal camouflage, concealment, searching and target indication.

DRESS AND STORES

2. Battle order, camouflage equipment, range cards.

NOTES

3. Choose a piece of ground with all sorts of cover on it. Make out an accurate range card to help you with the practice in target indication.

PRELIMINARIES

4. Safety precautions.

APPROACH

5. *Your lives may depend on your being able to see without being seen. You are now going to practice camouflage, concealment and observation.*

PRACTICE

6. Tell the men to camouflage themselves, working in pairs.

7. Divide the men into two teams; give the first team five minutes to conceal themselves in positions from which they can observe the second team; give them a piece of ground to work in, and tell them that their position must be between 50 and 100 yards away.

8. While the first team are getting into position, turn the second team about, and practise them in target indication. At the end of five minutes, get the second team to search the ground where the first team are concealed. When any of them spots a man of the first team, he should tell you and his team-mates, and say what it was that gave the man away.

9. If any members of the first team are not spotted after a reasonable time, signal to them to move about until they are.

10. Collect all the men together, discuss results, and repeat the practice with the teams changed round, and on different ground.

CONCLUSION

11. Questions from and to the squad.

12. Sum up what has been achieved.

## LESSON 7.—MOVING WITH AND WITHOUT RIFLES

AIM

1. To teach recruits how to move with and without rifles.

DRESS AND STORES

2. Battle order, rifles.

NOTES

3. You need a stretch of hard road for the men to practise walking silently on.

PRELIMINARIES

4. Safety precautions.

APPROACH

5. *You need to know how to move about in battle, and how to use ground, so that you can close with the enemy, and occupy and leave positions, without the enemy seeing you or being able to shoot at you.*

METHODS OF MOVEMENT

6.˙ Explain and demonstrate each method; then divide the men into pairs, and make them practise the method that they have just seen, as master and pupil, without equipment.

7. **The monkey run** (Fig 11):—

    *(a) It is simply crawling on hands and knees.*

    *(b) It is useful behind cover about two feet high.*

    *(c) You can go quite fast, but the faster you go, the more noise you make.*

    *(d) If you really want to be quiet, always choose a safe place (with no twigs to crack, etc) to put your hands, and then put your knees exactly where your hands have been.*

    *(e) Keep your backside and head down, but observe as you go.*

    *(f) If you have a rifle, hold it at the point of balance with your left hand, and see that no dirt gets into the muzzle.*

8. **The leopard crawl** (Fig 12):—

    *(a) It is crawling on elbows and the inside of the knees.*

    *(b) It is useful behind very low cover.*

    *(c) Propel yourself along by alternate elbows and knees, and roll your body a little as you bend each knee; or let one leg trail behind, and use only one knee. Keep your heels, head, body and elbows down, but observe as you go.*

    *(d) If you have a rifle, hold it either with your right hand on the small of the butt and your left hand at the point of balance, with the bolt uppermost, or by the front of the sling with your right hand, with the rifle rested on your right arm, and the muzzle forwards.*

Fig 11.—The monkey run, with and without a rifle.

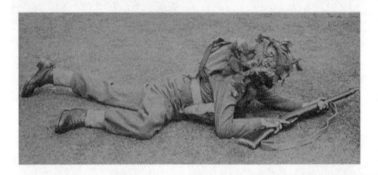

Fig 12.—The leopard crawl, with and without a rifle.

9. **The roll** (Fig 13):—

 (a) *It is often the quickest way of getting away from a spot, such as a crest line, where the enemy has seen you.*

 (b) *Roll with you arms, and your rifle, if you have one, close in to your side.*

Fig 13.—The roll, with and without a rifle.

10. **The walk** (Fig 14):—

    *(a) Hold your rifle so that you can use it instantly. Your whole attitude must be alert, with your head up so that you can observe*

    *(b) To be really quiet on hard ground, put the edge of the sole of your boot down first. To keep your balance, keep your knees slighty bent.*

Fig 14.—The walk.

11. Give the men more practice in all methods of moving, with equipment on.

CONCLUSION

    12. Questions from and to the squad.

    13. Sum up.

LESSON 8.—MOVING WITH LMGs

AIM

    1. To teach recruits how to move with LMGs.

STORES

2. LMGs with slings attached.

NOTES

3. When you demonstrate how two men can crawl with a gun, use a recruit as your assistant.

PRELIMINARIES

4. Safety precautions. Load guns.

APPROACH

5. *You move with an LMG much the same as you do with a rifle, and have to decide for yourself which crawl to use.*

6. *Only constant practice will make you good at it.*

METHODS OF MOVEMENT (ONE MAN ALONE)

7. Explain and demonstrate each method of movement; then divide the men into groups, and make them practise the method that they have just seen, as masters and pupils.

8. The leopard crawl (Fig 15):—
   (a) *The leopard crawl is very much the same as with a rifle.*
   (b) *Hold the small of the butt with your right hand, the folded bipod with your left.*

Fig 15.—The leopard crawl.

9. **The leopard crawl (second method).**—*Push the gun forward with both hands as far as you can; then use your knees, in the leopard crawl position, to move your body forward.*

10. **The side crawl (Fig 16):—**

    *(a) Lie on either side, hold the gun by its carrying handle with your upper hand, and rest the butt on your lower leg.*

    *(b) Use your upper foot and lower elbow to push you along.*

Fig 16.—The side crawl.

11. **The knee crawl (Fig 17):—**

    *(a) Use the knee crawl behind waist high cover.*

    *(b) Kneel on your right knee, with your right fist flat on the ground. Hold the gun with your left hand by the carrying handle; rest your thumb on your knee to take some of the weight of the gun off your arm.*

    *(c) To advance, move your left foot and right fist forwards together, and bring your right knee up to them, and so on.*

## METHODS OF MOVEMENT (IN PAIRS)

12. **The combined leopard crawl (Fig 18):—**

    *(a) The two men lie side by side, with No. 2 slightly in front; No. 1 holds the small of the butt with his left hand, No. 2 the bipod with his right. Keep the gun pointing forwards.*

    *(b) Both men leopard crawl as they would with rifles, but their inside legs and their outside legs must keep step.*

Fig 17.—The knee crawl.

13. **The combined leopard crawl (second method) (Fig 19):—**

   *(a) It is the same as the ordinary combined leopard crawl, except that the two men are level with each other, and they have the gun on its side, with the magazine to the front.*

   *(b) It takes longer to get the gun into action.*

14. **The combined leopard crawl by bounds.**—*It is the same as the ordinary combined leopard crawl, except that the men crawl forward as far as they can without letting go of the gun, and then lift the gun as far forward as they can, and so on.*

Fig 18.—The combined leopard crawl.

Fig. 19.—The combined leopard crawl (second method).

CONCLUSION

15. Questions from and to the squad.

16. Sum up.

## LESSON 9.—AIDS TO JUDGING DISTANCE

AIM

1. To teach and practise the use of aids to judging distance.

STORES

2. Rifles and range cards.

NOTES

3. All your ranges must be accurately measured.

4. One instructor can take several squads, while the others go out in front to illustrate the halving method.

5. Make the men practise in proper firing positions.

PRELIMINARIES

6. Safety precautions.

7. Revise judging distance by unit of measure and appearance (Lessons 2 and 3).

APPROACH

8. *You already know the two main ways of judging distance, but there are several other devices to help you.*

AIDS TO JUDGING DISTANCE

9. Explain and demonstrate each aid, and then make the men practise it.

10. **Halving.**—*Choose a point that you think is half way to your target; estimate the distance to that point, and double it.*

11. **Bracketing.**—*Say to yourself " The target could not be more than x yards, nor less than y yards, away "; add x to y and halve the result; the answer is the range. For instance, if x is 1,000 and y 600, the range is 800. The farther the target is away, the wider should be your bracket.*

12. **Key ranges.**—*If you know the range to any point in your arc, you can estimate the distance to other objects from it.*

13. **Unit average.**—*Get several men to judge a distance, and take the average of their answers.*

14. Practise the two methods and the aids, checking one against another.

CONCLUSION

15. Questions from and to the squad.

16. Sum up.

## PRACTICE 3.—MOVEMENT AND OBSERVATION

AIM

1. To give men practice in movement and observation.

DRESS AND STORES

2. Battle order. Rifles, flags, camouflage materials.

NOTES

3. The practice can be run as a competition.

4. Choose a course about 50 yards long, and divide it into four equal sections; mark the end of each section with a flag. The course should entail crawling on hands and knees, and on elbows and knees, and crossing a small gap. A skilful, agile man should be able to complete it in ten minutes without being seen. Give marks for each section that a man completes unseen; a suggestion is 2 for the first section, and 4, 6 and 8 for the other three.

PRELIMINARIES

5. Safety precautions and personal camouflage.

APPROACH

6. *The aim of this period is to give you realistic practice at moving and observing.*

CONDUCT OF THE PRACTICE

7. Paint a simple tactical picture, and point out the route and the flags, and that a NCO is observing from the last flag.

8. Explain the marking, how the competition will work, and the time limit.

9. Start the men off one by one at intervals. If a man is seen, tell him why, and let him try again. Men who succeed should stay near the last flag and observe.

CONCLUSION

10. Tell the men who has won.

11. Sum up the lessons learnt.

## LESSON 10.—LOCATING THE ENEMY

AIM

1. To accustom recruits to the sound of shots coming towards them, to teach them to locate the enemy by his fire, and to give them further practice in judging distances, and in recognizing and indicating targets.

DRESS AND STORES

2. Battle order. LMGs and tripods, rifles, SAA ball and tracer, thunderflashes.

# Other Books in the Series

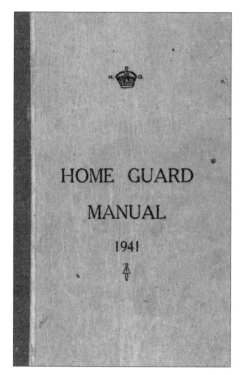

Home Guard
Manual 1941

ISBN: 978-0-7524-4471-0

It was May 1940, and Hitler stood on the cliffs at Calais and eyed up his next conquest: England! There was a call to arms that saw the founding of the Home Guard, a motley collection of men, poorly armed, many too old to fight in the war. The Home Guard was untried in war, often without weapons or training, and they were Britain's last-ditch defence against the Germans.

But all was not lost and, over the period of a few months, this rag-tag group was armed, uniformed and trained using the *Home Guard Manual*. Taught basic fieldcraft, how to survive in the open, how to destroy tanks, ambush the invaders, use weapons of varying sorts, make boobytraps, read maps and send signals, the fledgling volunteer was turned into a veritable fighting machine… or was he just another member of 'Dad's Army'? Read the manual and find out.

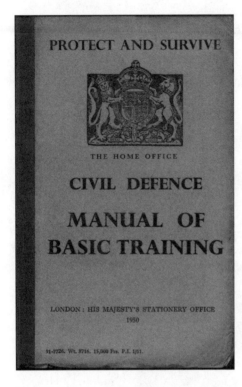

PROTECT AND SURVIVE

THE HOME OFFICE

CIVIL DEFENCE

MANUAL OF
BASIC TRAINING

LONDON : HIS MAJESTY'S STATIONERY OFFICE
1950

91-7726. Wt. 8716. 15,000 Prs. P.I. 1/51.

Protect and
Survive: The Civil
Defence Manual
of Basic Training

ISBN: 978-0-7524-4422-2

The end of the Second World War heralded the start of a new war. It was a war in name only, fought out by the superpowers through propaganda, and using smaller nations as pawns in the military build-up that became known as the Cold War. New and chilling phrases entered the vocabulary - mutually assured destruction, nuclear proliferation, hydrogen bomb, airburst and fallout. The UK Government, like that of many other nations, considered the effects on the population at large. Plans were drawn up, secret nuclear bunkers built and a new civil defence network created to counter the threat of all-out nuclear war.

Manuals were issued to those in the know and the civilian populace became used to the sounds of nuclear air-raid warning sirens being tested, of adverts informing them how to convert their house into a shelter, what to do with dead bodies, how to counteract radiation sickness, etc.

The government also issued a whole series of pamphlets and educational films for the masses. Out of these has come Protect & Survive - The Civil Defence Manual, which brings together, for the first time, the Government's own pamphlets for Civil Defence volunteers and the populace at large.

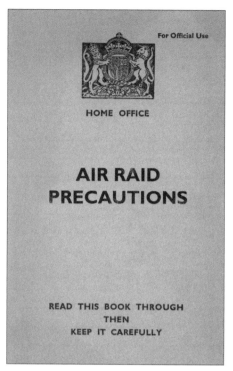

For Official Use

HOME OFFICE

# AIR RAID
# PRECAUTIONS

READ THIS BOOK THROUGH
THEN
KEEP IT CAREFULLY

Air Raid
Precautions

ISBN: 978-0-7524-4470-3

During the late 1930s it was finally realised that war with Hitler's Germany was a major possibility. As the armed forces began their re-arming, the Home Front was not neglected. In the intervening twenty years since the end of the First World War, war had changed for the worst. Aircraft had progressed and had become potent fighting machines, capable of flying huge distances with large payloads of bombs. The realities of 'Total War' and of the 'Blitz' were almost upon Britain and Air Raid Precautions was sent out to almost every home in the land. Filled with useful advice, much of which was to become second nature to those in our industrial heartland and large cities, Air Raid Precautions became a classic of wartime reading, so much so that Britain's Air Raid Precautions was printed in its entirety, with no changes, for the American, New Zealand and Australian householder too.

From protection from gas attack to preparing a safe refuge and even first aid for bomb victims, the book is a mine of invaluable advice for the Blitz-weary householder.

Notes

_____
_____
_____
_____
_____
_____
_____
_____
_____
_____
_____
_____
_____
_____
_____
_____
_____
_____
_____
_____
_____
_____
_____
_____
_____
_____
_____
_____
_____
_____
_____
_____

_____

_____

_____

_____

_____

_____

_____

_____

_____

_____

_____

_____

_____

_____

_____

_____

_____

_____

_____

_____

_____

_____

_____

_____

_____

_____

_____

_____

_____